John Ruskin

On the Old Road

A Collection of Miscellaneous Essays, Pamphlets, etc., etc.: Vol. I.-ART

John Ruskin

On the Old Road
A Collection of Miscellaneous Essays, Pamphlets, etc., etc.: Vol. I.-ART

ISBN/EAN: 9783337092115

Printed in Europe, USA, Canada, Australia, Japan

Cover: Foto ©Thomas Meinert / pixelio.de

More available books at **www.hansebooks.com**

ON THE OLD ROAD.

A COLLECTION

OF

MISCELLANEOUS ESSAYS, PAMPHLETS, Etc., Etc.,

PUBLISHED 1834—1885

BY

JOHN RUSKIN, LL.D., D.C.L.,

HONORARY STUDENT OF CHRIST CHURCH, AND HONORARY FELLOW OF
CORPUS CHRISTI COLLEGE, OXFORD.

VOLUME I.—ART.

GEORGE ALLEN,
SUNNYSIDE, ORPINGTON, KENT.
1885.

CONTENTS OF VOLUME I.

PAGE

EDITOR'S NOTE .   .   ix

PART I.

INTRODUCTORY.

MY FIRST EDITOR. 1878   3

ART.

I. HISTORY AND CRITICISM.

LORD LINDSAY'S "CHRISTIAN ART." 1847   . 21
EASTLAKE'S "HISTORY OF OIL PAINTING."
1848 133
SAMUEL PROUT. 1849 .   .   . 206
SIR JOSHUA AND HOLBEIN. 1860   . 221

II. PRE-RAPHAELITISM.

ITS PRINCIPLES, AND TURNER. 1851   . 239
ITS THREE COLOURS. 1878 .   . 310

III. ARCHITECTURE.

THE OPENING OF THE CRYSTAL PALACE. 1854 349
THE STUDY OF ARCHITECTURE IN OUR SCHOOLS.
1865   . 371

PART II.

PAGE

IV. INAUGURAL ADDRESS, CAMBRIDGE
SCHOOL OF ART. 1858 . . 405

V. THE CESTUS OF AGLAIA. 1865-66.

PREFATORY .	. .	. 439
CHAPTER I.	. .	. 452
,, II.	see p. 467, note
,, III.	.	. 468
,, IV.	.	. 483
,, V.	. .	. 498
,, VI. .	see p. 513, note
,, VII. .	. .	. 514
,, VIII.	. .	. 523
,, IX.	. .	. 534

APPENDICES.

I. PICTURE GALLERIES.

PARLIAMENTARY EVIDENCE :—

NATIONAL GALLERY SITE COMMISSION. 1857 549

SELECT COMMITTEE OF PUBLIC INSTITU-
TIONS. 1860 574

THE ROYAL ACADEMY COMMISSION. 1863 . 602

LETTERS ON A MUSEUM OR PICTURE GALLERY.
1880 . . 625

II. MINOR WRITINGS UPON ART.

THE CAVALLI MONUMENTS, VERONA. 1872 . 643

VERONA AND ITS RIVERS. 1870 . . . 654

,, ,, ,, CATALOGUE. 1870 . 665

PAGE

CHRISTIAN ART AND SYMBOLISM. 1872 . 674
ART SCHOOLS OF MEDIÆVAL CHRISTENDOM.
1876 677
THE EXTENSION OF RAILWAYS. 1876 . 682
THE STUDY OF BEAUTY. 1883 . . 689

III. NOTES ON NATURAL SCIENCE.
THE COLOUR OF THE RHINE. 1834 . 699
THE STRATA OF MONT BLANC. 1834 . . 701
THE INDURATION OF SANDSTONE. 1836 . 703
THE TEMPERATURE OF SPRING AND RIVER
WATER. 1836 . . 707
METEOROLOGY. 1839 . 713
TREE TWIGS. 1861 717
STRATIFIED ALPS OF SAVOY. 1863 . . . 721
INTELLECTUAL CONCEPTION AND ANIMATED
LIFE. 1871 728

CHRONOLOGICAL LIST OF CONTENTS OF VOLUME I. . 735

INDEX . . 743

EDITOR'S NOTE.

THE present volumes need little preface. Upon the publication in 1880 of *Arrows of the Chace*, the Editor of that book received many letters requesting the edition, there suggested, of a volume or volumes bearing the same relation to Mr. Ruskin's uncollected articles and essays which that work did to his till then scattered letters to the public press. To that request, widely made, these volumes are the reply, and the Editor has only to set before the reader the arrangement and contents of the work.

The book has been edited without reference to Mr. Ruskin, who is responsible for nothing but his sanction to its issue and the title it bears. The articles have been reprinted without any change of text, and with the addition of but very few editorial notes. In the case of *Arrows of the Chace* numerous notes were necessary, but the present volumes are of a different character, and most of the allusions in them stand no more in need of explanation now than when the articles containing them were originally published.

The first volume, which for the sake of lightness in the hand is published in two parts, consists mainly of articles on Art; the second, of those on other subjects. In view of this each volume has been separately indexed; the first containing an index dealing almost exclusively with Art; the second, on the other hand, one in which that subject finds scarcely any mention. This plan may, it is hoped, be found convenient to those readers who desire to study either volume without reference to the other.

As regards the contents of the book, it contains with few exceptions a complete collection of all Mr. Ruskin's minor writings. The papers on the "Poetry of Architecture," published (1837-38) in London's *Architectural Magazine*, and some contributions (1867-70) to the *Geological Magazine*, are omitted; the former as fitted to form of themselves a separate volume; the latter as possibly finding a place in the presently issuing *Deucalion*. The three papers some time since reprinted at the end of *A Joy for Ever* are also not included; but with these exceptions, and those of one or two brief contributions to very recent works, the collection is, it is believed, complete, and it only remains to acknowledge the ready grace with which the Editor of the *Nineteenth Century* and others in whose publications the articles first appeared have consented to their reproduction here.—ED.

December, 1885.

PART I.

INTRODUCTORY: MY FIRST EDITOR.

ART.

I. HISTORY AND CRITICISM.
II. PRERAPHAELITISM.
III. ARCHITECTURE.

INTRODUCTORY.

MY FIRST EDITOR.

AN AUTOBIOGRAPHICAL REMINISCENCE.

(University Magazine, April 1878.)

MY FIRST EDITOR.*

AN AUTOBIOGRAPHICAL REMINISCENCE.

1st February, 1878.

1. IN seven days more I shall be fifty-nine;—which (practically) is all the same as sixty; but, being asked by the wife of my dear old friend, W. H. Harrison, to say a few words of our old relations together, I find myself, in spite of all these years, a boy again,— partly in the mere thought of, and renewed sympathy with, the cheerful heart of my old literary master, and partly in instinctive terror lest, wherever he is in celestial circles, he should catch me writing bad grammar, or putting wrong stops, and should set the table turning, or the like. For he was inexorable in such matters, and many a sentence in "Modern

---

* This paper was written as a preface to a series of "Reminiscences" from the pen of the late Mr. W. H. Harrison, commenced in the *University Magazine* of May 1878. It was separately printed in that magazine in the preceding month, but owing to Mr. Ruskin's illness at the time, he was unable to see it through the press. A letter from Mr. Ruskin to Mr. Harrison, printed in "Arrows of the Chace" (ii. 278), may be found of interest in connection with the opening statements of this paper.—[ED.]

Painters," which I had thought quite beautifully turned out after a forenoon's work on it, had to be turned outside-in, after all, and cut into the smallest pieces and sewn up again, because he had found out there wasn't a nominative in it, or a genitive, or a conjunction, or something else indispensable to a sentence's decent existence and position in life. Not a book of mine, for good thirty years, but went, every word of it, under his careful eyes twice over—often also the last revises left to his tender mercy altogether on condition he wouldn't bother me any more.

2. "For good thirty years": that is to say, from my first verse-writing in "Friendship's Offering" at fifteen, to my last orthodox and conservative compositions at forty-five.* But when I began to utter radical sentiments, and say things derogatory to the clergy, my old friend got quite restive—absolutely refused sometimes to pass even my most grammatical and punctuated paragraphs, if their contents savoured of heresy or revolution ; and at last I was obliged to print all my philanthropy and political economy on the sly.

3. The heaven of the literary world through which Mr. Harrison moved in a widely cometary fashion,

---

* "Friendship's Offering" of 1835 included two poems, signed "J. R.," and entitled "Saltzburg" and "Fragments from a Metrical Journal; Andernacht and St. Goar."—[ED.]

circling now round one luminary and now submitting
to the attraction of another, not without a serenely
erubescent lustre of his own, differed *toto cœlo* from
the celestial state of authorship by whose courses
we have now the felicity of being dazzled and directed.
Then, the publications of the months being very nearly
concluded in the modest browns of *Blackwood* and
Fraser, and the majesty of the quarterlies being above
the range of the properly so-called "public" mind,
the simple family circle looked forward with chief
complacency to their New Year's gift of the Annual
—a delicately printed, lustrously bound, and elaborately
illustrated small octavo volume, representing, after its
manner, the poetical and artistic inspiration of the
age. It is not a little wonderful to me, looking back
to those pleasant years and their bestowings, to
measure the difficultly imaginable distance between
the periodical literature of that day and ours. In a
few words, it may be summed by saying that the
ancient Annual was written by meekly-minded persons,
who felt that they knew nothing about anything, and
did not want to know more. Faith in the usually
accepted principles of propriety, and confidence in
the Funds, the Queen, the English Church, the British
Army and the perennial continuance of England, of
her Annuals, and of the creation in general, were
necessary then for the eligibility, and important ele-

ments in the success, of the winter-blowing author. Whereas I suppose that the popularity of our present candidates for praise, at the successive changes of the moon, may be considered as almost proportionate to their confidence in the abstract principles of dissolution, the immediate necessity of change, and the inconvenience, no less than the iniquity, of attributing any authority to the Church, the Queen, the Almighty, or anything else but the British Press. Such constitutional differences in the tone of the literary contents imply still greater contrasts in the lives of the editors of these several periodicals. It was enough for the editor of the "Friendship's Offering" if he could gather for his Christmas bouquet a little pastoral story, suppose, by Miss Mitford, a dramatic sketch by the Rev. George Croly, a few sonnets or impromptu stanzas to music by the gentlest lovers and maidens of his acquaintance, and a legend of the Apennines or romance of the Pyrenees by some adventurous traveller who had penetrated into the recesses of their mountains, and would modify the traditions of the country to introduce a plate by Clarkson Stanfield or J. D. Harding. Whereas now-a-days the editor of a leading monthly is responsible to his readers for exhaustive views of the politics of Europe during the last fortnight; and would think himself distanced in the race with his lunarian rivals, if his numbers did not contain three distinct and entirely new theories of the system of the universe, and at least one hitherto unobserved piece of evidence of the nonentity of God.

4. In one respect, however, the humilities of that departed time were loftier than the prides of to-day— that even the most retiring of its authors expected to be admired, not for what he had discovered, but for what he was. It did not matter in our dynasties of determined noblesse how many things an industrious blockhead knew, or how curious things a lucky booby had discovered. We claimed, and gave no honour but for real rank of human sense and wit; and although this manner of estimate led to many various collateral mischiefs—to much toleration of misconduct in persons who were amusing, and of uselessness in those of proved ability, there was yet the essential and constant good in it, that no one hoped to snap up for himself a reputation which his friend was on the point of achieving, and that even the meanest envy of merit was not embittered by a gambler's grudge at his neighbour's fortune.

5. Into this incorruptible court of literature I was early brought, whether by good or evil hap, I know not; certainly by no very deliberate wisdom in my friends or myself. A certain capacity for rhythmic cadence (visible enough in all my later writings) and the cheerfulness of a much protected, but not foolishly

indulged childhood, made me early a rhymester; and a shelf of the little cabinet by which I am now writing is loaded with poetical effusions which were the delight of my father and mother, and I have not yet the heart to burn. A worthy Scottish friend of my father's, Thomas Pringle, preceded Mr. Harrison in the editorship of " Friendship's Offering," and doubtfully, but with benignant sympathy, admitted the dazzling hope that one day rhymes of mine might be seen in real print, on those amiable and shining pages.

6. My introduction by Mr. Pringle to the poet Rogers, on the ground of my admiration of the recently published " Italy," proved, as far as I remember, slightly disappointing to the poet, because it appeared on Mr. Pringle's unadvised cross-examination of me in the presence that I knew more of the vignettes than the verses; and also slightly discouraging to me because, this contretemps necessitating an immediate change of subject, I thenceforward understood none of the conversation, and when we came away was rebuked by Mr. Pringle for not attending to it. Had his grave authority been maintained over me, my literary bloom would probably have been early nipped; but he passed away into the African deserts; and the Favonian breezes of Mr. Harrison's praise revived my drooping ambition.

7. I know not whether most in that ambition, or

to please my father, I now began seriously to cultivate my skill in expression. I had always an instinct of possessing considerable word-power; and the series of essays written about this time for the "Architectural Magazine," under the signature of Kata Phusin, contain sentences nearly as well put together as any I have done since. But without Mr. Harrison's ready praise, and severe punctuation, I should have either tired of my labour, or lost it ; as it was, though I shall always think those early years might have been better spent, they had their reward. As soon as I had anything really to say, I was able sufficiently to say it ; and under Mr. Harrison's cheerful auspices, and balmy consolations of my father under adverse criticism, the first volume of " Modern Painters" established itself in public opinion, and determined the tenor of my future life.

8. Thus began a friendship, and in no unreal sense, even a family relationship, between Mr. Harrison, my father and mother, and me, in which there was no alloy whatsoever of distrust or displeasure on either side, but which remained faithful and loving, more and more conducive to every sort of happiness among us, to the day of my father's death.

But the joyfullest days of it for *us*, and chiefly for me, cheered with concurrent sympathy from other friends—of whom only one now is left—were in the

triumphal Olympiad of years which followed the publication of the second volume of "Modern Painters,"
when Turner himself had given to me his thanks,
to my father and mother his true friendship, and came
always for *their* honour, to keep my birthday with
them ; the constant dinner party of the day remaining
in its perfect chaplet from 1844 to 1850,—Turner,
Mr. Thomas Richmond, Mr. George Richmond, Samuel
Prout, and Mr. Harrison.

9. Mr. Harrison, as my literary godfather, who had
held me at the Font of the Muses, and was answerable
to the company for my moral principles and my
syntax, always made "the speech"; my father used
most often to answer for me in few words, but with
wet eyes: (there was a general understanding that
any good or sorrow that might come to me in literary
life were infinitely more his) and the two Mr. Richmonds
held themselves responsible to him for my at least
moderately decent orthodoxy in art, taking in that
matter a tenderly inquisitorial function, and warning
my father solemnly of two dangerous heresies in the
bud, and of things really passing the possibilities of
the indulgence- of the Church, said against Claude or
Michael Angelo.   The death of Turner and other
things, far more sad than death, clouded those early
days, but the memory of them returned again after
I had well won my second victory with the "Stones

of Venice"; and the two Mr. Richmonds, and Mr.
Harrison, and my father, ·were again happy on my
birthday, and so to the end.

10. In a far deeper sense than he himself knew,
Mr. Harrison was all this time influencing my thoughts
and opinions, by the entire consistency, contentment,
and practical sense of his modest life. My father
and he were both flawless types of the true London
citizen of olden days : incorruptible, proud with sacred
and simple pride, happy in their function and position ;
putting daily their total energy into the detail of their
business duties, and finding daily a refined and perfect
pleasure in the hearth-side poetry of domestic life.
Both of them, in their hearts, as romantic as girls ;
both of them inflexible as soldier recruits in any
matter of probity and honour, in business or out of
it ; both of them utterly hating radical newspapers,
and devoted to the House of Lords; my father only,
it seemed to me, slightly failing in his loyalty to
the Worshipful the Mayor and Corporation of London.
This disrespect for civic dignity was connected in my
father with some little gnawing of discomfort—deep
down in his heart—in his own position as a merchant,
and with timidly indulged hope that his son might
one day move in higher spheres ; whereas Mr. Harrison
was entirely placid and resigned to the will of Providence which had appointed him his desk in the Crown

Life Office, never in his most romantic visions pro-
jected a marriage for any of his daughters with a
British baronet or a German count, and pinned his
little vanities prettily and openly on his breast, like
a nosegay, when he went out to dinner. Most especially he shone at the Literary Fund, where he was
Registrar and had proper official relations, therefore,
always with the Chairman, Lord Mahon, or Lord
Houghton, or the Bishop of Winchester, or some other
magnificent person of that sort, with whom it was
Mr. Harrison's supremest felicity to exchange a not
unfrequent little joke—like a pinch of snuff—and to
indicate for them the shoals to be avoided and the
channels to be followed with flowing sail in the speech
of the year; after which, if perchance there were any
malignant in the company who took objection, suppose,
to the claims of the author last relieved to the charity
of the Society, or to any claim founded on the production of a tale for *Blackwood's Magazine*, and of
two sonnets for "Friendship's Offering"; or if perchance there were any festering sharp thorn in Mr.
Harrison's side in the shape of some distinguished
radical, Sir Charles Dilke, or Mr. Dickens, or anybody
who had ever said anything against taxation, or the
Post Office, or the Court of Chancery, or the Bench
of Bishops,—then would Mr. Harrison, if he had full
faith in his Chairman, cunningly arrange with him

some delicate little extinctive operation to be performed on that malignant or that radical in the course of the evening, and would relate to us exultingly the next day all the incidents of the power of arms, and vindictively (for him) dwell on the barbed points and double edge of the beautiful episcopalian repartee with which it was terminated.

11. Very seriously, in all such public duties, Mr. Harrison was a person of rarest quality and worth; absolutely disinterested in his zeal, unwearied in exertion, always ready, never tiresome, never absurd; bringing practical sense, kindly discretion, and a most wholesome element of good-humoured, but incorruptible honesty, into everything his hand found to do. Everybody respected, and the best men sincerely regarded him, and I think those who knew most of the world were always the first to acknowledge his fine faculty of doing exactly the right thing to exactly the right point—and so pleasantly. In private life, he was to me an object of quite special admiration, in the quantity of pleasure he could take in little things; and he very materially modified many of my gravest conclusions, as to the advantages or mischiefs of modern suburban life. To myself scarcely any dwelling-place and duty in this world would have appeared (until, perhaps, I had tried them) less eligible for a man of sensitive and fanciful mind than the

New Road, Camberwell Green, and the monotonous
office work in Bridge Street.   And to a certain extent,
I am still of the same mind as to these matters, and
do altogether, and without doubt or hesitation, repu-
diate the existence of New Road and Camberwell
Green in general, no less than the condemnation of
intelligent persons to a routine of clerk's work broken
only by a three weeks' holiday in the decline of the
year.   On less lively, fanciful, and amiable persons
than my old friend, the New Road and the daily
desk do verily exercise a degrading and much to be
regretted influence.   But Mr. Harrison brought the
freshness of pastoral simplicity into the most faded
corners of the Green, lightened with his cheerful heart
the most leaden hours of the office, and gathered
during his three weeks' holiday in the neighbourhood,
suppose, of Guildford, Gravesend, Broadstairs, or
Rustington, more vital recreation and speculative
philosophy than another man would have got on the
grand tour.

12. On the other hand, I, who had nothing to do
all day but what I liked, and could wander at will
among all the best beauties of the globe—nor that
without sufficient power to see and to feel them, was
habitually a discontented person, and frequently a
weary one ; and the reproachful thought which always
rose in my mind when in that unconquerable listless-

ness of surfeit from excitement I found myself unable
to win even a momentary pleasure from the fairest
scene, was always : " If but Mr. Harrison were here
instead of me!"

13. Many and many a time I planned very seriously
the beguiling of him over the water. But there was
always something to be done in a hurry—something
to be worked out—something to be seen, as I thought,
only in my own quiet way. I believe if I had but
had the sense to take my old friend with me, he
would have shown me ever so much more than I
found out by myself. But it was not to be ; and
year after year I went to grumble and mope at Venice,
or Lago Maggiore ; and Mr. Harrison to enjoy himself
from morning to night at Broadstairs or Box Hill.
Let me not speak with disdain of either. No blue
languor of tideless wave is worth the spray and sparkle
of a South-Eastern English beach, and no one will
ever rightly enjoy the pines of the Wengern Alp who
despises the boxes of Box Hill.

Nay, I remember me of a little rapture of George
Richmond himself on those fair slopes of sunny sward,
ending in a vision of Tobit and his dog—no less—
led up there by the helpful angel. (I have always
wondered, by the way, whether that blessed dog minded
what the angel said to him.)

14. But Mr. Harrison was independent of these mere

æthereal visions, and surrounded himself only with a halo of sublunary beatitude. Welcome always he, as on his side frankly coming to be well, with the farmer, the squire, the rector, the—I had like to have said, dissenting minister, but I think Mr. Harrison usually evaded villages for summer domicile which were in any wise open to suspicion of Dissent in the air,— but with hunting rector, and the High Church curate, and the rector's daughters, and the curate's mother— and the landlord of the Red Lion, and the hostler of the Red Lion stables, and the tapster of the Pig and Whistle, and all the pigs in the back-yard, and all the whistlers in the street—whether for want of thought or for gaiety of it, and all the geese on the common, ducks in the horse-pond, and daws in the steeple, Mr. Harrison was known and beloved by every bird and body of them before half his holiday was over, and the rest of it was mere exuberance of festivity about him, and applauding coronation of his head and heart. Above all, he delighted in the ways of animals and children. He wrote a birthday ode—or at least a tumble-out-of-the-nest-day ode— to our pet rook, Grip, which encouraged that bird in taking such liberties with the cook, and in addressing so many impertinences to the other servants, that he became the mere plague, or as the French would express it, the "Black-beast," of the kitchen at

Denmark Hill for the rest of his life. There was almost always a diary kept, usually, I think, in rhyme, of those summer hours of indolence; and when at last it was recognised, in due and reverent way, at the Crown Life Office, that indeed the time had drawn near when its constant and faithful servant should be allowed to rest, it was perhaps not the least of my friend's praiseworthy and gentle gifts to be truly capable of rest; withdrawing himself into the memories of his useful and benevolent life, and making it truly a holiday in its honoured evening. The idea then occurred to him (and it was now my turn to press with hearty sympathy the sometimes intermitted task) of writing these Reminiscences: valuable—valuable to whom, and for what, I begin to wonder.

15. For indeed these memories are of people who are passed away like the snow in harvest; and now, with the sharp-sickle reapers of full shocks of the fattening wheat of metaphysics, and fair novelists Ruth-like in the fields of barley, or more mischievously coming through the rye,—what will the public, so vigorously sustained by these, care to hear of the lovely writers of old days, quaint creatures that they were?—Merry Miss Mitford, actually living in the country, actually walking in it, loving it, and finding history enough in the life of the butcher's boy, and romance enough in the story of the miller's daughter,

2

to occupy all her mind with, innocent of troubles
concerning the Turkish question; steady-going old
Barham, confessing nobody but the Jackdaw of Rheims,
and fearless alike of Ritualism, Darwinism, or dis-
establishment; iridescent clearness of Thomas Hood
—the wildest, deepest infinity of marvellously jestful
men; manly and rational Sydney, inevitable, infallible,
inoffensively wise of wit * ;—they are gone their way,
and ours is far diverse; and they and all the less-
known, yet pleasantly and brightly endowed spirits
of that time, are suddenly as unintelligible to us as
the Etruscans—not a feeling they had that we can
share in; and these pictures of them will be to us
valuable only as the sculpture under the niches far
in the shade there of the old parish church, dimly
vital images of inconceivable creatures whom we shall
never see the like of more.

* In the "Life and Times of Sydney Smith," by Stuart J. Reid
(London, 1884, p. 374), appears a letter addressed to the author by
Mr. Ruskin, to whom the book is dedicated:—

"OXFORD, *Nov.* 15*th*, 1883.

"MY DEAR SIR, I wanted to tell you what deep respect I had for
Sydney Smith; but my time has been cut to pieces ever since your
note reached me.   He was the first in the literary circles of London
to assert the value of 'Modern Painters,' and he has always seemed
to me equally keen-sighted and generous in his estimate of literary
efforts.   His 'Moral Philosophy' is the only book on the subject
which I care that my pupils should read, and there is no man (whom
I have not personally known) whose image is so vivid in my constant
affection.

"Ever your faithful servant,

John Ruskin."- [ED.]

ART.

I.

HISTORY AND CRITICISM.

LORD LINDSAY'S "CHRISTIAN ART."
(Quarterly Review, June 1847.)

EASTLAKE'S "HISTORY OF OIL PAINTING."
(Quarterly Review, March 1848.)

SAMUEL PROUT.
(Art Journal, March 1849.)

SIR JOSHUA AND HOLBEIN.
(Cornhill Magazine, March 1860.)

"THE HISTORY OF CHRISTIAN ART." *

BY LORD LINDSAY.

16. THERE is, perhaps, no phenomenon connected
with the history of the first half of the nineteenth
century, which will become a subject of more curious
investigation in after ages, than the coincident development of the Critical faculty, and extinction of the
Arts of Design.   Our mechanical energies, vast though
they be, are not singular nor characteristic; such,
and so great, have before been manifested—and it
may perhaps be recorded of us with wonder rather
than respect, that we pierced mountains and excavated valleys, only to emulate the activity of the gnat

* This essay is a review of two books by Lord Lindsay, viz.,
"Progression by Antagonism," published in 1846, and the "Sketches
of the History of Christian Art," which appeared in the following
year. It is, with the paper on Sir C. Eastlake's "History of Oil
Painting," one of the very few anonymous writings of its author.
"I never felt at ease" (says Mr. Ruskin, in speaking of anonymous
criticism) "in my graduate incognito, and although I consented,
some nine years ago, to review Lord Lindsay's 'Christian Art,' and
Sir Charles Eastlake's 'Essay on Oil Painting,' in the *Quarterly*,
I have ever since steadily refused to write even for that once
respectable periodical" ("Academy Notes," No. II., 1856). For Mr.
Ruskin's estimate of Lord Lindsay's work, see the "Eagle's Nest,"
p. 49, § 46, and "Val d'Arno," p. 199, § 264, where he speaks of
him as his "first master in Italian art."—[ED.]

and the swiftness of the swallow. Our discoveries in science, however accelerated or comprehensive, are but the necessary development of the more wonderful reachings into vacancy of past centuries; and they who struck the piles of the bridge of Chaos will arrest the eyes of Futurity rather than we builders of its towers and gates—theirs the authority of Light, ours but the ordering of courses to the Sun and Moon.

17. But the Negative character of the age is distinctive. There has not before appeared a race like that of civilized Europe at this day, thoughtfully unproductive of all art—ambitious—industrious—investigative—reflective, and incapable. Disdained by the savage, or scattered by the soldier, dishonoured by the voluptuary, or forbidden by the fanatic, the arts have not, till now, been extinguished by analysis and paralyzed by protection. Our lecturers, learned in history, exhibit the descents of excellence from school to school, and clear from doubt the pedigrees of powers which they cannot re-establish, and of virtues no more to be revived: the scholar is early acquainted with every department of the Impossible, and expresses in proper terms his sense of the deficiencies of Titian and the errors of Michael Angelo: the metaphysician weaves from field to field his analogies of gossamer, which shake and glitter fairly in the sun, but must be torn asunder by the first plough that passes : geometry

measures out, by line and rule, the light which is to illustrate heroism, and the shadow which should veil distress; and anatomy counts muscles, and system- atizes motion, in the wrestling of Genius with its angel. Nor is ingenuity wanting—nor patience; apprehen- sion was never more ready, nor execution more exact—yet nothing is of us, or in us, accomplished; —the treasures of our wealth and will are spent in vain—our cares are as clouds without water—our creations fruitless and perishable; the succeeding Age will trample " sopra lor vanita che par persona," and point wonderingly back to the strange colourless tessera in the mosaic of human mind.

18. No previous example can be shown, in the career of nations not altogether nomad or barbarous, of so total an absence of invention,—of any material representation of the mind's inward yearning and desire, seen, as soon as shaped,. to be, though imper- fect, in its essence good, and worthy to be rested in with contentment, and consisting self-approval—the Sabbath of contemplation which confesses and con- firms the majesty of a style. All but ourselves have had this in measure; the Imagination has stirred herself in proportion to the requirements, capacity, and energy of each race: reckless or pensive, soaring or frivolous, still she has had life and influence; sometimes aiming at Heaven with brick for stone and

slime for mortar—anon bound down to painting of
porcelain, and carving of ivory, but always with an
inward consciousness of power which might indeed
be palsied or imprisoned, but not in operation vain.
Altars have been rent, many—ashes poured out,—
hands withered—but we alone have worshipped, and
received no answer—the pieces left in order upon the
wood, and our names writ in the water that runs
round about the trench.

19. It is easier to conceive than to enumerate the
many circumstances which are herein against us,
necessarily, and exclusive of all that wisdom might
avoid, or resolution vanquish. First, the weight of
mere numbers, among whom ease of communication
rather renders opposition of judgment fatal, than agree-
ment probable ; looking from England to Attica, or
from Germany to Tuscany, we may remember to what
good purpose it was said that the magnetism of iron
was found not in bars, but in needles. Together with
this adversity of number comes the likelihood of many
among the more available intellects being held back
and belated in the crowd, or else prematurely out-
wearied ; for it now needs both curious fortune and
vigorous effort to give to any, even the greatest, such
early positions of eminence and audience as may feed
their force with advantage ; so that men spend their
strength in opening circles, and crying for place, and

only come to speech of us with broken voices and shortened time. Then follows the diminution of importance in peculiar places and public edifices, as they engage national affection or vanity; no single city can now take such queenly lead as that the pride of the whole body of the people shall be involved in adorning her; the buildings of London or Munich are not charged with the fulness of the national heart as were the domes of Pisa and Florence :—their credit or shame is metropolitan, not acropolitan; central at the best, not dominant; and this is one of the chief modes in which the cessation of superstition, so far as it has taken place, has been of evil consequence to art, that the observance of local sanctities being abolished, meanness and mistake are anywhere allowed of, and the thoughts and wealth which were devoted and expended to good purpose in one place, are now distracted and scattered to utter unavailableness.

20. In proportion to the increasing spirituality of religion, the conception of worthiness in material offering ceases, and with it the sense of beauty in the evidence of votive labour; machine-work is substituted for hand-work, as if the value of ornament consisted in the mere multiplication of agreeable forms, instead of in the evidence of human care and thought and love about the separate stones; and— machine-work once tolerated—the eye itself soon loses

its sense of this very evidence, and no more perceives the difference between the blind accuracy of the engine, and the bright, strange play of the living stroke—a difference as great as between the form of a stone pillar and a springing fountain. And on this blindness follow all errors and abuses—hollowness and slightness of frame-work, speciousness of surface ornament, concealed structure, imitated materials, and types of form borrowed from things noble for things base; and all these abuses must be resisted with the more caution, and less success, because in many ways they are signs or consequences of improvement, and are associated both with purer forms of religious feeling and with more general diffusion of refinements and comforts; and especially because we are critically aware of all our deficiencies, too cognizant of all that is greatest to pass willingly and humbly through the stages that rise to it, and oppressed in every honest effort by the bitter sense of inferiority. In every previous development the power has been in advance of the consciousness, the resources more abundant than the knowledge—the energy irresistible, the discipline imperfect. The light that led was narrow and dim—streakings of dawn—but it fell with kindly gentleness on eyes newly awakened out of sleep. But we are now aroused suddenly in the light of an intolerable day—our limbs fail under the sun-stroke

—we are walled in by the great buildings of elder times, and their fierce reverberation falls upon us without pause, in our feverish and oppressive consciousness of captivity; we are laid bedridden at the Beautiful Gate, and all our hope must rest in acceptance of the "such as I have," of the passers by.

21. The frequent and firm, yet modest expression of this hope, gives peculiar value to Lord Lindsay's book on Christian Art; for it is seldom that a grasp of antiquity so comprehensive, and a regard for it so affectionate, have consisted with aught but gloomy foreboding with respect to our own times. As a contribution to the History of Art, his work is unquestionably the most valuable which has yet appeared in England. His research has been unwearied; he has availed himself of the best results of German investigation—his own acuteness of discernment in cases of approximating or derivative style is considerable—and he has set before the English reader an outline of the relations of the primitive schools of Sacred art which we think so thoroughly verified in all its more important ramifications, that, with whatever richness of detail the labour of succeeding writers may illustrate them, the leading lines of Lord Lindsay's chart will always henceforth be followed. The feeling which pervades the whole book is chastened, serious, and full of

reverence for the strength ordained out of the lips of
infant Art—accepting on its own terms its simplest
teaching, sympathizing with all kindness in its un-
reasoning faith ; the writer evidently looking back with
most joy and thankfulness to hours passed in gazing
upon the faded and faint touches of feeble hands, and
listening through the stillness of uninvaded cloisters
for fall of voices now almost spent; yet he is never
contracted into the bigot, nor inflamed into the enthu-
siast ; he never loses his memory of the outside
world, never quits nor compromises his severe and
reflective Protestantism, never gives ground of offence
by despite or forgetfulness of any order of merit or
period of effort. And the tone of his address to
our present schools is therefore neither scornful nor
peremptory; his hope, consisting with full apprehension of all that we have lost, is based on a strict
and stern estimate of our power, position, and
resource, compelling the assent even of the least
sanguine to his expectancy of the revelation of a
new world of Spiritual Beauty, of which whosoever

" will dedicate his talents, as the bondsman of love, to
his Redeemer's glory and the good of mankind, may
become the priest and interpreter, by adopting in the
first instance, and re-issuing with that outward investiture
which the assiduous study of all that is beautiful, either
in Grecian sculpture, or the later but less spiritual schools
of painting, has enabled him to supply, such of its bright

ideas as he finds imprisoned in the early and imperfect efforts of art—and secondly, by exploring further on his own account in the untrodden realms of feeling that lie before him, and calling into palpable existence visions as bright, as pure, and as immortal as those that have already, in the golden days of Raphael and Perugino, obeyed their creative mandate, Live!" (Vol. iii., p. 422).*

22. But while we thus defer to the discrimination, respect the feeling, and join in the hope of the author, we earnestly deprecate the frequent assertion, as we entirely deny the accuracy or propriety, of the metaphysical analogies, in accordance with which his work has unhappily been arranged. Though these had been as carefully, as they are crudely, considered, it had still been no light error of judgment to thrust them with dogmatism so abrupt into the forefront of a work whose purpose is assuredly as much to win to the truth as to demonstrate it. The writer has apparently forgotten that of the men to whom he must primarily look for the working out of his anticipations, the most part are of limited knowledge and inveterate habit, men dexterous in practice, idle in thought ; many of them compelled by ill-ordered patronage into directions of exertion at variance with their own best impulses, and regarding their art only as a means of life ; all of them conscious of practical difficulties

* With one exception (see pp. 32-3) the quotations from Lord Lindsay are always from the "Christian Art."—[ED.]

which the critic is too apt to under-estimate, and
probably remembering disappointments of early effort
rude enough to chill the most earnest heart. The
shallow amateurship of the circle of their patrons
early disgusts them with theories; they shrink back
to the hard teaching of their own industry, and would
rather read the book which facilitated their methods
than the one that rationalized their aims. Noble
exceptions there are, and more than might be deemed;
but the labour spent in contest with executive difficulties renders even these better men unapt receivers
of a system which looks with little respect on such
achievement, and shrewd discerners of the parts of
such system which have been feebly rooted, or
fancifully reared. Their attention should have been
attracted both by clearness and kindness of promise;
their impatience prevented by close reasoning and
severe proof of every statement which might seem
transcendental. Altogether void of such consideration
or care, Lord Lindsay never even so much as states
the meaning or purpose of his appeal, but, clasping
his hands desperately over his head, disappears on
the instant in an abyss of curious and unsupported
assertions of the philosophy of human nature: re-
appearing only, like a breathless diver, in the third
page, to deprecate the surprise of the reader whom
he has never addressed, at a conviction which he has

never stated; and again vanishing ere we can well
look him in the face, among the frankincensed clouds
of Christian mythology: filling the greater part of
his first volume with a *resumé* of its symbols and
traditions, yet never vouchsafing the slightest hint
of the objects for which they are assembled, or the
amount of credence with which he would have them
regarded; and so proceeds to the historical portion
of the book, leaving the whole theory which is its
key to be painfully gathered from scattered passages,
and in great part from the mere form of enumeration
adopted in the preliminary chart of the schools; and
giving as yet account only of that period to which
the mere artist looks with least interest—while the
work, even when completed, will be nothing more
than a single pinnacle of the historical edifice whose
ground-plan is laid in the preceding essay, " Progression by Antagonism :"—a plan, by the author's
confession, "too extensive for his own, or any single
hand to execute," yet without the understanding of
whose main relations it is impossible to receive the
intended teaching of the completed portion.

23. It is generally easier to plan what is beyond
the reach of others than to execute what is within
our own; and it had ·been well if the range of this
introductory essay had been something less extensive,
and its reasoning more careful. Its search after truth

is honest and impetuous, and its results would have
appeared as interesting as they are indeed valuable,
had they but been arranged with ordinary perspicuity,
and represented in simple terms. But the writer's
evil genius pursues him; the demand for exertion
of thought is remorseless, and continuous throughout,
and the statements of theoretical principle as short,
scattered, and obscure, as they are bold. We question
whether many readers may not be utterly appalled
by the aspect of an "Analysis of Human Nature"—
the first task proposed to them by our intellectual
Eurystheus—to be accomplished in the space of six
semi-pages, followed in the seventh by the "Development of the Individual Man," and applied in the eighth
to a "General Classification of Individuals": and we
infinitely marvel that our author should have thought
it unnecessary to support or explain a division of the
mental attributes on which the treatment of his entire
subject afterwards depends, and whose terms are repeated in every following page to the very dazzling of
eye and deadening of ear (a division, we regret to say,
as illogical as it is purposeless), otherwise than by a
laconic reference to the assumptions of Phrenology.

"The Individual Man, or Man considered by himself as
an unit in creation, is compounded of three distinct primary
elements.

　　1. Sense, or the animal frame, with its passions or
　　　affections;

2. Mind or Intellect;—of which the distinguishing faculties—rarely, if ever, equally balanced, and by their respective predominance determinative of his whole character, conduct, and views of life—are,

    i. Imagination, the discerner of Beauty,—

    ii. Reason, the discerner of Truth,—

the former animating and informing the world of Sense or Matter, the latter finding her proper home in the world of abstract or immaterial existences—the former receiving the impress of things Objectively, or *ab externo*, the latter impressing its own ideas on them Subjectively, or *ab interno*—the former a feminine or passive, the latter a masculine or active principle; and

    iii. Spirit—the Moral or Immortal principle, ruling through the Will, and breathed into Man by the Breath of God."—"Progression of Antagonism," pp. 2, 3.

24. On what authority does the writer assume that the moral is alone the *Immortal* principle—or the only part of the human nature bestowed by the breath of God? Are imagination, then, and reason perishable? Is the Body itself? Are not all alike immortal; and when distinction is to be made among them, is not the first great division between their active and passive immortality, between the supported body and supporting spirit; that spirit itself afterwards rather conveniently to be considered as either exercising intellectual function, or receiving moral influence, and, both in power and passiveness, de-

3

riving its energy and sensibility alike from the
sustaining breath of God—than actually divided into
intellectual and moral parts ? For if the distinction
between us and the brute be the test of the nature
of the living soul by that breath conferred, it is
assuredly to be found as much in the imagination
as in the moral principle. There is but one of the
moral sentiments enumerated by Lord Lindsay, the
sign of which is absent in the animal creation :—the
enumeration is a bald one, but let it serve the turn
—"Self-esteem and love of Approbation," eminent in
horse and dog; "Firmness," not wanting either to
ant or elephant; "Veneration," distinct as far as the
superiority of man can by brutal intellect be comprehended ; "Hope," developed as far as its objects
can be made visible ; and "Benevolence," or Love,
the highest of all, the most assured of all—together
with all the modifications of opposite feeling, rage,
jealousy, habitual malice, even love of mischief and
comprehension of jest :—the one only moral sentiment
wanting being that of responsibility to an Invisible
being, or conscientiousness. But where, among brutes,
shall we find the slightest trace of the Imaginative
faculty, or of that discernment of beauty which our
author most inaccurately confounds with it, or of
the discipline of memory, grasping this or that circumstance at will, or of the still nobler foresight of,

and respect towards, things future, except only instinctive and compelled ?

25. The fact is, that it is not in intellect added 𝒥
to the bodily sense, nor in moral sentiment superadded
to the intellect, that the essential difference between
brute and man consists : but in the elevation of all
three to that point at which each becomes capable
of communion with the Deity, and worthy therefore
of eternal life ;—the body more universal as an
instrument—more exquisite in its sense—this last
character carried out in the eye and ear to the perception of Beauty, in form, sound, and colour—and
herein distinctively raised above the brutal sense ;
intellect, as we have said, peculiarly separating and
vast ; the moral sentiments like in essence, but bound-
lessly expanded, as attached to an infinite object, and
labouring in an infinite field : each part mortal in its
shortcoming, immortal in the accomplishment of its perfection and purpose ; the opposition which we at first
broadly expressed as between body and spirit, being
more strictly between the natural and spiritual condition of the entire creature—body natural, sown in death,
body spiritual, raised in incorruption : Intellect natural,
leading to scepticism ; intellect spiritual, expanding into
faith : Passion natural, suffered from things spiritual ;
passion spiritual, centred on things unseen : and the
strife or antagonism which is throughout the subject of

Lord Lindsay's proof, is not, as he has stated it, between the moral, intellectual, and sensual elements, but
between the upward and downward tendencies of all
three—between the spirit of Man which goeth upward,
and the spirit of the Beast which goeth downward.

26. We should not have been thus strict in our
examination of these preliminary statements, if the
question had been one of terms merely, or if the inaccuracy of thought had been confined to the Essay
on Antagonism.   If upon receiving a writer's terms
of argument in the sense—however unusual or mistaken—which he chooses they should bear, we may
without further error follow his course of thought,
it is as unkind as unprofitable to lose the use of
his result in quarrel with its algebraic expression ;
and if the reader will understand by Lord Lindsay's
general term "Spirit" the susceptibility of right moral
emotion, and the entire subjection of the Will to
Reason ; and receive his term "Sense" as not including
the perception of Beauty either in sight or sound,
but expressive of animal sensation only, he may follow
without embarrassment to its close, his magnificently
comprehensive statement of the forms of probation
which the heart and faculties of man have undergone
from the beginning of time.   But it is far otherwise
when the theory is to be applied, in all its pseudo-
organization, to the separate departments of a particular

art, and analogies the most subtle and speculative traced between the mental character and artistical choice or attainment of different races of men. Such analogies are always treacherous, for the amount of expression of individual mind which Art can convey is dependent on so many collateral circumstances, that it even militates against the truth of any particular system of interpretation that it should seem at first generally applicable, or its results consistent. The passages in which such interpretation has been attempted in the work before us, are too graceful to be regretted, nor is their brilliant suggestiveness otherwise than pleasing and profitable too, so long as it is received on its own grounds merely, and affects not with its uncertainty the very matter of its foundation. But all oscillation is communicable, and Lord Lindsay is much to be blamed for leaving it entirely to the reader to distinguish between the determination of his research and the activity of his fancy—between the authority of his interpretation and the aptness of his metaphor. He who would assert the true meaning of a symbolical art, in an age of strict inquiry and tardy imagination, ought rather to surrender something of the fulness which his own faith perceives, than expose the fabric of his vision, too finely woven, to the hard handling of the materialist; and we sincerely regret that dis-

credit is likely to accrue to portions of our author's
well-grounded statement of real significances, once
of all men understood, because these are rashly
blended with his own accidental perceptions of disputable analogy. He perpetually associates the present
imaginative influence of Art with its ancient hiero-
glyphical teaching, and mingles fancies fit only for
the framework of a sonnet, with the deciphered
evidence which is to establish a serious point of
history; and this the more frequently and grossly,
in the endeavour to force every branch of his subject
into illustration of the false division of the mental
attributes which we have pointed out.

27. His theory is first clearly stated in the following
passage :—

"Man is, in the strictest sense of the word, a progressive
being, and with many periods of inaction and retrogression,
has still held, upon the whole, a steady course towards the
great end of his existence, the re-union and re-harmonizing
of the three elements of his being, dislocated by the Fall,
in the service of his God. Each of these three elements,
Sense, Intellect, and Spirit, has had its distinct development
at three distant intervals, and in the personality of the
three great branches of the human family. The race of
Ham, giants in prowess if not in stature, cleared the earth
of primeval forests and monsters, built cities, established
vast empires, invented the mechanical arts, and gave the
fullest expansion to the animal energies. After them, the
Greeks, the elder line of Japhet, developed the intellectual
faculties, Imagination and Reason, more especially the

former, always the earlier to bud and blossom; poetry
and fiction, history, philosophy, and science, alike look back
to Greece as their birthplace; on the one hand they put
a soul into Sense, peopling the world with their gay
mythology—on the other they bequeathed to us, in Plato
and Aristotle, the mighty patriarchs of human wisdom,
the Darius and the Alexander of the two grand armies
of thinking men whose antagonism has ever since divided
the battle-field of the human intellect :—While, lastly, the
race of Shem, the Jews, and the nations of Christendom,
their *locum tenentes* as the Spiritual Israel, have, by God's
blessing, been elevated in Spirit to as near and intimate
communion with Deity as is possible in this stage of being.
Now the peculiar interest and dignity of Art consists in
her exact correspondence in her three departments with
these three periods of development, and in the illustration
she thus affords—more closely and markedly even than
literature—to the all-important truth that men stand or
fall according as they look up to the Ideal or not. For
example, the Architecture of Egypt, her pyramids and
temples, cumbrous and inelegant, but imposing from their
vastness and their gloom, express the ideal of Sense or
Matter—elevated and purified indeed, and nearly approaching the Intellectual, but Material still; we think of them
as of natural scenery, in association with caves or mountains, or vast periods of time; their voice is as the voice
of the sea, or as that of "many peoples," shouting in
unison :—But the Sculpture of Greece is the voice of
Intellect and Thought, communing with itself in solitude,
feeding on beauty and yearning after truth :—While the
Painting of Christendom—(and we must remember that
the glories of Christianity, in the full extent of the term,
are yet to come)—is that of an immortal Spirit, conversing
with its God. And as if to mark more forcibly the fact
of continuous progress towards perfection, it is observable

that although each of the three arts peculiarly reflects and characterises one of the three epochs, each art of later growth has been preceded in its rise, progress, and decline, by an antecedent correspondent development of its elder sister or sisters—Sculpture, in Greece, by that of Architecture—Painting, in Europe, by that of Architecture and Sculpture. If Sculpture and Painting stand by the side of Architecture in Egypt, if Painting by that of Architecture and Sculpture in Greece, it is as younger sisters, girlish and unformed. In Europe alone are the three found linked together, in equal stature and perfection."—Vol. i., pp. xii.—xiv.

28. The reader must, we think, at once perceive the bold fallacy of this forced analogy—the comparison of the architecture of one nation with the sculpture of another, and the painting of a third, and the assumption as a proof of difference in moral character, of changes necessarily wrought, always in the same order, by the advance of mere mechanical experience. Architecture must precede sculpture, not because sense precedes intellect, but because men must build houses before they adorn chambers, and raise shrines before they inaugurate idols; and sculpture must precede painting, because men must learn forms in the solid before they can project them on a flat surface, and must learn to conceive designs in light and shade before they can conceive them in colour, and must learn to treat subjects under positive colour and in narrow groups, before they can treat

them under atmospheric effect and in receding masses and all these are mere necessities of practice, and have no more connexion with any divisions of the human mind than the equally paramount necessities that men must gather stones before they build walls, or grind corn before they bake bread. And that each following nation should take up either the same art at an advanced stage, or an art altogether more difficult, is nothing but the necessary consequence of its subsequent elevation and civilization. Whatever nation had succeeded Egypt in power and knowledge, after having had communication with her, must necessarily have taken up art at the point where Egypt left it—in its turn delivering the gathered globe of heavenly snow to the youthful energy of the nation next at hand, with an exhausted "à vous le dé!" In order to arrive at any useful or true estimate of the respective rank of each people in the scale of mind, the architecture of each must be compared with the architecture of the other—sculpture with sculpture— line with line; and to have done this broadly and with a surface glance, would have set our author's theory on firmer foundation, to outward aspect, than it now rests upon. Had he compared the accumulation of the pyramid with the proportion of the peristyle, and then with the aspiration of the spire ; had he set the colossal horror of the Sphinx beside

the Phidian Minerva, and this beside the Pietà of
M. Angelo; had he led us from beneath the iridescent capitals of Denderah, by the contested line
of Apelles, to the hues and the heaven of Perugino
or Bellini, we might have been tempted to assoilzie
from all staying of question or stroke of partizan
the invulnerable aspect of his ghostly theory; but,
if, with even partial regard to some of the circumstances which physically limited the attainments of
each race, we follow their individual career, we shall
find the points of superiority less salient, and the
connexion between heart and hand more embarrassed.

29. Yet let us not be misunderstood:—the great
gulf between Christian and Pagan art we cannot
bridge—nor do we wish to weaken one single sentence
wherein its breadth or depth is asserted by our author.
The separation is not gradual, but instant and final
—the difference not of degree, but of condition; it is
the difference between the dead vapours rising from
a stagnant pool, and the same vapours touched by a
torch. But we would brace the weakness which Lord
Lindsay has admitted in his own assertion of this
great inflaming instant by confusing its fire with the
mere phosphorescence of the marsh, and explaining
as a successive development of the several human
faculties, what was indeed the bearing of them all at

once, over a threshold strewed with the fragments of their idols, into the temple of the One God.

We shall therefore, as fully as our space admits, examine the application of our author's theory to Architecture, Sculpture, and Painting, successively, setting before the reader some of the more interesting passages which respect each art, while we at the same time mark with what degree of caution their conclusions are, in our judgment, to be received.

30. Accepting Lord Lindsay's first reference to Egypt, let us glance at a few of the physical accidents which influenced its types of architecture. The first of these is evidently the capability of carriage of large blocks of stone over perfectly level land. It was possible to roll to their destination along that uninterrupted plain, blocks which could neither by the Greek have been shipped in sea-worthy vessels, nor carried over mountain-passes, nor raised except by extraordinary effort to the height of the rock-built fortress or seaward promontory. A small undulation of surface, or embarrassment of road, makes large difference in the portability of masses, and of consequence, in the breadth of the possible intercolumniation, the solidity of the column, and the whole scale of the building. Again, in a hill-country, architecture can be important only by position, in a level country only by bulk. Under the overwhelming mass of

mountain-form it is vain to attempt the expression of
majesty by size of edifice—the humblest architecture
may become important by availing itself of the power
of nature, but the mightiest must be crushed in
emulating it: the watch-towers of Amalfi are more
majestic than the Superga of Piedmont; St. Peter's
would look like a toy if built beneath the Alpine
cliffs, which yet vouchsafe some communication of
their own solemnity to the smallest châlet that glitters
among their glades of pine. On the other hand, a
small building is in a level country lost, and the
impressiveness of bulk proportionably increased; hence
the instinct of nations has always led them to the
loftiest efforts where the masses of their labour might
be seen looming at incalculable distance above the
open line of the horizon—hence rose her foursquare
mountains above the flat of Memphis, while the Greek
pierced the recesses of Phigaleia with ranges of
columns, or crowned the sea-cliffs of Sunium with a
single pediment, bright, but not colossal.

31. The derivation of the Greek types of form from
the forest-hut is too direct to escape observation;
but sufficient attention has not been paid to the
similar petrifaction, by other nations, of the rude
forms and materials adopted in the haste of early
settlement, or consecrated by the purity of rural life.
The whole system of Swiss and German Gothic has

thus been most characteristically affected by the
structure of the intersecting timbers at the angels of
the châlet. This was in some cases directly and
without variation imitated in stone, as in the piers
of the old bridge at Aarburg; and the practice
obtained—partially in the German after-Gothic—
universally, or nearly so, in Switzerland—of causing
mouldings which met at an angle to appear to
interpenetrate each other, both being truncated immediately beyond the point of intersection. The pain-
fulness of this ill-judged adaptation was conquered
by association—the eye became familiarized to uncouth
forms of tracery—and a stiffness and meagreness, as
of cast-iron, resulted in the mouldings of much of
the ecclesiastical, and all the domestic Gothic of
central Europe; the mouldings of casements intersecting so as to form a small hollow square at the
angles, and the practice being further carried out
into all modes of decoration—pinnacles interpene-
trating crockets, as in a peculiarly bold design of
archway at Besançon. The influence at Venice has
been less immediate and more fortunate; it is with
peculiar grace that the majestic form of the ducal
palace reminds us of the years of fear and endurance
when the exiles of the Prima Venetia settled like
homeless birds on the sea-sand, and that its quad-
rangular range of marble wall and painted chamber,

raised upon multiplied columns of confused arcade,* presents but the exalted image of the first pile-supported hut that rose above the rippling of the lagoons.

32. In the chapter on the "Influence of Habit and Religion," of Mr. Hope's Historical Essay,† the reader will find further instances of the same feeling, and, bearing immediately on our present purpose, a clear account of the derivation of the Egyptian temple from the excavated cavern; but the point to which in all these cases we would direct especial attention, is, that the first perception of the great laws of architectural *proportion* is dependent for its acuteness less on the æsthetic instinct of each nation than on the mechanical conditions of stability and natural limitations of size in the primary type, whether hut, châlet, or tent.

As by the constant reminiscence of the natural proportions of his first forest-dwelling, the Greek would be restrained from all inordinate exaggeration of size—the Egyptian was from the first left without hint of any system of proportion, whether constructive, or of visible parts. The cavern—its level roof supported by amorphous piers—might be extended indefinitely into the interior of the hills, and its outer façade continued almost without term along their flanks

---

* The reader must remember that this arcade was originally quite open, the inner wall having been built after the fire, in 1574.

† "An Historical Essay on Architecture" by the late Thomas Hope. (Murray, 1835) chap. iv., pp. 23-31.

—the solid mass of cliff above forming one gigantic entablature, poised upon props instead of columns. Hence the predisposition to attempt in the built temple the expression of infinite extent, and to heap the ponderous architrave above the proportionless pier.

33. The less direct influences of external nature in the two countries were still more opposed. The sense of beauty, which among the Greek peninsulas was fostered by beating of sea and rush of river, by waving of forest and passing of cloud, by undulation of hill and poise of precipice, lay dormant beneath the shadowless sky and on the objectless plain of the Egyptians; no singing winds nor shaking leaves nor gliding shadows gave life to the line of their barren mountains—no Goddess of Beauty rose from the pacing of their silent and foamless Nile. One continual perception of stability, or changeless revolution, weighed upon their hearts—their life depended on no casual alternation of cold and heat—of drought and shower; their gift-Gods were the risen River and the eternal Sun, and the types of these were for ever consecrated in the lotus decoration of the temple and the wedge of the enduring Pyramid. Add to these influences, purely physical, those dependent on the superstitions and political constitution; of the over-flowing multitude of "populous No"; on their condition of prolonged peace—their simple habits of life

—their respect for the dead—their separation by
incommunicable privilege and inherited occupation—
and it will be evident to the reader that Lord Lindsay's
broad assertion of the expression of "the Ideal of
Sense or Matter" by their universal style, must be
received with severe modification, and is indeed thus
far only true, that the mass of Life supported upon
that fruitful plain could, when swayed by a despotic
ruler in any given direction, accomplish by mere
weight and number what to other nations had been
impossible, and bestow a pre-eminence, owed to mere
bulk and evidence of labour, upon public works which
among the Greek republics could be rendered admirable
only by the intelligence of their design.

34. Let us, for the present omitting consideration of
the debasement of the Greek types which took place
when their cycle of achievement had been fulfilled,
pass to the germination of Christian architecture, out
of one of the least important elements of those fallen
forms—one which, less than the least of all seeds, has
risen into the fair branching stature under whose
shadow we still dwell.

The principal characteristics of the new architecture, as exhibited in the Lombard cathedral, are well
sketched by Lord Lindsay:—

"The three most prominent features, the eastern aspect
of the sanctuary, the cruciform plan, and the soaring

octagonal cupola, are borrowed from Byzantium—the latter in an improved form—the cross with a difference—the nave, or arm opposite the sanctuary, being lengthened so as to resemble the supposed shape of the actual instrument of suffering, and form what is now distinctively called the Latin Cross. The crypt and absis, or tribune, are retained from the Romish basilica, but the absis is generally pierced with windows, and the crypt is much loftier and more spacious, assuming almost the appearance of a subterranean church. The columns of the nave, no longer isolated, are clustered so as to form compound piers, massive and heavy—their capitals either a rude imitation of the Corinthian, or, especially in the earlier structures, sculptured with grotesque imagery. Triforia, or galleries for women, frequently line the nave and transepts. The roof is of stone, and vaulted. The narthex, or portico, for excluded penitents, common alike to the Greek and Roman churches, and in them continued along the whole façade of entrance, is dispensed with altogether in the oldest Lombard ones, and when afterwards resumed, in the eleventh century, was restricted to what we should now call Porches, over each door, consisting generally of little more than a canopy open at the sides, and supported by slender pillars, resting on sculptured monsters. Three doors admit from the western front; these are generally covered with sculpture, which frequently extends in belts across the façade, and even along the sides of the building. Above the central door is usually seen, in the later Lombard churches, a S. Catherine's-wheel window. The roof slants at the sides, and ends in front sometimes in a single pediment, sometimes in three gables answering to three doors; while, in Lombardy at least, hundreds of slender pillars, of every form and device—those immediately adjacent to each other frequently interlaced in the true lover's

4

knot, and all supporting round or trefoliate arches—run along, in continuous galleries, under the eaves, as if for the purpose of supporting the roof—run up the pediment in front, are continued along the side-walls and round the eastern absis, and finally engirdle the cupola. Sometimes the western front is absolutely covered with these galleries, rising tier above tier. Though introduced merely for ornament, and therefore on a vicious principle, these fairylike colonnades win very much on one's affections. I may add to these general features the occasional and rare one, seen to peculiar advantage in the cathedral of Cremona, of numerous slender towers, rising, like minarets, in every direction, in front and behind, and giving the east end, specially, a marked resemblance to the mosques of the Mahometans.

"The Bapistery and the Campanile, or bell-tower, are in theory invariable adjuncts to the Lombard cathedral, although detached from it. The Lombards seem to have built them with peculiar zest, and to have had a keen eye for the picturesque in grouping them with the churches they belong to.

" I need scarcely add that the round arch is exclusively employed in pure Lombard architecture.

" To translate this new style into its symbolical language is a pleasurable task. The three doors and three gable ends signify the Trinity, the Catherine-wheel window (if I mistake not) the Unity, as concentrated in Christ, the Light of the Church, from whose Greek monogram its shape was probably adopted. The monsters that support the pillars of the porch stand there as talismans to frighten away evil spirits. The crypt (as in older buildings) signifies the moral death of man, the cross, the atonement, the cupola heaven ; and these three, taken in conjunction with the lengthened nave, express, reconcile, and give their due and balanced prominence to the leading ideas of the Militant and Triumph-

ant Church, respectively embodied in the architecture of
Rome and Byzantium. Add to this, the symbolism of the
Baptistery, and the Christian pilgrimage, from the Font to
the Door of Heaven, is complete."—Vol. ii., p. 8-11.

35. We have by-and-bye an equally comprehensive
sketch of the essential characters of the Gothic cathedral; but this we need not quote, as it probably
contains little that would be new to the reader. It
is succeeded by the following interpretation of the
spirit of the two styles :—

"Comparing, apart from enthusiasm, the two styles of
Lombard and Pointed Architecture, they will strike you,
I think, as the expression, respectively, of that alternate
repose and activity which characterise the Christian life,
exhibited in perfect harmony in Christ alone, who, on
earth, spent His night in prayer to God, His day in
doing good to man—in heaven, as we know by His own
testimony, "worketh hitherto," conjointly with the Father
—for ever, at the same time, reposing on the infinity of
His wisdom and of His power. Each, then, of these
styles has its peculiar significance, each is perfect in its
way. The Lombard Architecture, with its horizontal lines,
its circular arches and expanding cupola, soothes and calms
one; the Gothic, with its pointed arches, aspiring vaults
and intricate tracery, rouses and excites—and why ?
Because the one symbolises an infinity of Rest, the other
of Action, in the adoration and service of God. And
this consideration will enable us to advance a step
farther :—The aim of the one style is definite, of the
other indefinite; we look up to the dome of heaven and
calmly acquiesce in the abstract idea of infinity; but we
only realise the impossibility of conceiving it by the

flight of imagination from star to star, from firmament to firmament. Even so Lombard Architecture attained perfection, expressed its idea, accomplished its purpose—but Gothic never; the Ideal is unapproachable."—Vol. ii., p. 23.

36. This idea occurs not only in this passage :— it is carried out through the following chapters ;— at page 38, the pointed arch associated with the cupola is spoken of as a "fop interrupting the meditations of a philosopher"; at page 65, the "earlier contemplative style of the Lombards" is spoken of; at page 114, Giottesque art is "the expression of that Activity of the Imagination which produced Gothic Architecture"; and, throughout, the analogy is prettily expressed, and ably supported ; yet it is one of those against which we must warn the reader: it is altogether superficial, and extends not to the minds of those whose works it accidentally, and we think disputably, characterises. The transition from Romanesque (we prefer using the generic term) to Gothic is natural and straightforward, in many points traceable to mechanical and local necessities (of which one, the dangerous weight of snow on flat roofs, has been candidly acknowledged by our author), and directed by the tendency, common to humanity in all ages, to push every newly-discovered means of delight to its most fantastic extreme, to exhibit every newly-felt power in its most admirable achievement,

and to load with extrinsic decoration forms whose
essential varieties have been exhausted. The arch,
carelessly struck out by the Etruscan, forced by
mechanical expediencies on the unwilling, uninventive
Roman, remained unfelt by either. The noble form
of the apparent Vault of Heaven—the line which
every star follows in its journeying, extricated by
the Christian architect from the fosse, the aqueduct,
and the sudarium—grew into long succession of proportioned colonnade, and swelled into the white domes
that glitter above the plain of Pisa, and fretted channels
of Venice, like foam globes at rest.

37. But the spirit that was in these Aphrodites of
the earth was not then, nor in them, to be restrained.
Colonnade rose over colonnade ; the pediment of the
western front was lifted into a detached and scenic
wall ; story above story sprang the multiplied arches
of the Campanile, and the eastern pyramidal fire-
type, lifted from its foundation, was placed upon the
summit. With the superimposed arcades of the principal front arose the necessity, instantly felt by their
subtle architects, of a new proportion in the column ;
the lower wall enclosure, necessarily for the purposes
of Christian worship continuous, and needing no
peristyle, rendered the lower columns a mere facial
decoration, whose proportions were evidently no more
to be regulated by the laws hitherto observed in

detached colonnades. The column expanded into the
shaft, or into the huge pilaster rising unbanded from
tier to tier ; shaft and pilaster were associated in
ordered groups, and the ideas of singleness and limited
elevation once attached to them, swept away for ever ;
the stilted and variously centred arch existed already :
the pure ogive followed—where first exhibited we
stay not to inquire ;—finally, and chief of all, the
great mechanical discovery of the resistance of lateral
pressure by the weight of the superimposed flanking
pinnacle.   Daring concentrations of pressure upon
narrow piers were the immediate consequence, and
the recognition of the buttress as a feature in itself
agreeable and susceptible of decoration.   The glorious
art of painting on glass added its temptations ; the
darkness of northern climes both rendering the typical
character of Light more deeply felt than in Italy,
and necessitating its admission in larger masses ; the
Italian, even at the period of his most exquisite art
in glass, retaining the small Lombard window, whose
expediency will hardly be doubted by any one who
has experienced the transition from the scorching
reverberation of the white-hot marble front, to the
cool depth of shade within, and whose beauty will
not be soon forgotten by those who have seen the
narrow lights of the Pisan duomo announce by their
redder burning, not like transparent casements, but

like characters of fire searing the western wall, the decline of day upon Capraja.

38. Here, then, arose one great distinction between Northern and Transalpine Gothic, based, be it still observed, on mere necessities of climate. While the architect of Santa Maria Novella admitted to the frescoes of Ghirlandajo scarcely more of purple lancet light than had been shed by the morning sun through the veined alabasters of San Miniato; and looked to the rich blue of the quinquipartite vault above, as to the mosaic of the older concha, for conspicuous aid in the colour decoration of the whole; the northern builder burst through the walls of his apse, poured over the eastern altar one unbroken blaze, and lifting his shafts like pines, and his walls like precipices, ministered to their miraculous stability by an infinite phalanx of sloped buttress and glittering pinnacle. The spire was the natural consummation. Internally, the sublimity of space in the cupola had been superseded by another kind of infinity in the prolongation of the nave; externally, the spherical surface had been proved, by the futility of Arabian efforts, incapable of decoration; its majesty depended on its simplicity, and its simplicity and leading forms were alike discordant with the rich rigidity of the body of the building. The campanile became, therefore, principal and central; its pyramidal termination was

surrounded at the base by a group of pinnacles, and
the spire itself, banded, or pierced into aërial tracery,
crowned with its last enthusiastic effort the flamelike
ascent of the perfect pile.

39. The process of change was thus consistent
throughout, though at intervals accelerated by the
sudden discovery of resource, or invention of design ;
nor, had the steps been less traceable, do we think
the suggestiveness of Repose, in the earlier style,
or of Imaginative Activity in the latter, definite or
trustworthy. We much question whether the Duomo
of Verona, with its advanced guard of haughty gryphons
—the mailed peers of Charlemagne frowning from its
vaulted gate,—that vault itself ribbed with variegated
marbles, and peopled by a crowd of monsters—the
Evangelical types not the least stern or strange ;
its stringcourses replaced by flat cut friezes, combats
between gryphons and chain-clad paladins, stooping
behind their triangular shields and fetching sweeping
blows with two-handled swords ; or that of Lucca—
its fantastic columns clasped by writhing snakes and
winged dragons, their marble scales spotted with
inlaid serpentine, every available space alive with
troops of dwarfish riders, with spur on heel and
hawk in hood, sounding huge trumpets of chase, like
those of the Swiss Urus-horn, and cheering herds
of gaping dogs upon harts and hares, boars and

wolves, every stone signed with its grisly beast—
be one whit more soothing to the contemplative, or
less exciting to the imaginative faculties, than the
successive arch, and visionary shaft, and dreamy vault,
and crisped foliage, and colourless stone, of our own
fair abbeys, chequered with sunshine through the depth
of ancient branches, or seen far off, like clouds in the
valley, risen out of the pause of its river.

40. And with respect to the more fitful and fantastic expression of the " Italian Gothic," our author
is again to be blamed for his loose assumption, from
the least reflecting of preceding writers, of this general
term, as if the pointed buildings of Italy could in
any wise be arranged in one class, or criticised in
general terms. It is true that so far as the church
interiors are concerned, the system is nearly universal,
and always bad ; its characteristic features being arches
of enormous span, and banded foliage capitals divided
into three fillets, rude in design, unsuggestive of any
structural connection with the column, and looking consequently as if they might be slipped up or down, and
had been only fastened in their places for the tempo-
rary purposes of a festa. But the exteriors of Italian
pointed buildings display variations of principle and
transitions of type quite as bold as either the advance
from the Romanesque to the earliest of their forms,
or the recoil from their latest to the cinquecento.

41. The first and grandest style resulted merely
from the application of the pointed arch to the frequent Romanesque window, the large semicircular
arch divided by three small ones. Pointing both the
superior and inferior arches, and adding to the grace
of the larger one by striking another arch above it
with a more removed centre, and placing the voussoirs
at an acute angle to the curve, we have the truly
noble form of domestic Gothic, which—more or less
enriched by mouldings and adorned by penetration,
more or less open of the space between the including
and inferior arches—was immediately adopted in almost
all the proudest palaces of North Italy—in the Bro-
lettos of Como, Bergamo, Modena, and Siena—in the
palace of the Scaligers at Verona—of the Gambacorti
at Pisa—of Paolo Guinigi at Lucca—besides inferior
buildings innumerable :—nor is there any form of
civil Gothic except the Venetian, which can be for
a moment compared with it in simplicity or power.
The latest is that most vicious and barbarous style
of which the richest types are the lateral porches
and upper pinnacles of the Cathedral of Como, and
the whole of the Certosa of Pavia :—characterised
by the imitative sculpture of large buildings on a
small scale by way of pinnacles and niches; the
substitution of candelabra for columns ; and the covering of the surfaces with sculpture, often of classical

subject, in high relief and daring perspective, and
finished with delicacy which rather would demand
preservation in a cabinet, and exhibition under a lens,
than admit of exposure to the weather and removal
from the eye, and which, therefore, architecturally
considered, is worse than valueless, telling merely
as unseemly roughness and rustication.   But between
these two extremes are varieties nearly countless—
some of them both strange and bold, owing to the
brilliant colour and firm texture of the accessible
materials, and the desire of the builders to crowd the
greatest expression of value into the smallest space.

42. Thus it is in the promontories of serpentine
which meet with their polished and gloomy green
the sweep of the Gulf of Genoa, that we find the
first cause of the peculiar spirit of the Tuscan and
Ligurian Gothic—carried out in the Florentine duomo
to the highest pitch of coloured finish—adorned in
the upper story of the Campanile by a transformation,
peculiarly rich and exquisite, of the narrowly-pierced
heading of window already described, into a veil of
tracery—and aided throughout by an accomplished
precision of design in its mouldings which we believe
to be unique.   In St. Petronio of Bologna, another
and a barbarous type occurs; the hollow niche of
Northern Gothic wrought out with diamond-shaped
penetrations enclosed in squares; at Bergamo another,

remarkable for the same square penetrations of its
rich and daring foliation ;—while at Monza and Carrara
the square is adopted as the leading form of decoration on the west fronts, and a grotesque expression
results—barbarous still ;—which, however, in the latter
duomo is associated with the arcade of slender niches
—the translation of the Romanesque arcade into
pointed work, which forms the second perfect order
of Italian Gothic, entirely ecclesiastical, and well
developed in the churches of Santa Caterina and Santa
Maria della Spina at Pisa. The Veronese Gothic,
distinguished by the extreme purity and severity of
its ruling lines, owing to the distance of the centres
of circles from which its cusps are struck, forms
another, and yet a more noble school—and passes
through the richer decoration of Padua and Vicenza
to the full magnificence of the Venetian—distinguished
by the introduction of the ogee curve without pruriency
or effeminacy, and by the breadth and decision of
mouldings as severely determined in all examples of
the style as those of any one of the Greek orders.

43. All these groups are separated by distinctions
clear and bold—and many of them by that broadest
of all distinctions which lies between disorganization
and consistency—accumulation and adaptation, ex-
periment and design ;—yet to all one or two principles
are common, which again divide the whole series from

that of the Transalpine Gothic—and whose importance
Lord Lindsay too lightly passes over in the general
description, couched in somewhat ungraceful terms,
"the vertical principle snubbed, as it were, by the
horizontal." We have already alluded to the great
school of colour which arose in the immediate neighbourhood of the Genoa serpentine. The accessibility
of marble throughout North Italy similarly modified
the aim of all design, by the admission of undecorated
surfaces. A blank space of freestone wall is always
uninteresting, and sometimes offensive; there is no
suggestion of preciousness in its dull colour, and
the stains and rents of time upon it are dark, coarse,
and gloomy. But a marble surface receives in its age
hues of continually increasing glow and grandeur;
its stains are never foul nor dim; its undecomposing
surface preserves a soft, fruit-like polish for ever,
slowly flushed by the maturing suns of centuries.
Hence, while in the Northern Gothic the effort of
the architect was always so to diffuse his ornament
as to prevent the eye from permanently resting on
the blank material, the Italian fearlessly left fallow
large fields of uncarved surface, and concentrated the
labour of the chisel on detached portions, in which
the eye, being rather directed to them by their
isolation than attracted by their salience, required
perfect finish and pure design rather than force of

shade or breadth of parts; and further, the intensity
of Italian sunshine articulated by perfect gradations,
and defined by sharp shadows at the edge, such
inner anatomy and minuteness of outline as would
have been utterly vain and valueless under the gloom
of a northern sky; while again the fineness of material
both admitted of, and allured to, the precision of execution which the climate was calculated to exhibit.

44. All these influences working together, and with
them that of classical example and tradition, induced
a delicacy of expression, a slightness of salience, a
carefulness of touch, and refinement of invention, in
all, even the rudest, Italian decorations, utterly unrecognised in those of Northern Gothic: which, however
picturesquely adapted to their place and purpose,
depend for most of their effect upon bold undercutting,
accomplish little beyond graceful embarrassment of
the eye, and cannot for an instant be separately regarded as works of accomplished art. Even the later
and more imitative examples profess little more than
picturesque vigour or ingenious intricacy. The oak
leaves and acorns of the Beauvais mouldings are
superbly wreathed, but rigidly repeated in a constant
pattern; the stems are without character, and the
acorns huge, straight, blunt, and unsightly. Round
the southern door of the Florentine duomo runs a
border of fig-leaves, each leaf modulated as if dew

had just dried from off it—yet each alike, so as to secure the ordered symmetry of classical enrichment. But the Gothic fulness of thought is not therefore left without expression ; at the edge of each leaf is an animal, first a cicala; then a lizard, then a bird, moth, serpent, snail—all different, and each wrought to the very life—panting—plumy—writhing—glittering —full of breath and power. This harmony of classical restraint with exhaustless fancy, and of architectural propriety with imitative finish, is found throughout all the fine periods of the Italian Gothic, opposed to the wildness without invention, and exuberance without completion, of the North.

45. One other distinction we must notice, in the treatment of the Niche and its accessories. In Northern Gothic the niche frequently consists only of a bracket and canopy—the latter attached to the wall, independent of columnar support, pierced into openwork profusely rich, and often prolonged upwards into a crocketed pinnacle of indefinite height. But in the niche of pure Italian Gothic the classic principle of columnar support is never lost sight of. Even when its canopy is actually supported by the wall behind, it is apparently supported by two columns in front, perfectly formed with bases and capitals :—(the support of the Northern niche—if it have any—commonly takes the form of a buttress) :—when it appears as a de-

tached pinnacle, it is supported on four columns, the canopy trefoliated with very obtuse cusps, richly charged with foliage in the foliating space, but undecorated at the cusp points, and terminating above in a smooth pyramid, void of all ornament, and never very acute. This form, modified only by various grouping, is that of the noble sepulchral monuments of Verona, Lucca, Pisa, and Bologna; on a small scale it is at Venice associated with the cupola, in St. Mark's, as well as in Santa Fosca, and other minor churches. At Pisa, in the Spina chapel it occurs in its most exquisite form, the columns there being chased with chequer patterns of great elegance. The windows of the Florence cathedral are all placed under a flat canopy of the same form, the columns being elongated, twisted, and enriched with mosaic patterns. The reader must at once perceive how vast is the importance of the difference in system with respect to this member; the whole of the rich, cavernous chiaroscuro of Northern Gothic being dependent on the accumulation of its niches.

46. In passing to the examination of our Author's theory as tested by the progress of Sculpture, we are still struck by his utter want of attention to physical advantages or difficulties. He seems to have forgotten from the first, that the mountains of Syene are not the rocks of Paros. Neither the social

habits nor intellectual powers of the Greek had so
much share in inducing his advance in Sculpture
beyond the Egyptian, as the difference between
marble and syenite, porphyry or alabaster. Marble
not only gave the power, it actually introduced the
thought of representation or realization of form, as
opposed to the mere suggestive abstraction : its
translucency, tenderness of surface, and equality of
tint tempting by utmost reward to the finish which
of all substances it alone admits :—even ivory receiving not so delicately, as alabaster endures not
so firmly, the lightest, latest touches of the com-
pleting chisel. The finer feeling of the hand cannot
be put upon a hard rock like syenite—the blow
must be firm and fearless—the traceless, tremulous
difference between common and immortal sculpture
cannot be set upon it—it cannot receive the en-
chanted strokes which, like Aaron's incense, separate
the Living and the Dead. Were it otherwise, were
finish possible, the variegated and lustrous surface
would not exhibit it to the eye. The imagination
itself is blunted by the resistance of the material,
and by the necessity of absolute predetermination of
all it would achieve. Retraction of all thought into
determined and simple forms, such as might be
fearlessly wrought, necessarily remained the characteristic of the school. The size of the edifice induced

5

by other causes above stated, further limited the
efforts of the sculptor. No colossal figure can be
minutely finished; nor can it easily be conceived
except under an imperfect form. It is a representation of Impossibility, and every effort at completion
adds to the monstrous sense of Impossibility. Space
would altogether fail us were we even to name one-
half of the circumstances which influence the treatment of light and shade to be seen at vast distances
upon surfaces of variegated or dusky colour; or of
the necessities by which, in masses of huge proportion, the mere laws of gravity, and the difficulty
of clearing the substance out of vast hollows neither
to be reached nor entered, bind the realization of
absolute form. Yet all these Lord Lindsay ought
rigidly to have examined, before venturing to determine anything respecting the mental relations of the
Greek and Egyptian. But the fact of his overlooking these inevitablenesses of material is inti-
mately connected with the worst flaw of his theory
—his idea of a Perfection resultant from a balance
of elements; a perfection which all experience has
shown to be neither desirable nor possible.

47. His account of Niccola Pisano, the founder of
the first great school of middle age sculpture, is thus
introduced :—

"Niccola's peculiar praise is this,—that, in practice at

least, if not in theory, he first established the principle that the study of nature, corrected by the ideal of the antique, and animated by the spirit of Christianity, personal and social, can alone lead to excellence in art : —each of the three elements of human nature—Matter, Mind, and Spirit—being thus brought into union and co-operation in the service of God, in due relative harmony and subordination. I cannot over-estimate the import-ance of this principle ; it was on this that, consciously or unconsciously, Niccola himself worked—it has been by following it that Donatello and Ghiberti, Leonardo, Raphael, and Michael Angelo have risen to glory. The Sienese school and the Florentine, minds contemplative and dramatic, are alike beholden to it for whatever success has attended their efforts. Like a treble-stranded rope, it drags after it the triumphal car of Christian Art. But if either of the strands be broken, if either of the three elements be pursued disjointedly from the other two, the result is, in each respective case, grossness, pedantry, or weakness :—the exclusive imitation of Nature produces a Caravaggio, a Rubens, a Rembrandt—that of the Antique, a Pellegrino di Tibaldo and a David ; and though there be a native chastity and taste in religion, which restrains those who worship it too abstractedly from Intellect and Sense, from running into such extremes, it cannot at least supply that mechanical apparatus which will enable them to soar :—such devotees must be content to gaze up into heaven, like angels cropt of their wings." —Vol. ii., pp. 102-3.

48. This is mere Bolognese eclecticism in other terms, and those terms incorrect. We are amazed to find a writer usually thoughtful, if not accurate, thus indolently adopting the worn-out falsities of our

weakest writers on Taste. Does he—can he for an
instant suppose that the ruffian Caravaggio, distinguished only by his preference of candlelight and
black shadows for the illustration and reinforcement
of villany, painted nature—mere nature—exclusive
nature, more painfully or heartily than John Bellini
or Raphael? Does he not see that whatever men
imitate must be nature of some kind, material nature
or spiritual, lovely or foul, brutal or human, but
nature still? Does he himself see in mere, external,
copyable nature, no more than Caravaggio saw, or
in the Antique no more than has been comprehended
by David? The fact is, that all artists are primarily
divided into the two great groups of Imitators and
Suggestors—their falling into one or other being dependent partly on disposition, and partly on the
matter they have to subdue—(thus Perugino imitates
line by line with pencilled gold, the hair which Nino
Pisano can only suggest by a gilded marble mass,
both having the will of representation alike). And
each of these classes is again divided into the
faithful and unfaithful imitators and suggestors ; and
that is a broad question of blind eye and hard
heart, or seeing eye and serious heart, always co-
existent ; and then the faithful imitators and suggestors
—artists proper, are appointed, each with his peculiar
gift and affection, over the several orders and classes

of things natural, to be by them illumined and set forth.

49. And that is God's doing and distributing; and none is rashly to be thought inferior to another, as if by his own fault; nor any of them stimulated to emulation, and changing places with others, although their allotted tasks be of different dignities, and their granted instruments of differing keenness; for in none of them can there be a perfection or balance of all human attributes;—the great colourist becomes gradually insensible to the refinements of form which he at first intentionally omitted; the master of line is inevitably dead to many of the delights of colour; the study of the true or ideal human form is inconsistent with the love of its most spiritual expressions. To one it is intrusted to record the historical realities of his age; in him the perception of character is subtle, and that of abstract beauty in measure diminished; to another, removed to the desert, or enclosed in the cloister, is given, not the noting of things transient, but the revealing of things eternal. Ghirlandajo and Titian painted men, but could not angels; Duccio and Angelico painted Saints, but could not senators. One is ordered to copy material form lovingly and slowly—his the fine finger and patient will: to another are sent visions and dreams upon the bed—his the hand fearful and swift, and impulse

of passion irregular and wild. We may have occasion
further to insist upon this great principle of the
incommunicableness and singleness of all the highest
powers; but we assert it here especially, in opposition
to the idea, already so fatal to art, that either the aim
of the antique may take place together with the purposes, or its traditions become elevatory of the power,
of Christian art; or that the glories of Giotto and the
Sienese are in any wise traceable through Niccola
Pisano to the venerable relics of the Campo Santo.

50. Lord Lindsay's statement, as far as it regards
Niccola himself, is true.

"His improvement in Sculpture is attributable, in the
first instance, to the study of an ancient sarcophagus,
brought from Greece by the ships of Pisa in the eleventh
century, and which, after having stood beside the door of
the Duomo for many centuries as the tomb of the Countess
Beatrice, mother of the celebrated Matilda, has been recently removed to the Campo Santo. The front is sculptured
in bas-relief, in two compartments, the one representing
Hippolytus rejecting the suit of Phædra, the other his
departure for the chase :—such at least is the most plausible
interpretation. The sculpture, if not super-excellent, is
substantially good, and the benefit derived from it by
Niccola is perceptible on the slightest examination of his
works. Other remains of antiquity are preserved at Pisa,
which he may have also studied, but this was the classic
well from which he drew those waters which became wine
when poured into the hallowing chalice of Christianity. I
need scarcely add that the mere presence of such models

would have availed little, had not nature endowed him with the quick eye and the intuitive apprehension of genius, together with a purity of taste which taught him how to select, how to modify and how to reinspire the germs of excellence thus presented to him."—Vol. ii., pp. 104, 105.

51. But whatever characters peculiarly classical were impressed upon Niccola by this study, died out gradually among his scholars; and in Orcagna the Byzantine manner finally triumphed, leading the way to the purely Christian sculpture of the school of Fiesole, in its turn swept away by the returning wave of classicalism. The sculpture of Orcagna, Giotto, and Mino da Fiesole, would have been what it was, if Niccola had been buried in his sarcophagus; and this is sufficiently proved by Giotto's remaining entirely uninfluenced by the educated excellence of Andrea Pisano, while he gradually bent the Pisan down to his own uncompromising simplicity. If, as Lord Lindsay asserts, "Giotto had learned from the works of Niccola the grand principle of Christian art," the sculptures of the Campanile of Florence would not now have stood forth in contrasted awfulness of simplicity, beside those of the south door of the Baptistery.

52. "Andrea's merit was indeed very great; his works, compared with those of Giovanni and Niccola Pisano, exhibit a progress in design, grace, composition and mechanical execution, at first sight unaccountable—a chasm yawns between them, deep and broad, over which the younger artist seems to have leapt at a bound,—the stream

that sank into the earth at Pisa emerges a river at Florence.
The solution of the mystery lies in the peculiar plasticity
of Andrea's genius, and the ascendancy acquired over it
by Giotto, although a younger man, from the first moment
they came into contact.   Giotto had learnt from the works
of Niccola the grand principle of Christian art, imperfectly
apprehended by Giovanni and his other pupils, and by
following up which he had in the natural course of things
improved upon his prototype.   He now repaid to Sculpture,
in the person of Andrea, the sum of improvement in which
he stood her debtor in that of Niccola:—so far, that is to
say, as the treasury of Andrea's mind was capable of taking
it in, for it would be an error to suppose that Andrea
profited by Giotto in the same independent manner or
degree that Giotto profited by Niccola.   Andrea's was not
a mind of strong individuality; he became completely
Giottesque in thought and style, and as Giotto and he
continued intimate friends through life, the impression
never wore off:—most fortunate, indeed, that it was so,
for the welfare of Sculpture in general, and for that of the
buildings in decorating which the friends worked in concert.

   " Happily, Andrea's most important work, the bronze
door of the Baptistery, still exists, and with every prospect
of preservation.   It is adorned with bas-reliefs from the
history of S. John, with allegorical figures of virtues and
heads of prophets, all most beautiful,—the historical compositions distinguished by simplicity and purity of feeling
and   design,   the   allegorical   virtues   perhaps   still   more
expressive, and full of poetry in their symbols and attitudes;
the whole series is executed with a delicacy of workmanship till then unknown in bronze, a precision yet softness
of touch resembling that of a skilful performer on the
pianoforte.   Andrea was occupied upon it for nine years,
from 1330 to 1339, and when finished, fixed in its place,

and exposed to view, the public enthusiasm exceeded all
bounds; the Signoria, with unexampled condescension,
visited it in state, accompanied by the ambassadors of
Naples and Sicily, and bestowed on the fortunate artist
the honour and privilege of citizenship, seldom accorded
to foreigners unless of lofty rank or exalted merit. The
door remained in its original position—facing the Cathedral
—till superseded in that post of honour by the 'Gate of
Paradise,' cast by Ghiberti. It was then transferred to the
Southern entrance of the Baptistery, facing the Miseri-
cordia."—Vol. ii., pp. 125—128.

53. A few pages farther on, the question of *Giotto's*
claim to the authorship of the designs for this door
is discussed at length, and, to the annihilation of the
honour here attributed to *Andrea*, determined affirma-
tively, partly on the testimony of Vasari, partly on
internal evidence—these designs being asserted by
our author to be "thoroughly Giottesque." But, not
to dwell on Lord Lindsay's inconsistency, in the
ultimate decision his discrimination seems to us
utterly at fault. Giotto has, we conceive, suffered
quite enough in the abduction of the work in the
Campo Santo, which was worthy of him, without
being made answerable for these designs of Andrea.
That he gave a rough draft of many of them,
is conceivable; but if even he did this, Andrea has
added cadenzas of drapery, and other scholarly commonplace, as a bad singer puts ornament into an
air. It was not of such teaching that came the

"Jabal" of Giotto. Sitting at his tent door, he withdraws its rude drapery with one hand: three sheep
only are feeding before him, the watchdog sitting
beside them; but he looks forth like a Destiny, be-
holding the ruined cities of the earth become places,
like the valley of Achor, for herds to lie down in.

54. We have not space to follow our author through
his very interesting investigation of the comparatively
unknown schools of Teutonic sculpture. With one
beautiful anecdote, breathing the whole spirit of the
time—the mingling of deep piety with the modest,
manly pride of art—our readers must be indulged :—

"The Florentine Ghiberti gives a most interesting account
of a sculptor of Cologne in the employment of Charles
of Anjou, King of Naples, whose skill he parallels with
that of the statuaries of ancient Greece; his heads, he
says, and his design of the naked, were 'maravigliosa-
mente bene,' his style full of grace, his sole defect the
somewhat curtailed stature of his figures. He was no
less excellent in minuter works as a goldsmith, and in
that capacity had worked for his patron a 'tavola d'oro,'
a tablet or screen (apparently) of gold, with his utmost
care and skill; it was a work of exceeding beauty—but
in some political exigency his patron wanted money, and
it was broken up before his eyes. Seeing his labour vain
and the pride of his heart rebuked, he threw himself on
the ground, and uplifting his eyes and hands to heaven,
prayed in contrition, 'Lord God Almighty, Governor and
disposer of heaven and earth! Thou hast opened mine
eyes that I follow from henceforth none other than Thee—

Have mercy upon me!'—He forthwith gave all he had to the poor for the love of God, and went up into a mountain where there was a great hermitage, and dwelt there the rest of his days in penitence and sanctity, surviving down to the days of Pope Martin, who reigned from 1281 to 1284. 'Certain youths,' adds Ghiberti, 'who sought to be skilled in statuary, told me how he was versed both in painting and sculpture, and how he had painted in the Romitorio where he lived; he was an excellent draughtsman and very courteous. When the youths who wished to improve visited him, he received them with much humility, giving them learned instructions, showing them various proportions, and drawing for them many examples, for he was most accomplished in his art. And thus,' he concludes, 'with great humility, he ended his days in that hermitage."—Vol. iii., pp. 257—259.

55. We could have wished that Lord Lindsay had further insisted on what will be found to be a characteristic of all the truly Christian or spiritual, as opposed to classical, schools of sculpture—the scenic or painter-like management of effect. The marble is not cut into the actual form of the thing imaged, but oftener into a perspective suggestion of it—the bas-reliefs sometimes almost entirely undercut, and sharp-edged, so as to come clear off a dark ground of shadow; even heads the size of life being in this way rather shadowed out than carved out, as the Madonna of Benedetto da Majano in Santa Maria Novella, one of the cheeks being advanced half an inch out of its proper place—and often the

most audacious violations of proportion admitted, as
in the limbs of Michael Angelo's sitting Madonna in
the Uffizii; all artifices, also, of deep and sharp
cutting being allowed, to gain the shadowy and
spectral expressions about the brow and lip which
the mere actualities of form could not have conveyed ;—the sculptor never following a material model,
but feeling after the most momentary and subtle
aspects of the countenance—striking these out sometimes suddenly, by rude chiselling, and stopping the
instant they are attained—never risking the loss of
thought by the finishing of flesh surface. The heads
of the Medici sacristy we believe to have been thus
left unfinished, as having already the utmost expression which the marble could receive, and incapable
of anything but loss from further touches. So with
Mino da Fiesole and Jacopo della Quercia, the workmanship is often hard, sketchy, and angular, having
its full effect only at a little distance; but at that
distance the statue becomes ineffably alive, even to
startling, bearing an aspect of change and uncertainty, as if it were about to vanish, and withal
having a light, and sweetness, and incense of passion
upon it that silences the looker-on, half in delight,
half in expectation. This daring stroke—this trans-
figuring tenderness—may be shown to characterize
all truly Christian sculpture, as compared with the

antique, or the pseudo-classical of subsequent periods.
We agree with Lord Lindsay in thinking the Psyche
of Naples the nearest approach to the Christian ideal
of all ancient efforts; but even in this the approximation is more accidental than real—a fair type of
feature, further exalted by the mode in which the
imagination supplies the lost upper folds of the hair.
The fountain of life and emotion remains sealed; nor
was the opening of that fountain due to any study
of the far less pure examples accessible by the Pisan
sculptors. The sound of its waters had been heard
long before in the aisles of the Lombard; nor was it
by Ghiberti, still less by Donatello, that the bed of
that Jordan was dug deepest, but by Michael Angelo
(the last heir of the Byzantine traditions descending
through Orcagna), opening thenceforward through
thickets darker and more dark, and with waves ever
more soundless and slow, into the Dead Sea wherein
its waters have been stayed.

56. It is time for us to pass to the subject which
occupies the largest portion of the work—the History

"of Painting, as developed contemporaneously with her
sister, Sculpture, and (like her) under the shadow of the
Gothic Architecture, by Giotto and his successors throughout
Italy, by Mino, Duccio, and their scholars at Siena, by
Orcagna and Fra Angelico da Fiesole at Florence, and by
the obscure but interesting primitive school of Bologna,
during the fourteenth and the early years of the fifteenth

century. The period is one, comparatively speaking, of repose and tranquillity,—the storm sleeps and the winds are still, the currents set in one direction, and we may sail from isle to isle over a sunny sea, dallying with the time, secure of a cloudless sky and of the greetings of innocence and love wheresoever the breeze may waft us. There is in truth a holy purity, an innocent naïveté, a child-like grace and simplicity, a freshness, a fearlessness, an utter freedom from affectation, a yearning after all things truthful, lovely and of good report, in the productions of this early time, which invest them with a charm peculiar in its kind, and which few even of the most perfect works of the maturer era can boast of,—and hence the risk and danger of becoming too passionately attached to them, of losing the power of discrimination, of admiring and imitating their defects as well as their beauties, of running into affectation in seeking after simplicity and into exaggeration in our efforts to be in earnest,—in a word, of forgetting that in art, as in human nature, it is the balance, harmony, and co-equal development of Sense, Intellect, and Spirit, which constitute perfection."—Vol. ii., pp. 161—163.

57. To the thousand islands, or how many soever they may be, we shall allow ourselves to be wafted with all willingness, but not in Lord Lindsay's three-masted vessel, with its balancing topmasts of Sense, Intellect, and Spirit. We are utterly tired of the triplicity; and we are mistaken if its application here be not as inconsistent as it is arbitrary. Turning back to the introduction, which we have quoted, the reader will find that while Architecture is there taken

for the exponent of Sense, Painting is chosen as the peculiar expression of Spirit. "The painting of Christendom is that of an immortal spirit conversing with its God." But in a note to the first chapter of the second volume, he will be surprised to find painting become a "twin of intellect," and architecture suddenly advanced from a type of sense to a type of spirit :—

"Sculpture and Painting, twins of Intellect, rejoice and breathe freest in the pure ether of Architecture, or Spirit, like Castor or Pollux under the breezy heaven of their father Jupiter."—Vol. ii., p. 14.

58. Prepared by this passage to consider painting either as spiritual or intellectual, his patience may pardonably give way on finding in the sixth letter— (what he might, however, have conjectured from the heading of the third period in the chart of the schools)—that the peculiar prerogative of painting— colour, is to be considered as a *sensual* element, and the exponent of sense, in accordance with a new analogy, here for the first time proposed, between spirit, intellect, and sense, and expression, form, and colour. Lord Lindsay is peculiarly unfortunate in his adoptions from previous writers. He has taken this division of art from Fuseli and Reynolds, without perceiving that in those writers it is one of convenience merely, and, even so considered, is as injudicious as illogical. In what does expression consist but in form and

colour ? It is one of the ends which these accomplish, and may be itself an attribute of both. Colour may be expressive or inexpressive, like music ; form expressive or inexpressive, like words ; but expression by itself cannot exist ; so that to divide painting into colour, form, and expression, is precisely as rational as to divide music into notes, words, and expression. Colour may be pensive, severe, exciting, appalling, gay, glowing, or sensual ; in all these modes it is expressive : form may be tender or abrupt, mean or majestic, attractive or overwhelming, discomfortable or delightsome ; in all these modes, and many more, it is expressive ; and if Lord Lindsay's analogy be in anywise applicable to either form or colour, we should have colour sensual (Correggio), colour intellectual (Tintoret), colour spiritual (Angelico)—form sensual (French sculpture), form intellectual (Phidias), form spiritual (Michael Angelo). Above all, our author should have been careful how he attached the epithet "sensual" to the element of colour—not only on account of the glaring inconsistency with his own previous assertion of the spirituality of painting— (since it is certainly not merely by being flat instead of solid, representative instead of actual, that painting is—if it be—more spiritual than sculpture) ; but also, because this idea of sensuality in colour has had much share in rendering abortive the efforts of the modern

German religious painters, inducing their abandonment of its consecrating, kindling, purifying power.

59. Lord Lindsay says, in a passage which we shall presently quote, that the most sensual as well as the most religious painters have always loved the brightest colours. Not so; no painters ever were more sensual than the modern French, who are alike insensible to, and incapable of colour—depending altogether on morbid gradation, waxy smoothness of surface, and lusciousness of line, the real elements of sensuality wherever it eminently exists. So far from good colour being sensual, it saves, glorifies, and guards from all evil: it is with Titian, as with all great masters of flesh-painting, the redeeming and protecting element; and with the religious painters, it is a baptism with fire, an under-song of holy Litanies. Is it in sensuality that the fair flush opens upon the cheek of Francia's chanting angel,* until we think it comes, and fades, and returns, as his voice and his harping are louder or lower—or that the silver light rises upon wave after wave of his lifted hair; or that the burning of the blood is seen on the unclouded brows of the three angels of the Campo Santo, and of folded fire within their wings; or that the hollow blue of the highest heaven mantles the Madonna with its depth, and falls around her

* At the feet of his Madonna, in the Gallery of Bologna.

6

like raiment, as she sits beneath the throne of the
Sistine Judgment ?   Is it in sensuality that the visible
world about us is girded with an eternal iris ?—is
there pollution in the rose and the gentian more than
in the rocks that are trusted to their robing ?—is
the sea-blue a stain upon its water, or the scarlet
spring of day upon the mountains less holy than
their snow ?   As well call the sun itself, or the
firmament, sensual, as the colour which flows from
the one, and fills the other.

60. We deprecate this rash assumption, however,
with more regard to the forthcoming portion of the
history, in which we fear it may seriously diminish
the value of the author's account of the school of
Venice, than to the part at present executed.   This
is written in a spirit rather sympathetic than critical,
and rightly illustrates the feeling of early art, even
where it mistakes, or leaves unanalyzed, the technical
modes of its expression.   It will be better, perhaps,
that we confine our attention to the accounts of the
three men who may be considered as sufficient repre-
sentatives not only of the art of their time, but of
all subsequent ; Giotto, the first of the great line of
dramatists, terminating in Raffaelle ; Orcagna, the
head of that branch of the contemplative school which
leans towards sadness or terror, terminating in Michael
Angelo ; and Angelico, the head of the contemplatives

concerned with the heavenly ideal, around whom may
be grouped first Duccio, and the Sienese, who preceded
him, and afterwards Pinturiccio, Perugino, and Leonardo
da Vinci.

61. The fourth letter opens in the fields of Ves-
pignano. The circumstances of the finding of Giotto
by Cimabue are well known. Vasari's anecdote of
the fly painted upon the nose of one of Cimabue's
figures might, we think, have been spared, or at least
not instanced as proof of study from nature "nobly
rewarded." Giotto certainly never either attempted
or accomplished any small imitation of this kind ;
the story has all the look of one of the common
inventions of the ignorant for the ignorant ; nor, if
true, would Cimabue's careless mistake of a black
spot in the shape of a fly for one of the living
annoyances of which there might probably be some
dozen or more upon his panel at any moment, have
been a matter of much credit to his young pupil.
The first point of any real interest is Lord Lindsay's
confirmation of Förster's attribution of the Campo
Santo Life of Job, till lately esteemed Giotto's, to
Francesco da Volterra. Förster's evidence appears
incontrovertible ; yet there is curious internal evidence, we think, in favour of the designs being
Giotto's, if not the execution. The landscape is
especially Giottesque, the trees being all boldly massed

first with dark brown, within which the leaves are
painted separately in light: this very archaic treatment
had been much softened and modified by the Giotteschi
before the date assigned to these frescoes by Förster.
But, what is more singular, the figure of Eliphaz,
or the foremost of the three friends, occurs in a
tempera picture of Giotto's in the Academy of Florence,
the Ascension, among the apostles on the left; while
the face of another of the three friends is again
repeated in the "Christ disputing with the Doctors"
of the small tempera series, also in the Academy;
the figure of Satan shows much analogy to that of
the Envy of the Arena chapel; and many other portions of the design are evidently either sketches of
this very subject by Giotto himself, or dexterous
compilations from his works by a loving pupil. Lord
Lindsay has not done justice to the upper division—
the Satan before God: it is one of the very finest
thoughts ever realized by the Giotteschi. The serenity
of power in the principal figure is very noble; no
expression of wrath, or even of scorn, in the look
which commands the evil spirit. The position of the
latter, and countenance, are less grotesque and more
demoniacal than is usual in paintings of the time;
the triple wings expanded—the arms crossed over
the breast, and holding each other above the elbow,
the claws fixing in the flesh; a serpent buries its

head in a cleft in the bosom, and the right hoof is
lifted, as if to stamp.

62. We should have been glad if Lord Lindsay
had given us some clearer idea of the internal evidence
on which he founds his determination of the order
or date of the works of Giotto. When no trustworthy
records exist, we conceive this task to be of singular
difficulty, owing to the differences of execution universally existing between the large and small works
of the painter. The portrait of Dante in the chapel
of the Podestà is proved by Dante's exile, in 1302,
to have been painted before Giotto was six and twenty;
yet we remember no head in any of his works which
can be compared with it for carefulness of finish and
truth of drawing; the crudeness of the material van-
quished by dexterous hatching; the colour not only
pure, but deep—a rare virtue with Giotto; the eye soft
and thoughtful, the brow nobly modelled. In the fresco
of the Death of the Baptist, in Santa Croce, which we
agree with Lord Lindsay in attributing to the same
early period, the face of the musician is drawn with
great refinement, and considerable power of rounding
surfaces—(though in the drapery may be remarked a
very singular piece of archaic treatment : it is warm
white, with yellow stripes ; the dress itself falls in deep
folds, but the striped pattern does not follow the fold-
ings—it is drawn across, as if with a straight ruler).

63. But passing from these frescoes, which are
nearly the size of life, to those of the Arena chapel at
Padua, erected in 1303, decorated in 1306, which are
much smaller, we find the execution proportionably less
dexterous. Of this famous chapel Lord Lindsay says—
" nowhere (save in the Duomo of Orvieto) is the legendary
history of the Virgin told with such minuteness.

"The heart must indeed be cold to the charms of
youthful art that can enter this little sanctuary without
a glow of delight. From the roof, with its sky of ultramarine, powdered with stars and interspersed with
medallions containing the heads of our Saviour, the
Virgin and the Apostles, to the mock panelling of the
nave, below the windows, the whole is completely covered
with frescoes, in excellent preservation, and all more or
less painted by Giotto's own hand, except six in the
tribune, which however have apparently been executed
from his cartoons . . . .

"These frescoes form a most important document in
the history of Giotto's mind, exhibiting all his peculiar
merits, although in a state as yet of immature development. They are full of fancy and invention ; the composition is almost always admirable, although sometimes
too studiously symmetrical ; the figures are few and
characteristic, each speaking for itself, the impersonation
of a distinct idea, and most dramatically grouped and
contrasted ; the attitudes are appropriate, easy, and natural ;
the action and gesticulation singularly vivid ; the expression
is excellent, except when impassioned grief induces caricature :—devoted to the study of Nature as he is, Giotto
had not yet learnt that it is suppressed feeling which
affects one most. The head of our Saviour is beautiful
throughout—that of the Virgin not so good—she is modest,

but not very graceful or celestial;—it was long before
he succeeded in his Virgins—they are much too matronly :
among the accessory figures, graceful female forms occasionally appear, foreshadowing those of his later works
at Florence and Naples, yet they are always clumsy
about the waist and bust, and most of them are under-
jawed, which certainly detracts from the sweetness of the
female countenance. His delineation of the naked is excellent, as compared with the works of his predecessors,
but far unequal to what he attained in his later years,—
the drapery, on the contrary, is noble, majestic, and
statuesque; the colouring is still pale and weak,—it was
long ere he improved in this point; the landscape displays little or no amendment upon the Byzantine; the
architecture, that of the fourteenth century, is to the
figures that people it in the proportion of dolls' houses
to the children that play with them,—an absurdity long
unthinkingly acquiesced in, from its occurrence in the
classic bas-reliefs from which it had been traditionally
derived ;—and, finally, the lineal perspective is very fair,
and in three of the compositions an excellent effect is
produced by the introduction of the same background
with varied *dramatis personæ*, reminding one of Retzsch's
illustrations of Faust. The animals too are always excellent, full of spirit and character."—Vol. ii., pp. 183—199.

64. This last characteristic is especially to be noticed.
It is a touching proof of the influence of early years.
Giotto was only ten years old when he was taken
from following the sheep. For the rest, as we have
above stated, the manipulation of these frescoes is
just as far inferior to that of the Podestà chapel as
their dimensions are less; and we think it will be

found generally that the smaller the work the more
rude is Giotto's hand. In this respect he seems to
differ from all other masters.

"It is not difficult, gazing on these silent but eloquent
walls, to repeople them with the group once, as we
know—five hundred years ago—assembled within them,—
Giotto intent upon his work, his wife Ciuta admiring his
progress, and Dante, with abstracted eye, alternately conversing with his friend and watching the gambols of the
children playing on the grass before the door. It is
generally affirmed that Dante, during this visit, inspired
Giotto with his taste for allegory, and that the Virtues
and Vices of the Arena were the first fruits of their intercourse; it is possible, certainly, but I doubt it,—allegory
was the universal language of the time, as we have seen in
the history of the Pisan school."—Vol. ii., pp. 199, 200.

It ought to have been further mentioned, that the
representation of the Virtues and Vices under these
Giottesque figures continued long afterwards. We
find them copied, for instance, on the capitals of the
Ducal Palace at Venice, with an amusing variation
on the "Stultitia," who has neither Indian dress nor
club, as with Giotto, but is to the Venetians sufficiently distinguished by riding a horse.

65. The notice of the frescoes at Assisi consists
of little more than an enumeration of the subjects,
accompanied by agreeable translations of the traditions respecting St. Francis, embodied by St. Buona-
ventura. Nor have we space to follow the author

through his examination of Giotto's works at Naples
and Avignon. The following account of the erection
of the Campanile of Florence is too interesting to be
omitted :—

"Giotto was chosen to erect it, on the ground avowedly
of the universality of his talents, with the appointment
of Capo-maestro, or chief architect of the Cathedral and
its dependencies, a yearly salary of one hundred gold
florins, and the privilege of citizenship, and under the
special understanding that he was not to quit Florence.
His designs being approved of, the republic passed a
decree in the spring of 1334, that 'the Campanile should
be built so as to exceed in magnificence, 'height and excellence of workmanship whatever in that kind had been
achieved of old by the Greeks and Romans in the time
of their utmost power and greatness—"della loro più
florida potenza."' The first stone was laid accordingly,
with great pomp, on the 18th of July following, and the
work prosecuted with such vigour and with such costli-
ness and utter disregard of expense, that a citizen of
Verona, looking on, exclaimed that the republic was
taxing her strength too far,—that the united resources of
two great monarchs would be insufficient to complete it;
a *criticism which the Signoria resented by confining him
for two months in prison*, and afterwards conducting him
through the public treasury, to teach him that the
Florentines could build their whole city of marble, and
not one poor steeple only, were they so inclined.

"Giotto made a model of his proposed structure, on
which every stone was marked, and the successive
courses painted red and white, according to his design,
so as to match with the Cathedral and Baptistery; this
model was of course adhered to strictly during the short

remnant of his life, and the work was completed in strict conformity to it after his death, with the exception of the spire, which, the taste having changed, was never added. He had intended it to be one hundred *braccia*, or one hundred and fifty feet high."—Vol. ii., pp. 247—249.

The deficiency of the spire Lord Lindsay does not regret :—

"Let the reader stand before the Campanile, and ask himself whether, with Michael Scott at his elbow, or Aladdin's lamp in his hand, he would supply the deficiency? I think not."—p. 38.

We have more faith in Giotto than our author—and we will reply to his question by two others— whether, looking down upon Florence from the hill of San Miniato, his eye rested oftener and more affectionately on the Campanile of Giotto, or on the simple tower and spire of Santa Maria Novella ?— and whether, in the backgrounds of Perugino, he would willingly substitute for the church spires invariably introduced, flat-topped campaniles like the unfinished tower of Florence ?

66. Giotto sculptured with his own hand two of the bas-reliefs of this campanile, and probably might have executed them all. But the purposes of his life had been accomplished ; he died at Florence on the 8th of January, 1337. The concluding notice of his character and achievement is highly valuable.

67. "Painting indeed stands indebted to Giotto beyond

any of her children. His history is a most instructive one. Endowed with the liveliest fancy, and with that facility which so often betrays genius, and achieving in youth a reputation which the age of Methuselah could not have added to, he had yet the discernment to perceive how much still remained to be done, and the resolution to bind himself (as it were) to Nature's chariot wheel, confident that she would ere long emancipate and own him as her son. Calm and unimpassioned, he seems to have commenced his career with a deliberate survey of the difficulties he had to encounter and of his resources for the conflict, and then to have worked upon a system steadily and perseveringly, prophetically sure of victory. His life was indeed one continued triumph,—and no conqueror ever mounted to the Capitol with a step more equal and sedate. We find him, at first, slowly and cautiously endeavouring to infuse new life into the tradi tional compositions, by substituting the heads, attitudes, and drapery of the actual world for the spectral forms and conventional types of the mosaics and the Byzantine painters,—idealising them when the personages represented were of higher mark and dignity, but in none ever out-stepping truth. Advancing in his career, we find year by year the fruits of continuous unwearied study in a consistent and equable contemporary improvement in all the various minuter though most important departments of his art, in his design, his drapery, his colouring, in the dignity and expression of his men and in the grace of his women—asperities softened down, little graces unexpectedly born and playing about his path, as if to make amends for the deformity of his actual offspring— touches, daily more numerous, of that nature which makes the world akin—and ever and always a keen yet cheerful sympathy with life, a playful humour mingling with his graver lessons, which affects us the more as coming from one who, knowing himself an object personally of disgust and ridicule, could yet satirise with a smile.

"Finally, throughout his works, we are conscious of an earnest, a lofty, a religious aim and purpose, as of one who felt himself a pioneer of civilization in a newly-discovered world, the Adam of a new Eden freshly planted in the earth's wilderness, a mouthpiece of God and a preacher of righteousness to mankind.—And here we must establish a distinction very necessary to be recognised before we can duly appreciate the relative merits of the elder painters in this, the most important point in which we can view their character. Giotto's genius, however universal, was still (as I have repeatedly observed) Dramatic rather than Contemplative,—a tendency in which his scholars and successors almost to a man resembled him. Now, just as in actual life—where, with a few rare exceptions, all men rank under two great categories according as Imagination or Reason predominates in their intellectual character—two individuals may be equally impressed with the truths of Christianity and yet differ essentially in its outward manifestation, the one dwelling in action, the other in contemplation, the one in strife, the other in peace, the one (so to speak) in hate, the other in love, the one struggling with devils, the other communing with angels, yet each serving as a channel of God's mercies to man, each (we may believe) offering Him service equally acceptable in His sight—even so shall we find it in art and with artists; few in whom the Dramatic power predominates will be found to excel in the expression of religious emotions of the more abstract and enthusiastic cast, even although men of indisputably pure and holy character themselves; and *vice versâ*, few of the more Contem-

plative but will feel bewildered and at fault, if they
descend from their starry region of light into the grosser
atmosphere that girdles in this world of action. The
works of artists are their minds' mirror; they cannot
express what they do not feel; each class dwells apart
and seeks its ideal in a distinct sphere of emotion,—
their object is different, and their success proportioned
to the exclusiveness with which they pursue that object.
A few indeed there have been in all ages, monarchs of
the mind and types of our Saviour, who have lived a
two-fold existence of action and contemplation in art, in
song, in politics, and in daily life; of these have been
Abraham, Moses, David, and Cyrus in the elder world—
Alfred, Charlemagne, Dante, and perhaps Shakspeare, in
the new,—and in art, Niccola Pisano, Leonard da Vinci
and Michael Angelo. But Giotto, however great as the
patriarch of his peculiar tribe, was not of these few, and
we ought not therefore to misapprehend him, or be dis-
appointed at finding his Madonnas (for instance) less exquisitely spiritual than the Sienese, or those of Fra
Angelico and some later painters, who seem to have
dipped their pencils in the rainbow that circles the
throne of God,—they are pure and modest, but that is
all; on the other hand, where his Contemplative rivals
lack utterance, he speaks most feelingly to the heart in
his own peculiar language of Dramatic composition—he
glances over creation with the eye of love, all the
charities of life follow in his steps, and his thoughts are
as the breath of the morning. A man of the world,
living in it and loving it, yet with a heart that it could
not spoil nor wean from its allegiance to God—'non
meno buon Cristiano che eccellente pittore,' as Vasari
emphatically describes him—his religion breathes of the
free air of heaven rather than the cloister, neither en-

thusiastic nor superstitious, but practical, manly and
healthy—and this, although the picturesque biographer
of S. Francis!"—Vol. ii., pp. 260—264.

68. This is all as admirably felt as expressed, and
to those acquainted with and accustomed to love the
works of the painter, it leaves nothing to be asked
for ; but we must again remind Lord Lindsay, that
he has throughout left the *artistical* orbit of Giotto
undefined, and the offence of his manner unremoved,
as far as regards the uninitiated spectator. We
question whether from all that he has written, the
untravelled reader could form any distinct idea of
the painter's peculiar merits or methods, or that the
estimate, if formed, might not afterwards expose him
to severe disappointment. It ought especially to
have been stated, that the Giottesque system of
chiaroscuro is one of pure, quiet, pervading daylight.
No *cast* shadows ever occur, and this remains a
marked characteristic of all the works of the Giotteschi. Of course, all subtleties of reflected light or
raised colour are unthought of. Shade is only given
as far as it is necessary to the articulation of simple
forms, nor even then is it rightly adapted to the
colour of the light ; the folds of the draperies are
well drawn, but the entire rounding of them always
missed—the general forms appearing flat, and terminated by equal and severe outlines, while the

masses of ungradated colour often seem to divide the figure into fragments. Thus, the Madonna in the small tempera series of the Academy of Florence, is usually divided exactly in half by the dark mass of her blue robe, falling in a vertical line. In consequence of this defect, the grace of Giotto's composition can hardly be felt until it is put into outline. The colours themselves are of good quality, never glaring, always gladdening, the reds inclining to orange more than purple, yellow frequent, the prevalent tone of the colour groups warm ; the sky always blue, the whole effect somewhat resembling that of the Northern painted glass of the same century—and chastened in the same manner by noble neutral tints or greens ; yet all somewhat unconsidered and unsystematic, painful discords not unfrequent. The material and ornaments of dress are never particularized, no imitations of texture or jewellery, yet shot stuffs of two colours frequent. The drawing often powerful, though of course uninformed ; the mastery of mental expression by bodily motion, and of bodily motion, past and future, by a single gesture, altogether unrivalled even by Raffaelle ;—it is obtained chiefly by throwing the emphasis always on the right line, admitting straight lines of great severity, and never dividing the main drift of the drapery by inferior folds ; neither are

accidents allowed to interfere — the garments fall
heavily and in marked angles—nor are they affected
by the wind, except under circumstances of very
rapid motion. The ideal of the face is often solemn—
seldom beautiful; occasionally ludicrous failures occur:
in the smallest designs the face is very often a
dead letter, or worse: and in all, Giotto's handling
is generally to be distinguished from that of any of
his followers by its bluntness. In the school work
we find sweeter types of feature, greater finish,
stricter care, more delicate outline, fewer errors, but
on the whole less life.

69. Finally, and on this we would especially insist,
Giotto's genius is not to be considered as struggling
with difficulty and repressed by ignorance, but as
appointed, for the good of men, to come into the
world exactly at the time when its rapidity of invention was not likely to be hampered by demands
for imitative dexterity or neatness of finish; and
when, owing to the very ignorance which has been
unwisely regretted, the simplicity of his thoughts
might be uttered with a childlike and innocent
sweetness, never to be recovered in times of prouder
knowledge. The dramatic power of his works,
rightly understood, could receive no addition from
artificial arrangement of shade, or scientific exhibition of anatomy, and we have reason to be deeply

grateful when afterwards "inland far" with Buonaroti and Titian, that we can look back to the
Giotteschi—to see those children

"Sport upon the shore
And hear the mighty waters rolling evermore."

We believe Giotto himself felt this—unquestionably
he could have carried many of his works much
farther in finish, had he so willed it; but he chose
rather to multiply motives than to complete details.
Thus we recur to our great principle of Separate gift.
The man who spends his life in toning colours must
leave the treasures of his invention untold—let each
have his perfect work; and while we thank Bellini
and Leonardo for their deeply wrought dyes, and
life-laboured utterance of passionate thought; let us
remember also what cause, but for the remorseless
destruction of myriads of his works, we should have
had to thank Giotto, in that, abandoning all proud
effort, he chose rather to make the stones of Italy
cry out with one voice of pauseless praise, and to
fill with perpetual remembrance of the Saints he
loved, and perpetual honour of the God he worshipped,
palace chamber and convent cloister, lifted tower and
lengthened wall, from the utmost blue of the plain
of Padua to the Southern wildernesses of the hermit-
haunted Apennine.

70. From the head of the Dramatic branch of Art,

7

we turn to the first of the great Contemplative Triad,
associated, as it most singularly happens in name as
well as in heart; Orcagna=Arcagnuolo; Fra Giovanni
—detto Angelico; and Michael Angelo :—the first two
names being bestowed by contemporary admiration.

"Orcagna was born apparently about the middle of the
(14th) century, and was christened Andrea, by which name,
with the addition of that of his father, Cione, he always
designated himself; that, however, of Orcagna, a corruption
of Arcagnuolo, or 'The Archangel,' was given him by his
contemporaries, and by this he has become known to
posterity.

"The earliest works of Orcagna will be found in that
sanctuary of Semi-Byzantine art, the Campo Santo of Pisa.
He there painted three of the four 'Novissima,' Death,
Judgment, Hell, and Paradise—the two former entirely
himself, the third with the assistance of his brother Ber-
nardo, who is said to have coloured it after his designs.
The first of the series, a most singular performance, had
for centuries been popularly known as the 'Trionfo della
Morte.' It is divided by an immense rock into two irregular portions. In that to the right, Death, personified as
a female phantom, bat-winged, claw-footed, her robe of
linked mail [?] and her long hair streaming on the wind,
swings back her scythe in order to cut down a company
of the rich ones of the earth, Castruccio Castracani and
his gay companions, seated under an orange-grove, and
listening to the music of a troubadour and a female min-
strel; little genii or Cupids, with reversed torches, float
in the air above them; one young gallant caresses his
hawk, a lady her lap-dog,—Castruccio alone looks abstractedly away, as if his thoughts were elsewhere. But all
are alike heedless and unconscious, though the sand is run

out, the scythe falling and their doom sealed. Meanwhile the lame and the halt, the withered and the blind, to whom the heavens are brass and life a burthen, cry on Death with impassioned gestures, to release them from their misery,—but in vain ; she sweeps past, and will not hear them. Between these two groups lie a heap of corpses, mown down already in her flight—kings, queens, bishops, cardinals, young men and maidens, secular and ecclesiastical—ensigned by their crowns, coronets, neck-laces, mitres and helmets—huddled together in hideous confusion ; some are dead, others dying,—angels and devils draw the souls out of their mouths ; that of a nun (in whose hand a purse, firmly clenched, betokens her besetting sin) shrinks back aghast at the unlooked-for sight of the demon who receives it—an idea either inherited or adopted from Andrea Tafi. The whole upper half of the fresco, on this side, is filled with angels and devils carrying souls to heaven or to hell ; sometimes a struggle takes place, and a soul is rescued from a demon who has unwar-rantably appropriated it ; the angels are very graceful, and their intercourse with their spiritual charge is full of tenderness and endearment ; on the other hand, the wicked are hurried off by the devils and thrown headlong into the mouths of hell, represented as the crater of a volcano, belching out flames nearly in the centre of the compo-sition. These devils exhibit every variety of horror in form and feature."—Vol. iii., pp. 130—134.

71. We wish our author had been more specific in his account of this wonderful fresco. The portrait of Castruccio ought to have been signalized as a severe disappointment to the admirers of the heroic Lucchese : the face is flat, lifeless, and sensual, though

fine in feature. The group of mendicants occupying
the centre are especially interesting, as being among
the first existing examples of hard study from the
model : all are evidently portraits—and the effect of
deformity on the lines of the countenance rendered
with appalling truth ; the retractile muscles of the
mouth wrinkled and fixed—the jaws projecting—the
eyes hungry and glaring—the eyebrows grisly and
stiff, the painter having drawn each hair separately :
the two stroppiati with stumps instead of arms are
especially characteristic, as the observer may at once
determine by comparing them with the descendants of
the originals, of whom he will at any time find two,
or more, waiting to accompany his return across the
meadow in front of the Duomo : the old woman also,
nearest of the group, with grey dishevelled hair and
grey coat, with a brown girdle and gourd flask, is
magnificent, and the archetype of all modern conceptions of witch. But the crowning stroke of feeling
is dependent on a circumstance seldom observed. As
Castruccio and his companions are seated under the
shade of an orange grove, so the mendicants are
surrounded by a thicket of *teazles*, and a branch of
ragged thorn is twisted like a crown about their
sickly temples and weedy hair.

72. We do not altogether agree with our author
in thinking that the devils exhibit every variety of

horror; we rather fear that the spectator might at
first be reminded by them of what is commonly
known as the Dragon pattern of Wedgwood ware.
There is invention in them however—and energy;
the eyes are always terrible, though simply drawn—
a black ball set forward, and two-thirds surrounded
by a narrow crescent of white, under a shaggy brow;
the mouths are frequently magnificent; that of a
demon accompanying a thrust of a spear with a growl,
on the right of the picture, is interesting as an example
of the development of the canine teeth noticed by Sir
Charles Bell ('Essay on Expression,' p. 138)—its
capacity of laceration is unlimited : another, snarling
like a tiger at an angel who has pulled a soul out
of his claws, is equally well conceived; we know
nothing like its ferocity except Rembrandt's sketches
of wounded wild beasts. The angels we think generally disappointing; they are for the most part
diminutive in size, and the crossing of the extremities
of the two wings that cover the feet, gives them a
coleopterous, cockchafer look, which is not a little
undignified; the colours of their plumes are somewhat coarse and dark—one is covered with silky hair,
instead of feathers. The souls they contend for are
indeed of sweet expression; but exceedingly earthly
in contour, the painter being unable to deal with the
nude form. On the whole, he seems to have reserved

his highest powers for the fresco which follows next in order, the scene of Resurrection and Judgment.

"It is, in the main, the traditional Byzantine composition, even more rigidly symmetrical than usual, singularly contrasting in this respect with the rush and movement of the preceding compartment. Our Saviour and the Virgin, seated side by side, each on a rainbow and within a vesica piscis, appear in the sky—Our Saviour uttering the words of malediction with uplifted arm, showing the wound in his side, and nearly in the attitude of Michael Angelo, but in wrath, not in fury—the Virgin timidly drawing back and gazing down in pity and sorrow. I never saw this co-equal juxta-position in any other representation of the Last Judgment."—Vol. iii., p. 136.

73. The positions of our Saviour and of the Virgin are not strictly co-equal; the glory in which the Madonna is seated is both lower and less; but the equality is more complete in the painting of the same subject in Santa M. Novella. We believe Lord Lindsay is correct in thinking Orcagna the only artist who has dared it. We question whether even wrath be intended in the countenance of the principal figure; on the contrary, we think it likely to disappoint at first, and appear lifeless in its exceeding tranquillity; the brow is indeed slightly knit, but the eyes have no local direction. They comprehend all things—are set upon all spirits alike, as in that *word-fresco* of our own, not unworthy to be set side by side with this, the Vision of the Trembling Man in the House

of the Interpreter. The action is as majestic as the
countenance—the right hand seems raised rather to
show its wound (as the left points at the same
instant to the wound in the side), than in condemnation, though its gesture has been adopted as one of
threatening—first (and very nobly) by Benozzo Gozzoli,
in the figure of the Angel departing, looking towards
Sodom—and afterwards, with unfortunate exaggeration, by Michael Angelo. Orcagna's Madonna we think
a failure, but his strength has been more happily displayed in the Apostolic circle. The head of St. John
is peculiarly beautiful. The other Apostles look forward or down as in judgment—some in indignation,
some in pity, some serene—but the eyes of St. John
are fixed upon the Judge Himself with the stability of
love—intercession and sorrow struggling for utterance
with awe—and through both is seen a tremor of sub-
missive astonishment, that the lips which had once
forbidden his to call down fire from heaven should now
themselves burn with irrevocable condemnation.

74. "One feeling for the most part pervades this side
of the composition,—there is far more variety in the
other; agony is depicted with fearful intensity and in
every degree and character; some clasp their hands, some
hide their faces, some look up in despair, but none towards
Christ; others seem to have grown idiots with horror:
—a few gaze, as if fascinated, into the gulf of fire towards
which the whole mass of misery are being urged by the
ministers of doom—the flames bite them, the devils fish for

and catch them with long grappling-hooks :—in sad contrast
to the group on the opposite side, a queen, condemned
herself but self-forgetful, vainly struggles to rescue her
daughter from a demon who has caught her by the gown
and is dragging her backwards into the abyss—her sister,
wringing her hands, looks on in agony—it is a fearful scene.

"A vast rib or arch in the walls of pandemonium
admits one into the contiguous gulf of Hell, forming the
third fresco, or rather a continuation of the second—in
which Satan sits in the midst, in gigantic terror, cased
in armour and crunching sinners — of whom Judas,
especially, is eaten and ejected, re-eaten and re-ejected
again and again for ever. The punishments of the wicked
are portrayed in circles numberless around him. But in
everything save horror this compartment is inferior to
the preceding, and it has been much injured and repainted."—Vol. iii., p. 138.

75. We might have been spared all notice of this
last compartment. Throughout Italy, owing, it may
be supposed, to the interested desire of the clergy
to impress upon the populace as forcibly as possible
the verity of purgatorial horrors, nearly every representation of the Inferno has been repainted, and
vulgar butchery substituted for the expressions of
punishment which were too chaste for monkish
purposes. The infernos of Giotto at Padua, and of
Orcagna at Florence, have thus been destroyed ; but
in neither case have they been replaced by anything
so merely disgusting as these restorations by Solazzino in the Campo Santo. Not a line of Orcagna's

remains, except in one row of figures halfway up the wall, where his firm black drawing is still distinguish-able : throughout the rest of the fresco, hillocks of pink flesh have been substituted for his severe forms —and for his agonized features, puppets' heads with roaring mouths and staring eyes, the whole as coarse and sickening, and quite as weak, as any scrabble on the lowest booths of a London Fair.

76. Lord Lindsay's comparison of these frescoes of Orcagna with the great work in the Sistine, is, as a specimen of his writing, too good not to be quoted.

" While Michael Angelo's leading idea seems to be the self-concentration and utter absorption of all feeling into the one predominant thought, *Am I, individually, safe ?* resolving itself into two emotions only, doubt and despair —all diversities of character, all kindred sympathies annihilated under their pressure—those emotions uttering themselves, not through the face but the form, by bodily contortion, rendering the whole composition, with all its overwhelming merits, a mighty hubbub—Orcagna's on the contrary embraces the whole world of passions that make up the economy of man, and these not confused or crushed into each other, but expanded and enhanced in quality and intensity commensurably with the ' change ' attendant upon the resurrection—variously expressed indeed, and in reference to the diversities of individual character, which will be nowise compromised by that change, yet from their very intensity suppressed and subdued, stilling the body and informing only the soul's index, the countenance. All therefore is calm ; the saved have acquiesced in all things, they can mourn no more—

the damned are to them as if they had never been ;—
among the lost, grief is too deep, too settled for caricature,
and while every feeling of the spectator, every key of the
soul's organ, is played upon by turns, tenderness and
pity form the under-song throughout and ultimately
prevail; the curse is uttered in sorrow rather than
wrath, and from the pitying Virgin and the weeping
archangel above, to the mother endeavouring to rescue
her daughter below, and the young secular led to paradise
under the approving smile of S. Michael, all resolves
itself into sympathy and love.—Michael Angelo's conception may be more efficacious for teaching by terror—it
was his object, I believe, as the heir of Savonarola and
the representative of the Protestant spirit within the
bosom of Catholicism ; but Orcagna's is in better taste,
truer to human nature, sublimer in philosophy, and (if
I mistake not) more scriptural."—Vol. iii., pp. 139—141.

77. We think it somewhat strange that the object of
teaching by terror should be attributed to M. Angelo
more than to Orcagna, seeing that the former, with
his usual dignity, has refused all representation of
infernal punishment — except in the figure dragged
down with the hand over the face, the serpent biting
the thigh, and in the fiends of the extreme angle ;
while Orcagna, whose intention may be conjectured
even from Solazzino's restoration, exhausted himself
in detailing Dante's distribution of torture, and brings
into successive prominence every expedient of pain ;
the prong, the spit, the rack, the chain, venomous
fang and rending beak, harrowing point and dividing

edge, biting fiend and calcining fire. The objects of the two great painters were indeed opposed, but not in this respect. Orcagna's, like that of every great painter of his day, was to write upon the wall, as in a book, the greatest possible number of those religious facts or doctrines which the Church desired should be known to the people. This he did in the simplest and most straightforward way, regardless of artistical reputation, and desiring only to be read and under-stood. But Michael Angelo's object was from the beginning that of an artist. He addresses not the sympathies of his day, but the understanding of all time, and he treats the subject in the mode best adapted to bring every one of his own powers into full play. As might have been expected, while the self-forgetfulness of Orcagna has given, on the one hand, an awfulness to his work, and verity, which are wanting in the studied composition of the Sistine, on the other it has admitted a puerility commensurate with the narrowness of the religion he had to teach.

78. Greater differences still result from the opposed powers and idiosyncrasies of the two men. Orcagna was unable to draw the nude—on this inability followed a coldness to the value of flowing lines, and to the power of unity in composition—neither could he indicate motion or buoyancy in flying or floating figures, nor express violence of action in the limbs

—he cannot even show the difference between pulling and pushing in the muscles of the arm. In M. Angelo these conditions were directly reversed. Intense sensibility to the majesty of writhing, flowing, and connected lines, was in him associated with a power, unequalled except by Angelico, of suggesting aërial motion—motion deliberate or disturbed, inherent or impressed, impotent or inspired—gathering into glory, or gravitating to death. Orcagna was therefore compelled to range his figures symmetrically in ordered lines, while Michael Angelo bound them into chains, or hurled them into heaps, or scattered them before him as the wind does leaves. Orcagna trusted for all his expression to the countenance, or to · rudely explained gesture aided by grand fall of draperies, though in all these points he was still immeasurably inferior to his colossal rival. As for his "embracing the whole world of passions which make up the economy of man," he had no such power of delineation—nor, we believe, of conception. The expressions on the inferno side are all of them varieties of grief and fear, differing merely in degree, not in character or operation : there is something dramatic in the raised hand of a man wearing a green bonnet with a white plume—but the only really far-carried effort in the group is the head of a Dominican monk (just above the queen in green), who, in the midst of the close crowd, struggling, shuddering, and howling on every side, is fixed in quiet, total despair, insensible to all things, and seemingly poised in existence and sensation upon that one point in his past life when his steps first took hold on hell; this head, which is opposed to a face distorted by horror beside it, is, we repeat, the only highly wrought piece of expression in the group.

79. What Michael Angelo could do by expression of countenance alone, let the Pietà of Genoa tell, or the Lorenzo, or the parallel to this very head of Orcagna's, the face of the man borne down in the Last Judgment with the hand clenched over one of the eyes. Neither in that fresco is he wanting in dramatic episode; the adaptation of the Niobe on the spectator's left hand is far finer than Orcagna's condemned queen and princess; the groups rising below, side by side, supporting each other, are full of tenderness, and reciprocal devotion ; the contest in the centre for the body which a demon drags down by the hair is another kind of quarrel from that of Orcagna between a feathered angel and bristly fiend for a diminutive soul—reminding us, as it forcibly did at first, of a vociferous difference in opinion between a cat and a cockatoo. But Buonaroti knew that it was useless to concentrate interest in the countenances, in a picture of enormous size, ill

lighted; and he preferred giving full play to the powers of line-grouping, for which he could have found no nobler field. Let us not by unwise comparison mingle with our admiration of these two sublime works any sense of weakness in the naïveté of the one, or of coldness in the science of the other. Each painter has his own sufficient dominion, and he who complains of the want of knowledge in Orcagna, or of the display of it in Michael Angelo, has probably brought little to his judgment of either.

80. One passage more we must quote, well worthy of remark in these days of hollowness and haste, though we question the truth of the particular fact stated in the second volume respecting the shrine of Or San Michele. Cement is now visible enough in all the joints, but whether from recent repairs we cannot say:—

"There is indeed another, a technical merit, due to Orcagna, which I would have mentioned earlier, did it not partake so strongly of a moral virtue. Whatever he undertook to do, he did well—by which I mean, better than anybody else. His Loggia, in its general structure and its provisions against injury from wet and decay, is a model of strength no less than symmetry and elegance; the junction of the marbles in the tabernacle of Or San Michele, and the exquisite manual workmanship of the bas-reliefs, have been the theme of praise for five centuries; his colours in the Campo Santo have maintained a freshness unrivalled by those of any of his successors there;—

nay, even had his mosaics been preserved at Orvieto, I am confident the *commettitura* would be found more compact and polished than any previous to the sixteenth century. The secret of all this was that he made himself thoroughly an adept in the mechanism of the respective arts, and therefore his works have stood. Genius is too apt to think herself independent of form and matter—never was there such a mistake ; she cannot slight either without hamstringing herself. But the rule is of universal application ; without this thorough mastery of their respective tools, this determination honestly to make the best use of them, the divine, the soldier, the statesman, the philosopher, the poet—however genuine their enthusiasm, however lofty their genius—are mere empirics, pretenders to crowns they will not run for, children not men—sporters with Imagination, triflers with Reason, with the prospects of humanity, with Time, and with God."—Vol. iii., pp. 148, 149.

81. A noble passage this, and most true, provided we distinguish always between mastery of tool together with thorough strength of workmanship, and mere neatness of outside polish or fitting of measurement, of which ancient masters are daringly scornful.

None of Orcagna's pupils, except Francisco Traini, attained celebrity—

"nothing in fact is known of them except their names. Had their works, however inferior, been preserved, we might have had less difficulty in establishing the links between himself and his successor in the supremacy of the Semi-Byzantine school at Florence, the Beato Fra Angelico da Fiesole. . . . . He was born at Vicchio, near Florence, it is said in 1387, and was baptized by the name of Guido.

Of a gentle nature, averse to the turmoil of the world, and
pious to enthusiasm, though as free from fanaticism as his
youth was innocent of vice, he determined, at the age of
twenty, though well provided for in a worldly point of
view, to retire to the cloister ; he professed himself accordingly a brother of the monastery of S. Domenico at Fiesole
in 1407, assuming his monastic name from the Apostle of
love, S. John. He acquired from his residence there the
distinguishing surname ' da Fiesole ;' and a calmer retreat
for one weary of earth and desirous of commerce with
heaven would in vain be sought for ;—the purity of the
atmosphere, the freshness of the morning breeze, the
starry clearness and delicious fragrance of the nights, the
loveliness of the valley at one's feet, lengthening out, like
a life of happiness, between the Apennine and the sea—
with the intermingling sounds that ascend perpetually from
below, softened by distance into music, and by an agreeable
compromise at once giving a zest to solitude and cheating
it of its loneliness—rendering Fiesole a spot which angels
might alight upon by mistake in quest of paradise, a spot
where it would be at once sweet to live and sweet to die."
—Vol. iii., pp. 151—153.

82. Our readers must recollect that the convent
where Fra Giovanni first resided is not that whose
belfry tower and cypress grove crown the "top of
Fésole." The Dominican convent is situated at the
bottom of the slope of olives, distinguished only by its
narrow and low spire ; a cypress avenue recedes from
it towards Florence—a stony path, leading to the
ancient Badia of Fiesole, descends in front of the
three-arched loggia which protects the entrance to the

church. No extended prospect is open to it ; though over the low wall, and through the sharp, thickset olive leaves, may be seen one silver gleam of the Arno, and, at evening, the peaks of the Carrara mountains, purple against the twilight, dark and calm, while the fire-flies glance beneath, silent and intermittent, like stars upon the rippling of mute, soft sea.

"It is by no means an easy task to adjust the chronology of Fra Angelico's works ; he has affixed no dates to them, and consequently, when external evidence is wanting, we are thrown upon internal, which in his case is unusually fallacious. It is satisfactory therefore to possess a fixed date in 1433, the year in which he painted the great taber-nacle for the Company of Flax-merchants, now removed to the gallery of the Uffizii. It represents the Virgin and child, with attendant Saints, on a gold ground—very dignified and noble, although the Madonna has not attained the exquisite spirituality of his later efforts. Round this tabernacle as a nucleus, may be classed a number of paint-ings, all of similar excellence—admirable that is to say, but not of his very best, and in which, if I mistake not, the type of the Virgin bears throughout a strong family resemblance."—Vol. iii., pp. 160, 161.

83. If the painter ever increased in power after this period (he was then forty-three), we have been unable to systematize the improvement. We much doubt whether, in his modes of execution, advance were possible. Men whose merit lies in record of natural facts, increase in knowledge ; and men whose merit is in dexterity of hand increase in facility ; but we much

8

doubt whether the faculty of design, or force of feeling, increase after the age of twenty-five. By Fra Angelico, who drew always in fear and trembling, dexterous execution had been from the first repudiated ; he neither needed nor sought technical knowledge of the form, and the inspiration, to which his power was owing, was not less glowing in youth than in age. The inferiority traceable (we grant) in this Madonna results not from its early date, but from Fra Angelico's incapability, always visible, of drawing the head of life size. He is, in this respect, the exact reverse of Giotto ; he was essentially a miniature painter, and never attained the mastery of muscular play in the features necessary in a full-sized drawing. His habit, almost constant, of surrounding the iris of the eye by a sharp black line, is, in small figures, perfectly successful, giving a transparency and tenderness not otherwise expressible. But on a larger scale it gives a stony stare to the eyeball, which not all the tenderness of the brow and mouth can conquer or redeem.

84. Further, in this particular instance, the ear has by accident been set too far back—(Fra Angelico, drawing only from feeling, was liable to gross errors of this kind,—often, however, more beautiful than other men's truths)—and the hair removed in consequence too far off the brow ; in other respects the face is very noble—still more so that of the Christ. The

child *stands* upon the Virgin's knees,* one hand raised in the usual attitude of benediction, the other holding a globe. The face looks straightforward, quiet, Jupiter-like, and very sublime, owing to the smallness of the features in proportion to the head, the eyes being placed at about three-sevenths of the whole height, leaving four-sevenths for the brow, and themselves only in length about one-sixth of the breadth of the face, half closed, giving a peculiar appearance of repose. The hair is short, golden, symmetrically curled, statuesque in its contour ; the mouth tender and full of life : the red cross of the glory about the head of an intense ruby enamel, almost fire colour ; the dress brown, with golden girdle. In all the treatment Fra Angelico maintains his assertion of the authority of abstract imagination, which, depriving his subject of all material or actual being, contemplates it as retain= ing qualities eternal only—adorned by incorporeal splendour. The eyes of the beholder are super-naturally unsealed : and to this miraculous vision whatever is of the earth vanishes, and all things are seen endowed with an harmonious glory—the garments falling with strange, visionary grace, glowing with indefinite gold—the walls of the chamber dazzling as of a heavenly city—the mortal forms themselves

---

* In many pictures of Angelico, the Infant Christ appears self-supported - the Virgin not touching the child.

impressed with divine changelessness—no domesticity
—no jest—no anxiety—no expectation—no variety of
action or of thought.   Love, all fulfilling, and various
modes of power, are alone expressed; the Virgin
never shows the complacency or petty watchfulness
of maternity; she sits serene, supporting the child
whom she ever looks upon, as a stranger among
strangers; "Behold the handmaid of the Lord" for
ever written upon her brow.

85. An approach to an exception in treatment is
found in the Annunciation of the upper corridor of
St. Mark's, most unkindly treated by our author :—

"Probably the earliest of the series—full of faults, but im-
bued with the sweetest feeling; there is a look of naïve
curiosity, mingling with the modest and meek humility of
the Virgin, which almost provokes a smile."—iii., 176.

Many a Sabbath evening of bright summer have we
passed in that lonely corridor—but not to the finding
of faults, nor the provoking of smiles.   The angel is
perhaps something less majestic than is usual with
the painter; but the Virgin is only the more to be
worshipped, because here, for once, set before us in
the verity of life.   No gorgeous robe is upon her;
no lifted throne set for her; the golden border
gleams faintly on the dark blue dress; the seat is
drawn into the shadow of a lowly loggia.   The face
is of no strange, far-sought loveliness; the features

might even be thought hard, and they are worn
with watching, and severe, though innocent. She
stoops forward with her arms folded on her bosom :
no casting down of eye nor shrinking of the frame
in fear ; she is too earnest, too self-forgetful for
either : wonder and inquiry are there, but chastened
and free from doubt ; meekness, yet mingled with a
patient majesty ; peace, yet sorrowfully sealed, as if
the promise of the Angel were already underwritten
by the prophecy of Simeon. They who pass and
repass in the twilight of that solemn corridor, need
not the adjuration inscribed beneath :—

> " Virginis intactae cum veneris ante figuram
> Praetereundo cave ne sileatur Ave."*

We in general allow the inferiority of Angelico's
fresco to his tempera works ; yet even that which of
all these latter we think the most radiant, the Annunciation on the reliquary of Santa Maria Novella,
would, we believe, if repeatedly compared with this
of St. Mark's, in the end have the disadvantage.
The eminent value of the tempera paintings results
partly from their delicacy of line, and partly from
the purity of colour and force of decoration of which
the material is capable.

---

* The upper inscription Lord Lindsay has misquoted—it runs thus :—
> " Salve Mater Pietatis
> Et Totius Trinitatis
> Nobile Triclinium."

86. The passage, to which we have before alluded, respecting Fra Angelico's colour in general, is one of the most curious and fanciful in the work :—

" His colouring, on the other hand, is far more beautiful, although of questionable brilliancy. This will be found invariably the case in minds constituted like his. Spirit and Sense act on each other with livelier reciprocity the closer their approximation, the less intervention there is of Intellect. Hence the most religious and the most sensual painters have always loved the brightest colours—Spiritual Expression and a clearly defined (however inaccurate) outline forming the distinction of the former class ; Animal Expression and a confused and uncertain outline (reflecting that lax morality which confounds the limits of light and darkness, right and wrong) of the latter. On the other hand, the more that Intellect, or the spirit of Form, intervenes in its severe precision, the less pure, the paler grow the colours, the nearer they tend to the hue of marble, of the bas-relief. We thus find the purest and brightest colours only in Fra Angelico's pictures, with a general predominance of blue, which we have observed to prevail more or less in so many of the Semi-Byzantine painters, and which, fanciful as it may appear, I cannot but attribute, independently of mere tradition, to an inherent, instinctive sympathy between their mental constitution and the colour in question ; as that of red, or of blood, may be observed to prevail among painters in whom Sense or Nature predominates over Spirit—for in this, as in all things else, the moral and the material world respond to each other as closely as shadow and substance. But, in Painting as in Morals, perfection implies the due intervention of Intellect between Spirit and Sense—of Form between Expression and Colouring—as a power at once controlling and controlled — and therefore, although acknowledging its fascination, I cannot unreservedly praise the Colouring of Fra Angelico."—Vol. iii., pp. 193, 194.

87. There is much ingenuity, and some truth, here, but the reader, as in other of Lord Lindsay's speculations, must receive his conclusions with qualification. It is the natural character of strong effects of colour, as of high light, to confuse outlines ; and it is a necessity. in all fine harmonies of colour that many tints should merge imperceptibly into their following or succeeding ones :—we believe Lord Lindsay himself would hardly wish to mark the hues of the rainbow into divided zones, or to show its edge, as of an iron arch, against the sky, in order that it might no longer reflect (a reflection of which we profess ourselves up to this moment altogether unconscious) "that lax morality which confounds the limits of right and wrong." Again, there is a character of energy in all warm colours, as of repose in cold, which necessarily causes the former to be preferred by painters of savage subject—that is to say, commonly by the coarsest and most degraded ;—but when sensuality is free from ferocity, it leans to blue more than to red (as especially in the flesh tints of Guido), and when intellect prevails over this sensuality, its first step is invariably to put more red into every

colour, and so "rubor est virtutis color." We
hardly think Lord Lindsay would willingly include
Luca Giordano among his spiritual painters, though
that artist's servant was materially enriched by
washing the ultramarine from the brushes which with
he painted the Ricardi palace ; nor would he, we
believe, degrade Ghirlandajo to fellowship with the
herd of the sensual, though in the fresco of the
vision of Zacharias there are seventeen different
reds in large masses, and not a shade of blue. The
fact is, there is no colour of the spectrum, as there
is no note of music, whose key and prevalence may
not be made pure in expression, and elevating in
influence, by a great and good painter, or degraded
to unhallowed purpose by a base one.

88. We are sorry that our author "cannot unreservedly praise the colouring of Angelico ;" but he
is again curbed by his unhappy system of balanced
perfectibility, and must quarrel with the gentle monk
because he finds not in him the flames of Giorgione,
nor the tempering of Titian, nor the melody of
Cagliari. This curb of perfection we took between
our teeth from the first, and we will give up our
hearts to Angelico without drawback or reservation.
His colour is, in its sphere and to its purpose, as
perfect as human work may be : wrought to radiance
beyond that of the ruby and opal, its inartificialness

prevents it from arresting the attention it is intended only to direct; were it composed with more science it would become vulgar from the loss of its unconsciousness; if richer, it must have parted with its purity, if deeper, with its joyfulness, if more subdued, with its sincerity. Passages are, indeed, sometimes unsuccessful; but it is to be judged in its rapture, and forgiven in its fall: he who works by law and system may be blamed when he sinks below the line above which he proposes no elevation, but to him whose eyes are on a mark far off, and whose efforts are impulsive, and to the utmost of his strength, we may not unkindly count the slips of his sometime descent into the valley of humiliation.

89. The concluding notice of Angelico is true and interesting, though rendered obscure by useless recurrence to the favourite theory.

"Such are the surviving works of a painter, who has recently been as unduly extolled as he had for three centuries past been unduly depreciated,—depreciated, through the amalgamation during those centuries of the principle of which he was the representative with baser, or at least less precious matter—extolled, through the recurrence to that principle, in its pure, unsophisticated essence, in the present—in a word, to the simple Imaginative Christianity of the middle ages, as opposed to the complex Reasoning Christianity of recent times. Creeds therefore are at issue, and no exclusive partisan, neither Catholic nor Protestant in the absolute sense of the terms, can fairly appreciate Fra Angelico. Nevertheless, to those who regard society as progressive through the gradual development of the component elements of human nature, and who believe that Providence has accommodated the mind of man, individually, to the perception of half-truths only, in order to create that antagonism from which Truth is generated in the abstract, and by which the progression is effected, his rank and position in art are clear and definite. All that Spirit could achieve by herself, anterior to that struggle with Intellect and Sense which she must in all cases pass through in order to work out her destiny, was accomplished by him. Last and most gifted of a long and imaginative race—the heir of their experience, with collateral advantages which they possessed not—and flourishing at the moment when the transition was actually taking place from the youth to the early manhood of Europe, he gave full, unreserved, and enthusiastic expression to that Love and Hope which had winged the Faith of Christendom in her flight towards heaven for fourteen centuries,—to those yearnings of the Heart and the Imagination which ever precede, in Universal as well as Individual development, the severer and more chastened intelligence of Reason."—Vol. iii., pp. 188—190.

90. We must again repeat that if our author wishes to be truly serviceable to the schools of England, he must express himself in terms requiring less laborious translation. Clearing the above statement of its mysticism and metaphor, it amounts only to this,—that Fra Angelico was a man of (humanly speaking) *perfect* piety—humility, charity, and faith—that he never employed his art but as a means of expressing

his love to God and man, and with the view, single,
simple, and straightforward, of glory to the Creator,
and good to the Creature. Every quality or subject
of art by which these ends were not to be attained,
or to be attained secondarily only, he rejected; from
all study of art, as such, he withdrew; whatever
might merely please the eye, or interest the intellect,
he despised, and refused; he used his colours and
lines, as David his harp, after a kingly fashion, for
purposes of praise and not of science. To this
grace and gift of holiness were added, those of a
fervent imagination, vivid invention, keen sense of
loveliness in lines and colours, unwearied energy,
and to all these gifts the crowning one of quietness of
life and mind, while yet his convent-cell was at first
within view, and afterwards in the centre, of a city
which had lead of all the world in Intellect, and in
whose streets he might see daily and hourly the noblest
setting of manly features. It would perhaps be well
to wait until we find another man thus actuated, thus
endowed, and thus circumstanced, before we speak of
"unduly extolling" the works of Fra Angelico.

91. His artistical attainments, as might be conjectured, are nothing more than the development,
through practice, of his natural powers in accordance
with his sacred instincts. His power of expression
by bodily gesture is greater even than Giotto's,

wherever he could feel or comprehend the passion
to be expressed ; but so inherent in him was his
holy tranquillity of mind, that he could not by any
exertion, even for a moment, conceive either agita-
tion, doubt, or fear—and all the actions proceeding
from such passions, or, à *fortiori*, from any yet more
criminal, are absurdly and powerlessly pourtrayed by
him ; while contrariwise, every gesture, consistent
with emotion pure and saintly, is rendered with an
intensity of truth to which there is no existing
parallel ; the expression being carried out into every
bend of the hand, every undulation of the arm,
shoulder, and neck, every fold of the dress and
every wave of the hair. His drawing of movement
is subject to the same influence ; vulgar or vicious
motion he cannot represent ; his running, falling, or
struggling figures are drawn with childish incapability ; but give him for his scene the pavement of
heaven, or pastures of Paradise, and for his subject
the " inoffensive pace " of glorified souls, or the
spiritual speed of Angels, and Michael Angelo alone
can contend with him in majesty,—in grace and
musical continuousness of motion, no one. The inspiration was in some degree caught by his pupil
Benozzo, but thenceforward for ever lost. The
angels of Perugino appear to be let down by cords
and moved by wires ; that of Titian, in the sacrifice

of Isaac, kicks like an awkward swimmer; Raphael's
Moses and Elias of the Transfiguration are cramped
at the knees; and the flight of Domenichino's angels
is a sprawl paralyzed. The authority of Tintoret
over movement is, on the other hand, too unlimited;
the descent of his angels is the swoop of a whirl-
wind or the fall of a thunderbolt; his mortal impulses are oftener impetuous than pathetic, and
majestic more than melodious.

92. But it is difficult by words to convey to the
reader unacquainted with Angelico's works, any idea
of the thoughtful variety of his rendering of movement—Earnest haste of girded faith in the Flight
into Egypt, the haste of obedience, not of fear; and
unweariedness, but through spiritual support, and
not in human strength—Swift obedience of passive
earth to the call of its Creator, in the Resurrection
of Lazarus—March of meditative gladness in the
following of the Apostles down the Mount of Olives
—Rush of adoration breaking through the chains
and shadows of death, in the Spirits in Prison.
Pacing of mighty angels above the Firmament,
poised on their upright wings, half opened, broad,
bright, quiet, like eastern clouds before the sun is
up;—or going forth, with timbrels and with dances,
of souls more than conquerors, beside the shore of
the last great Red Sea, the sea of glass mingled

with fire, hand knit with hand, and voice with voice, the joyful winds of heaven following the measure of their motion, and the flowers of the new earth looking on, like stars pausing in their courses.

93. And yet all this is but the lowest part and narrowest reach of Angelico's conceptions. Joy and gentleness, patience and power, he could indicate by gesture—but Devotion could be told by the countenance only. There seems to have been always a stern limit by which the thoughts of other men were stayed; the religion that was painted even by Perugino, Francia, and Bellini, was finite in its spirit—the religion of earthly beings, checked, not indeed by the corruption, but by the veil and the sorrow of clay. But with Fra Angelico the glory of the countenance reaches to actual transfiguration; eyes that see no more darkly, incapable of all tears, foreheads flaming, like Belshazzar's marble wall, with the writing of the Father's name upon them, lips tremulous with love, and crimson with the light of the coals of the altar—and all this loveliness, thus enthusiastic and ineffable, yet sealed with the stability which the coming and going of ages as countless as sea-sand cannot dim nor weary, and bathed by an ever flowing river of holy thought, with God for its source, God for its shore, and God for its ocean.

94. We speak in no inconsiderate enthusiasm.

We feel assured that to any person of just feeling
who devotes sufficient time to the examination of
these works, all terms of description must seem
derogatory. Where such ends as these have been
reached, it ill becomes us to speak of minor deficiencies as either to be blamed or regretted : it
cannot be determined how far even what we deprecate may be accessory to our delight, nor by what
intricate involution what we deplore may be connected with what we love. Every good that Nature
herself bestows, or accomplishes, is given with a
counterpoise, or gained at a sacrifice ; nor is it to
be expected of Man that he should win the hardest
battles and tread the narrowest paths, without the
betrayal of a weakness, or the acknowledgment of
an error.

95. With this final warning against our author's
hesitating approbation of what is greatest and best,
we must close our specific examination of the mode in
which his design has been worked out. We have
done enough to set the reader upon his guard
against whatever appears slight or inconsiderate in
his theory or statements, and with the more severity,
because this was alone wanting to render the book
one of the most valuable gifts which Art has ever
received. Of the translations from the lives of the
saints we have hardly spoken ; they are gracefully

rendered, and all of them highly interesting—but we could wish to see these, and the enumerations of fresco subjects* with which the other volumes are in great part occupied, published separately for the convenience of travellers in Italy. They are something out of place in a work like that before us. For the rest, we might have more interested the reader, and gratified ourselves, by setting before him some of the many passages of tender feeling and earnest eloquence with which the volumes are replete—but we felt it necessary rather to anticipate the hesitation with which they were liable to be received, and set limits to the halo of fancy by which their light is obscured—though enlarged. One or two paragraphs, however, of the closing chapter must be given before we part :—

96. "What a scene of beauty, what a flower-garden of art—how bright and how varied—must Italy have presented at the commencement of the sixteenth cen-

---

* We have been much surprised by the author's frequent reference to Lasinio's engravings of various frescoes, unaccompanied by any warning of their inaccuracy. No work of Lasinio's can be trusted for *anything* except the number and relative position of the figures. All masters are by him translated into one monotony of commonplace : –he dilutes eloquence, educates naïveté, prompts ignorance, stultifies intelligence, and paralyses power ; takes the chill off horror, the edge off wit, and the bloom off beauty. In all artistical points he is utterly valueless, neither drawing nor expression being ever preserved by him. Giotto, Benozzo, or Ghirlandajo are all alike to him ; and we hardly know whether he injures most when he robs or when he redresses.

tury, at the death of Raphael! The sacrileges we lament took place for the most part after that period; hundreds of frescoes, not merely of Giotto and those other elders of Christian Art, but of Gentile da Fabriano, Pietro della Francesca, Perugino and their compeers, were still existing, charming the eye, elevating the mind, and warming the heart. Now alas! few comparatively and fading are the relics of those great and good men. While Dante's voice rings as clear as ever, communing with us as friend with friend, theirs is dying gradually away, fainter and fainter, like the farewell of a spirit. Flaking off the walls, uncared for and neglected save in a few rare instances, scarce one of their frescoes will survive the century, and the labours of the next may not improbably be directed to the recovery and restoration of such as may still slumber beneath the whitewash and the daubs with which the Bronzinos and Zuccheros 'et id genus omne' have unconsciously sealed them up for posterity—their best title to our gratitude.—But why not begin at once? at all events in the instances numberless, where merely whitewash interposes between us and them.

"It is easy to reply—what need of this? They—the artists—have Moses and the prophets, the frescoes of Raphael and Michael Angelo—let them study them. Doubtless,—but we still reply, and with no impiety—they will not repent, they will not forsake their idols and their evil ways—they will not abandon Sense for Spirit, oils for fresco—unless these great ones of the past, these Sleepers of Ephesus, arise from the dead. . . . It is not by studying art in its perfection—by worshipping Raphael and Michael Angelo exclusively of all other excellence—that we can expect to rival them, but by re-ascending to the fountain-head—by planting ourselves as acorns in the ground those oaks are rooted

9

in, and growing up to their level—in a word, by
studying Duccio and Giotto that we may paint like
Taddeo di Bartolo and Masaccio, Taddeo di Bartolo and
Masaccio that we may paint like Perugino and Luca
Signorelli, Perugino and Luca Signorelli that we may
paint like Raphael and Michael Angelo. And why despair of this, or even of shaming the Vatican? For
with genius and God's blessing nothing is impossible.

"I would not be a blind partizan, but, with all their
faults, the old masters I plead for knew how to touch
the heart. It may be difficult at first to believe this;
like children, they are shy with us—like strangers, they
bear an uncouth mien and aspect—like ghosts from the
other world, they have an awkward habit of shocking
our conventionalities with home truths. But with the
dead as with the living all depends on the frankness with
which we greet them, the sincerity with which we credit
their kindly qualities; sympathy is the key to truth—we
must love, in order to appreciate."—iii., p. 418.

97. These are beautiful sentences; yet this let the
young painter of these days remember always, that
whomsoever he may love, or from whomsoever
learn, he can now no more go back to those hours
of infancy and be born again.* About the faith,

---

* We do not perhaps enough estimate the assistance which was
once given both to purpose and perception, by the feeling of wonder
which with us is destroyed partly by the ceaseless calls upon it,
partly by our habit of either discovering or anticipating a reason for
everything. Of the simplicity and ready surprise of heart which
supported the spirit of the older painters, an interesting example is
seen in the diary of Albert Dürer, lately published in a work every
way valuable, but especially so in the carefulness and richness of its
illustrations, "Divers Works of Early Masters in Christian Decoration," edited by John Weale, London, 2 vols. folio, 1846.

the questioning and the teaching of childhood there is a joy and grace, which we may often envy, but can no more assume :—the voice and the gesture must not be imitated when the innocence is lost. Incapability and ignorance in the act of being struggled against and cast away are often endowed with a peculiar charm—but both are only contemptible when they are pretended. Whatever we have now to do, we may be sure, first, that its strength and life must be drawn from the real nature with us and about us always, and secondly, that, if worth doing, it will be something altogether different from what has ever been done before. The visions of the cloister must depart with its superstitious peace—the quick, apprehensive symbolism of early Faith must yield to the abstract teaching of disciplined Reason. Whatever else we may deem of the Progress of Nations, one character of that progress is determined and discernible. As in the encroaching of the land upon the sea, the strength of the sandy bastions is raised out of the sifted ruin of ancient inland hills—for every tongue of level land that stretches into the deep, the fall of Alps has been heard among the clouds, and as the fields of industry enlarge, the intercourse with Heaven is shortened. Let it not be doubted that as this change is inevitable, so it is expedient, though the

form of teaching adopted and of duty prescribed be
less mythic and contemplative, more active and un-
assisted: for the light of Transfiguration on the
Mountain is substituted the Fire of Coals upon the
Shore, and on the charge to hear the Shepherd,
follows that to feed the Sheep. Doubtful we may
be for a time, and apparently deserted; but if, as
we wait, we still look forward with steadfast will
and humble heart, so that our Hope for the Future
may be fed, not dulled or diverted by our Love for
the Past, we shall not long be left without a Guide:
—the way will be opened, the Precursor appointed
—the Hour will come, and the Man.

EASTLAKE'S HISTORY OF OIL-PAINTING.*

98. THE stranger in Florence who for the first time passes through the iron gate which opens from the Green Cloister of Santa Maria Novella into the Spezieria, can hardly fail of being surprised, and that perhaps painfully, by the suddenness of the transition from the silence and gloom of the monastic enclosure, its pavement rough with epitaphs, and its walls retaining, still legible, though crumbling and mildewed, their imaged records of Scripture History, to the activity of a traffic not less frivolous than

---

* A review of the following books :—

1. "Materials for a History of Oil-Painting." By Charles Lock Eastlake, R.A., F.R.S., F.S.A., Secretary to the Royal Commission for promoting the Fine Arts in Connection with the Rebuilding of the Houses of Parliament, etc., etc. London, 1847.

2. "Theophili, qui et Rugerus, Presbyteri et Monachi, Libri III. de Diversis Artibus ; seu Diversarum Artium Schedula. (An Essay upon Various Arts, in Three Books, by Theophilus, called also Rugerus, Priest and Monk, forming an Encyclopædia of Christian Art of the Eleventh Century." Translated, with Notes, by Robert Hendrie.) London, 1847.

flourishing, concerned almost exclusively with the appliances of bodily adornment or luxury. Yet perhaps, on a moment's reflection, the rose-leaves scattered on the floor, and the air filled with odour of . myrtle and myrrh, aloes and cassia, may arouse associations of a different and more elevated character; the preparation of these precious perfumes may seem not altogether unfitting the hands of a religious brotherhood—or if this should not be conceded, at all events it must be matter of rejoicing to observe the evidence of intelligence and energy interrupting the apathy and languor of the cloister; nor will the institution be regarded with other than respect, as well as gratitude, when it is remembered that, as to the convent library we owe the preservation of ancient literature, to the convent laboratory we owe the duration of mediæval art.

99. It is at first with surprise not altogether dissimilar, that we find a painter of refined feeling and deep thoughtfulness, after manifesting in his works the most sincere affection for what is highest in the reach of his art, devoting himself for years (there is proof of this in the work before us) to the study of the mechanical preparation of its appliances, and whatever documentary evidence exists respecting their ancient use. But it is with a revulsion of feeling more entire, that we perceive the value of the results

obtained—the accuracy of the varied knowledge by which their sequence has been established—and above all, their immediate bearing upon the practice and promise of the schools of our own day.

Opposite errors, we know not which the least pardonable, but both certainly productive of great harm, have from time to time possessed the masters of modern art. It has been held by some that the great early painters owed the larger measure of their power to secrets of material and method, and that the discovery of a lost vehicle or forgotten process might at any time accomplish the regeneration of a fallen school. By others it has been asserted that all questions respecting materials or manipulation are idle and impertinent ; that the methods of the older masters were either of no peculiar value, or are still in our power ; that a great painter is independent of all but the simplest mechanical aids, and demonstrates his greatness by scorn of system and carelessness of means.

100. It is evident that so long as incapability could shield itself under the first of these creeds, or presumption vindicate itself by the second ; so long as the feeble painter could lay his faults on his palette and his panel ; and the self-conceited painter, from the assumed identity of materials proceed to infer equality of power—(for we believe that in most instances those

who deny the evil of our present methods will deny
also the weakness of our present works)—little good
could be expected from the teaching of the abstract
principles of the art; and less, if possible, from the
example of any mechanical qualities, however admirable, whose means might be supposed irrecoverable
on the one hand, or indeterminate on the other, or of
any excellence conceived to have been either summoned
by an incantation, or struck out by an accident. And
of late, among our leading masters, the loss has not
been merely of the system of the ancients, but of all
system whatsoever: the greater number paint as if
the virtue of oil pigment were its opacity, or as if its
power depended on its polish; of the rest, no two
agree in use or choice of materials; not many are
consistent even in their own practice; and the most
zealous and earnest, therefore the most discontented,
reaching impatiently and desperately after better things,
purchase the momentary satisfaction of their feelings
by the sacrifice of security of surface and durability
of hue. The walls of our galleries are for the most
part divided between pictures whose dead coating of
consistent paint, laid on with a heavy hand and a
cold heart, secures for them the stability of dulness
and the safety of mediocrity; and pictures whose
reckless and experimental brilliancy, unequal in its
result as lawless in its means, is as evanescent as

the dust of an insect's wing, and presents in its chief perfections so many subjects of future regret.

101. But if these evils now continue, it can only be through rashness which no example can warn, or through apathy which no hope can stimulate, for Mr. Eastlake has alike withdrawn licence from experimentalism and apology from indolence. He has done away with all legends of forgotten secrets; he has shown that the masters of the great Flemish and early Venetian schools possessed no means, followed no methods, but such as we may still obtain and pursue; but he has shown also, among all these masters, the most admirable care in the preparation of materials and the most simple consistency in their use; he has shown that their excellence was reached, and could only have been reached, by stern and exact science, condescending to the observance, care, and conquest of the most minute physical particulars and hindrances; that the greatest of them never despised an aid nor avoided a difficulty. The loss of imaginative liberty sometimes involved in a too scrupulous attention to methods of execution is trivial compared to the evils resulting from a careless or inefficient practice. The modes in which, with every great painter, realization falls short of conception are necessarily so many and so grievous, that he can ill afford to undergo the additional discouragement caused

by uncertain methods and bad materials. Not only
so, but even the choice of subjects, the amount of
completion attempted, nay, even the modes of conception and measure of truth are in no small degree
involved in the great question of materials. On the
habitual use of a light or dark ground may depend
the painter's preference of a broad and faithful, or
partial and scenic chiaroscuro; correspondent with
the facility or fatality of alterations, may be the
exercise of indolent fancy, or disciplined invention;
and to the complexities of a system requiring time,
patience, and succession of process, may be owing
the conversion of the ready draughtsman into the
resolute painter. Farther than this, who shall say
how unconquerable a barrier to all self-denying effort
may exist in the consciousness that the best that is
accomplished can last but a few years, and that the
painter's travail must perish with his life?

102. It cannot have been without strong sense of
this, the true dignity and relation of his subject, that
Mr. Eastlake has gone through a toil far more irksome,
far less selfish than any he could have undergone in
the practice of his art. The value which we attach
to the volume depends, however, rather on its pre-
ceptive than its antiquarian character. As objects of
historical inquiry merely, we cannot conceive any
questions less interesting than those relating to

mechanical operations generally, nor any honours less worthy of prolonged dispute than those which are grounded merely on the invention or amelioration of processes and pigments. The subject can only become historically interesting when the means ascertained to have been employed at any period are considered in their operation upon or procession from the artistical aim of such period, the character of its chosen subjects, and the effects proposed in their treatment upon the national mind. Mr. Eastlake has as yet refused himself the indulgence of such speculation ; his book is no more than its modest title expresses. For ourselves, however, without venturing in the slightest degree to anticipate the expression of his ulterior views—though we believe that we can trace their extent and direction in a few suggestive sentences, as pregnant as they are unobtrusive—we must yet, in giving a rapid sketch of the facts established, assume the privilege of directing the reader to one or two of their most obvious consequences, and, like honest 'prentices, not suffer the abstracted retirement of our master in the back parlour to diminish the just recommendation of his wares to the passers-by.

103. Eminently deficient in works representative of the earliest and purest tendencies of art, our National Gallery nevertheless affords a characteristic and sufficient series of examples of the practice of the

various schools of painting, after oil had been finally substituted for the less manageable glutinous vehicles which, under the general name of tempera, were principally employed in the production of easel pictures up to the middle of the fifteenth century. If the reader were to make the circuit of this collection for the purpose of determining which picture represented with least disputable fidelity the first intention of its painter, and united in its modes of execution the highest reach of achievement with the strongest assurance of durability, we believe that—after hesitating long over hypothetical degrees of blackened shadow and yellowed light, of lost outline and buried detail, of chilled lustre, dimmed transparency, altered colour, and weakened force—he would finally pause before a small picture on panel, representing two quaintly dressed figures in a dimly lighted room—dependent for its interest little on expression, and less on treatment—but eminently remarkable for reality of substance, vacuity of space, and vigour of quiet colour ; nor less for an elaborate finish, united with energetic freshness, which seem to show that time has been much concerned in its production, and has had no power over its fate.

104. We do not say that the total force of the material is exhibited in this picture, or even that it in any degree possesses the lusciousness and fulness which

are among the chief charms of oil-painting ; but that upon the whole it would be selected as uniting imperishable firmness with exquisite delicacy ; as approaching more unaffectedly and more closely than any other work to the simple truths of natural colour and space ; and as exhibiting, even in its quaint and minute treatment, conquest over many of the difficulties which the boldest practice of art involves.

This picture, bearing the inscription " Johannes Van Eyck (fuit ?) hic, 1434," is probably the portrait, certainly the work, of one of those brothers to whose ingenuity the first invention of the art of oil-painting has been long ascribed.   The volume before us is occupied chiefly in determining the real extent of the improvements they introduced, in examining the processes they employed, and in tracing the modifications of those processes adopted by later Flemings, especially Rubens, Rembrandt, and Vandyck.   Incidental notices of the Italian system occur, so far as, in its earlier stages, it corresponded with that of the north ; but the consideration of its separate character is reserved for a following volume, and though we shall expect with interest this concluding portion of the treatise, we believe that, in the present condition of the English school, the choice of the methods of Van Eyck, Bellini, or Rubens, is as much as we could modestly ask or prudently desire.

105. It would have been strange indeed if a technical perfection like that of the picture above described (equally characteristic of all the works of those brothers), had been at once reached by the first inventors of the art. So far was this from being the case, and so distinct is the evidence of the practice of oil-painting in antecedent periods, that of late years the discoveries of the Van Eycks have not unfrequently been treated as entirely fabulous; and Raspe, in particular, rests their claims to gratitude on the contingent introduction of amber-varnish and poppy-oil :—"Such *perhaps*," he says, "might have been the misrepresented discovery of the Van Eycks." That tradition, however, for which the great painters of Italy, and their sufficiently vain historian, had so much respect as never to put forward any claim in opposition to it, is not to be clouded by incautious suspicion. Mr. Eastlake has approached it with more reverence, stripped it of its exaggeration, and shown the foundations for it in the fact that the Van Eycks, though they did not create the art, yet were the first to enable it for its function; that having found it in servile office and with dormant power—laid like the dead Adonis on his lettuce-bed—they gave it vitality and dominion. And fortunate it is for those who look for another such reanimation, that the method of the Van Eycks was

not altogether their own discovery. Had it been so, that method might still have remained a subject of conjecture ; but after being put in possession of the principles commonly acknowledged before their time, it is comparatively easy to trace the direction of their inquiry and the nature of their improvements.

106. With respect to remote periods of antiquity, we believe that the use of a hydrofuge oil-varnish for the protection of works in tempera, the only fact insisted upon by Mr. Eastlake, is also the only one which the labour of innumerable ingenious writers has established : nor up to the beginning of the twelfth century is there proof of any practice of painting except in tempera, encaustic (wax applied by the aid of heat), and fresco. Subsequent to that period, notices of works executed in solid colour mixed with oil are frequent, but all that can be proved respecting earlier times is a gradually in- creasing acquaintance with the different kinds of oil and the modes of their adaptation to artistical uses.

Several drying oils are mentioned by the writers of the first three centuries of the Christian era— walnut by Pliny and Galen, walnut, poppy, and castor-oil (afterwards used by the painters of the twelfth century as a varnish) by Dioscorides—yet these notices occur only with reference to medicinal or culinary purposes. But at length a drying oil is mentioned in connection with works of art by Aetius, a medical writer of the fifth century.   His words are :—

"Walnut oil is prepared like that of almonds, either by pounding or pressing the nuts, or by throwing them, after they have been bruised, into boiling water.   The (medicinal) uses are the same : but it has a use besides these, being employed by gilders or encaustic painters; for it dries, and preserves gildings and encaustic paintings for a long time."

"It is therefore clear," says Mr. Eastlake, "that an oil varnish, composed either of inspissated nut oil, or of nut oil combined with a dissolved resin, was employed on gilt surfaces and pictures, with a view to preserve them, at least as early as the fifth century.   It may be added that a writer who could then state, as if from his own experience, that such varnishes had the effect of preserving works 'for a long time,' can hardly be understood to speak of a new invention."—P. 22.

Linseed-oil is also mentioned by Aetius, though still for medicinal uses only ; but a varnish, composed of linseed-oil mixed with a variety of resins, is described in a manuscript at Lucca, belonging probably to the eighth century :—

"The age of Charlemagne was an era in the arts; and the addition of linseed-oil to the materials of the varnisher and decorator may on the above evidence be assigned to it. From this time, and during many ages, the linseed oil varnish, though composed of simpler materials (such as sandarac and mastic resin boiled in the oil), alone appears in the recipes hitherto brought to light."—*Ib.*, p. 24.

107. The modes of bleaching and thickening oil in

the sun, as well as the siccative power of metallic
oxides, were known to the classical writers, and
evidence exists of the careful study of Galen, Dioscorides, and others by the painters of the twelfth
and thirteenth centuries : the loss (recorded by
Vasari) of Antonio Veneziano to the arts, "per che
studio in Dioscoride le cose dell' erbe," is a remarkable instance of its less fortunate results. Still,
the immixture of solid colour with the oil, which
had been commonly used as a varnish for tempera
paintings and gilt surfaces, was hitherto unsug-
gested ; and no distinct notice seems to occur of
the first occasion of this important step, though in
the twelfth century, as above stated, the process is
described as frequent both in Italy and England.
Mr. Eastlake's instances have been selected, for the
most part, from four treatises, two of which, though
in an imperfect form, have long been known to the
public ; the third, translated by Mrs. Merrifield, is in
course of publication ; the fourth, "Tractatus de
Coloribus Illuminatorum," is of less importance.

Respecting the dates of the first two, those of
Eraclius and Theophilus, some difference of opinion
exists between Mr. Eastlake and their respective
editors. The former MS. was published by Raspe,*
who inclines to the opinion of its having been written

* "A Critical Essay on Oil-Painting," London, 1781.

10

soon after the time of St. Isidore of Seville, probably therefore in the eighth century, but insists
only on its being prior to the thirteenth. That of
Theophilus, published first by M. Charles de l'Es-
calopier, and lately from a more perfect MS. by Mr.
Hendrie, is ascribed by its English editor (who
places Eraclius in the tenth) to the early half of
the eleventh century. Mr. Hendrie maintains his
opinion with much analytical ingenuity, and we are
disposed to think that Mr. Eastlake attaches too
much importance to the absence of reference to oil-
painting in the Mappæ Clavicula (a MS. of the
twelfth century), in placing Theophilus a century
and a half later on that ground alone. The question
is one of some importance in an antiquarian point of
view, but the general reader will perhaps be satisfied
with the conclusion that in MSS. which cannot possibly be later than the close of the twelfth century,
references to oil-painting are clear and frequent.

108. Nothing is known of the personality of either
Eraclius or Theophilus, but what may be collected
from their works ; amounting, in the first case, to the
facts of the author's "language being barbarous, his
credulity exceptionable, and his knowledge superficial,"
together with his written description as " vir sapien-
tissimus ; " while all that is positively known of
Theophilus is that he was a monk, and that Theo-

philus was not his real name. The character, however, of which the assumed name is truly expressive, deserves from us no unrespectful attention : we shall best possess our readers of it by laying before them one or two passages from the preface. We shall make some use of Mr. Hendrie's translation ; it is evidently the work of a tasteful man, and in most cases renders the feeling of the original faithfully ; but the Latin, monkish though it be, deserved a more accurate following, and many of Mr. Hendrie's deviations bear traces of unsound scholarship. An awkward instance occurs in the first paragraph :—

"Theophilus, humilis presbyter, servus servorum Dei, indignus nomine et professione monachi, omnibus mentis desidiam animique vagationem utili manuum occupatione, et delectabili novitatum meditatione declinare et calcare volentibus, retributionem cœlestis præmii ! "

"I, Theophilus, an humble priest, servant of the servants of God, unworthy of the name and profession of a monk, to all wishing to overcome and avoid sloth of the mind or wandering of the soul, by useful manual occupation and the delightful contemplation of novelties, send a recompense of heavenly price."—*Theophilus*, p. 1.

Præmium is not " price," nor is the verb understood before *retributionem* "send." Mr. Hendrie seems even less familiar with Scriptural than with monkish language, or in this and several other cases he would have recognised the adoption of apostolic

formulæ. The whole paragraph is such a greeting
and prayer as stands at the head of the sacred
epistles :—" Theophilus, to all who desire to overcome
wandering of the soul, etc., etc. (wishes) recompense
of heavenly reward." Thus also the dedication of
the Byzantine manuscript, lately translated by M.
Didron, commences " A tous les peintres, et à tous
ceux qui, aimant l'instruction, étudieront ce livre, salut
dans le Seigneur." So, presently afterwards, in the
sentence, " divina dignatio quæ dat omnibus affluenter
et non improperat " (translated, " divine *authority*
which affluently and not precipitately gives to all "),
though Mr. Hendrie might have perhaps been ex-
cused for not perceiving the transitive sense of
dignatio after *indignus* in the previous text, which
indeed, even when felt, is sufficiently difficult to
render in English; and might not have been aware
that the word *impropero* frequently bears the sense
of *opprobro ;* he ought still to have recognised the
Scriptural " who giveth to all men liberally and *up-
braideth* not." " Qui," in the first page, translated
" wherefore," mystifies a whole sentence ; " ut mere-
retur," rendered with a school-boy's carelessness " as
he merited," reverses the meaning of another ; " jac-
tantia," in the following page, is less harmfully but
not less singularly translated "jealousy." We have
been obliged to alter several expressions in the

following passages, in order to bring them near
enough to the original for our immediate purpose :

" Which knowledge, when he has obtained, let no one
magnify himself in his own eyes, as if it had been received from himself, and not from elsewhere ; but let him
rejoice humbly in the Lord, from whom and by whom
are all things, and without whom is nothing ; nor let him
wrap his gifts in the folds of envy, nor hide them in the
closet of an avaricious heart ; but all pride of heart being
repelled, let him with a cheerful mind give with simplicity
to all who ask of him, and let him fear the judgment of
the Gospel upon that merchant, who, failing to return to
his lord a talent with accumulated interest, deprived of all
reward, merited the censure from the mouth of his judge
of 'wicked servant.'

" Fearing to incur which sentence, I, a man unworthy
and almost without name, offer gratuitously to all desirous
with humility to learn, that which the divine condescension, which giveth to all men liberally and up-
braideth not, gratuitously conceded to me : and I
admonish them that in me they acknowledge the goodness, and admire the generosity of God ; and I would
persuade them to believe that if they also add their labour,
the same gifts are within their reach.

" Wherefore, gentle son, whom God has rendered perfectly happy in this respect, that those things are offered to
thee gratis, which many, ploughing the sea waves with the
greatest danger to life, consumed by the hardship of hunger
and cold, or subjected to the weary servitude of teachers,
and altogether worn out by the desire of learning, yet
acquire with intolerable labour, covet with greedy looks
this ' BOOK OF VARIOUS ARTS,' read it through with a tenacious memory, embrace it with an ardent love.

"Should you carefully peruse this, you will there find
out whatever Greece possesses in kinds and mixtures of
various colours ; whatever Tuscany knows of in mosaic-
work, or in variety of enamel; whatever Arabia shows
forth in work of fusion, ductility, or chasing ; whatever
Italy ornaments with gold, in diversity of vases and
sculpture of gems or ivory; whatever France loves in a
costly variety of windows; whatever industrious Germany
approves in work of gold, silver, copper, and iron, of
woods and of stones.

"When you shall have re-read this often, and have committed it to your tenacious memory, you shall thus recompense me for this care of instruction, that as often as you
shall have successfully made use of my work, you pray for
me for the pity of Omnipotent God, who knows that I have
written these things, which are here arranged, neither
through love of human approbation, nor through desire of
temporal reward, nor have I stolen anything precious or rare
through envious jealousy, nor have I kept back anything
reserved for myself alone; but in augmentation of the honour
and glory of His name, I have consulted the progress and
hastened to aid the necessities of many men."—*Ib.* pp.
xlvii.-li.

109. There is perhaps something in the naïve seriousness with which these matters of empiricism, to us of
so small importance, are regarded by the good monk,
which may at first tempt the reader to a smile. It is,
however, to be kept in mind that some such mode of
introduction was customary in all works of this order
and period. The Byzantine MS., already alluded to,
is prefaced still more singularly: "Que celui qui veut
apprendre la science de la peinture commence à s'y

préparer d'avance quelque temps en dessinant sans
relache . . . . . puis qu'il adresse à Jesus Christ la
prière et oraison suivante," etc. :—the prayer being
followed by a homily respecting envy, much resembling
that of Theophilus. And we may rest assured that
until we have again begun to teach and to learn in this
spirit, art will no more recover its true power or place
than springs which flow from no heavenward hills can
rise to useful level in the wells of the plain. The
tenderness, tranquillity, and resoluteness which we feel
in such men's words and thoughts found a correspondent expression even in the movements of the
hand; precious qualities resulted from them even in
the most mechanical of their works, such as no reward
can evoke, no academy teach, nor any other merits
replace. What force can be summoned by authority,
or fostered by patronage, which could for an instant
equal in intensity the labour of this humble love,
exerting itself for its own pleasure, looking upon its
own works by the light of thankfulness, and finishing
all, offering all, with the irrespective profusion of
flowers opened by the wayside, where the dust may
cover them, and the foot crush them ?

110. Not a few passages conceived in the highest
spirit of self-denying piety would, of themselves, have
warranted our sincere thanks to Mr. Hendrie for his
publication of the manuscript. The practical value of

its contents is however very variable; most of the
processes described have been either improved or
superseded, and many of the recipes are quite as illus-
trative of the writer's credulity in reception, as generosity in communication.   The references to the " land of
Havilah " for gold, and to " Mount Calybe " for iron, are
characteristic of monkish geographical science ;   the
recipe for the making of Spanish gold is interesting,
as affording us a clue to the meaning of the mediæval
traditions respecting the basilisk.   Pliny says nothing
about the hatching of this chimera from cocks' eggs,
and ascribes the power of killing at sight to a different
animal, the catoblepas, whose head, fortunately, was so
heavy that it could not be held up.   Probably the word
" basiliscus " in   Theophilus   would   have   been   better
translated " cockatrice."

   " There is also a gold called Spanish gold, which is composed from red copper, powder of basilisk, and human
blood, and acid.   The Gentiles, whose skilfulness in this
art is commendable, make basilisks in this manner.   They
have, underground, a house walled with stones everywhere, above and below, with two very small windows,
so narrow that scarcely any light can appear through
them ; in this house they place two old cocks of twelve or
fifteen years, and they give them plenty of food.   When
these have become fat, through the heat of their good
condition, they agree together and lay eggs.   Which being
laid, the cocks are taken out and toads are placed in, which
may hatch the eggs, and to which bread is given for food.
The eggs being hatched, chickens issue out, like hens'

chickens, to which after seven days grow the tails of
serpents, and immediately, if there were not a stone pavement to the house, they would enter the earth. Guarding
against which, their masters have round brass vessels of
large size, perforated all over, the mouths of which are
narrow, in which they place these chickens, and close the
mouths with copper coverings and inter them underground,
and they are nourished with the fine earth entering through
the holes for six months. After this they uncover them
and apply a copious fire, until the animals' insides are completely burnt. Which done, when they have become cold,
they are taken out and carefully ground, adding to them a
third part of the blood of a red man, which blood has been
dried and ground. These two compositions are tempered
with sharp acid in a clean vessel; they then take very thin
sheets of the purest red copper, and anoint this composition
over them on both sides, and place them in the fire. And
when they have become glowing, they take them out and
quench and wash them in the same confection; and they
do this for a long time, until this composition eats through
the copper, and it takes the colour of gold. This gold is
proper for all work."—*Ib.* p. 267.

Our readers will find in Mr. Hendrie's interesting
note the explanation of the symbolical language of this
recipe; though we cannot agree with him in supposing
Theophilus to have so understood it. We have no
doubt the monk wrote what he had heard in good faith,
and with no equivocal meaning; and we are even ourselves much disposed to regret and resist the transformation of toads into nitrates of potash, and of
basilisks into sulphates of copper.

111. But whatever may be the value of the recipes of Theophilus, couched in the symbolical language of the alchemist, his evidence is as clear as it is conclusive, as far as regards the general processes adopted in his own time. The treatise of Peter de St. Audemar, contained in a volume transcribed by Jehan le Begue in 1431, bears internal evidence of being nearly coeval with that of Theophilus. And in addition to these MSS., Mr. Eastlake has examined the records of Ely and Westminster, which are full of references to decorative operations. From these sources it is not only demonstrated that oil-painting, at least in the broadest sense (striking colours mixed with oil on surfaces of wood or stone), was perfectly common both in Italy and England in the 12th, 13th, and 14th centuries, but every step of the process is determinable. Stone surfaces were primed with white lead mixed with linseed oil, applied in successive coats, and carefully smoothed when dry. Wood was planed smooth (or, for delicate work, covered with leather of horse-skin or parchment), then coated with a mixture of white lead, wax, and pulverized tile, on which the oil and lead priming was laid. In the successive application of the coats of this priming, the painter is warned by Eraclius of the danger of letting the superimposed coat be more oily than that beneath, the shrivelling of the surface being a necessary consequence.

"The observation respecting the cause, or one of the causes, of a wrinkled and shrivelled surface, is not unimportant. Oil, or an oil varnish, used in abundance with the colours over a perfectly dry preparation, will produce this appearance : the employment of an oil varnish is even supposed to be detected by it. . . . . As regards the effect itself, the best painters have not been careful to avoid it. Parts of Titian's St. Sebastian (now in the Gallery of the Vatican) are shrivelled ; the Giorgione in the Louvre is so ; the drapery of the figure of Christ in the Duke of Wellington's Correggio exhibits the same appearance ; a Madonna and Child by Reynolds, at Petworth, is in a similar state, as are also parts of some pictures by Greuze.   It is the reverse of a cracked surface, and is unquestionably the less evil of the two."—" Eastlake," pp. 36-38.

112. On the white surface thus prepared, the colours, ground finely with linseed oil, were applied, according to the advice of Theophilus, in not less than three successive coats, and finally protected with amber or sandarac varnish : each coat of colour being carefully dried by the aid of heat or in the sun before a second was applied, and the entire work before varnishing. The practice of carefully drying each coat was continued in the best periods of art, but the necessity of exposure to the sun intimated by Theophilus appears to have arisen only from his careless preparation of the linseed oil, and ignorance of a proper drying medium. Consequent on this necessity is the restriction in Theophilus, St. Audemar, and in the British Museum MS., of oil-painting to wooden surfaces, because mov-

able panels could be dried in the sun ; while, for walls,
the colours are to be mixed with water, wine, gum, or
the usual tempera vehicles, egg and fig-tree juice;
white lead and verdigris, themselves driers, being the
only pigments which could be mixed with oil for walls.
But the MS. of Eraclius and the records of our English
cathedrals imply no such absolute restriction. They
mention the employment of oil for the painting or
varnishing of columns and interior walls, and in
quantity very remarkable.   Among the entries relating
to St. Stephen's chapel, occur—" For 19 flagons of
painter's oil, at 3s. 4d. the flagon, 43s. 4d." (It might
be as well, in the next edition, to correct the copyist's
reverse of the position of the X and L, lest it should be
thought that the principles of the science of arithmetic
have been progressive, as well as those of art.)   And
presently afterwards, in May of the same year, "to
John de Hennay, for *seventy* flagons and a half of
painter's oil for the painting of the same chapel, at 20d.
the flagon, 117s. 6d." The expression " painter's oil "
seems to imply more careful preparation than that
directed by Theophilus, probably purification from its
mucilage in the sun ; but artificial heat was certainly
employed to assist the drying, and after reading of
flagons supplied by the score, we can hardly be surprised at finding charcoal furnished by the cartload—
see an entry relating to the Painted Chamber.   In one

MS. of Eraclius, however, a distinct description of a drying oil in the modern sense, occurs, white lead and lime being added, and the oil thickened by exposure to the sun, as was the universal practice in Italy.

113. Such was the system of oil-painting known before the time of Van Eyck ; but it remains a question in what kind of works and with what degree of refinement this system had been applied.   The passages in Eraclius refer only to ornamental work, imitations of marble, etc. ; and although, in the records of Ely cathedral, the words " pro ymaginibus super columnas depingendis " may perhaps be understood as referring to paintings of figures, the applications of oil, which are distinctly determinable from these and other English documents, are merely decorative ; and "the large supplies of it which appear in the Westminster and Ely records indicate the coarseness of the operations for which it was required."   Theophilus, indeed, mentions tints for faces—*mixturas vultuum ;* but it is to be remarked that Theophilus painted with a liquid oil, the drying of which in the sun he expressly says "in *ymaginibus* et aliis picturis diuturnum et tædiosum nimis est."   The oil generally employed was thickened to the consistence of a varnish.   Cennini recommends that it be kept in the sun until reduced one half ; and in the Paris copy of Eraclius we are told that "the longer the oil remains in the sun the better it will

be." Such a vehicle entirely precluded delicacy of execution.

"Paintings entirely executed with the thickened vehicle, at a time when art was in the very lowest state, and when its votaries were ill qualified to contend with unnecessary difficulties, must have been of the commonest description. Armorial bearings, patterns, and similar works of mechanical decoration, were perhaps as much as could be attempted.

"Notwithstanding the general reference to flesh-painting, 'e cosi fa dello incarnare,' in Cennini's directions, there are no certain examples of pictures of the fourteenth century, in which the flesh is executed in oil colours. This leads us to inquire what were the ordinary applications of oil-painting in Italy at that time. It appears that the method, when adopted at all, was considered to belong to the complemental and merely decorative parts of a picture. It was employed in portions of the work only, on draperies, and over gilding and foils. Cennini describes such operations as follows. 'Gild the surface to be occupied by the drapery; draw on it what ornaments or patterns you please; glaze the unornamented intervals with verdigris ground in oil, shading some folds twice. Then, when this is dry, glaze the same colour over the whole drapery, both ornaments and plain portions.'

"These operations, together with the gilt field round the figures, the stucco decorations, and the carved framework, tabernacle, or *ornamento* itself of the picture, were completed first; the faces and hands, which in Italian pictures of the fourteenth century were always in tempera, were added afterwards, or at all events after the draperies and background were finished. Cennini teaches the practice of all but the carving. In later times the work was divided, and the decorator or gilder was sometimes a more im-

portant person than the painter. Thus some works of an
inferior Florentine artist were ornamented with stuccoes,
carving, and gilding, by the celebrated Donatello, who, in
his youth, practised this art in connection with sculpture.
Vasari observed the following inscription under a picture :—
'Simone Cini, a Florentine, wrought the carved work ;
Gabriello Saracini executed the gilding ; and Spinello di
Luca, of Arezzo, painted the picture, in the year 1385.' "—
Ib. pp. 71, 72, and 80.

114. We may pause to consider for a moment what
effect upon the mental habits of these earlier schools
might result from this separate and previous completion of minor details. It is to be remembered that the
painter's object in the backgrounds of works of this
period (universally, or nearly so, of religious subject)
was not the deceptive representation of a natural scene,
but the adornment and setting forth of the central
figures with precious work—the conversion of the
picture, as far as might be, into a gem, flushed with
colour and alive with light. The processes necessary
for this purpose were altogether mechanical ; and those
of stamping and burnishing the gold, and of enamelling,
were necessarily performed before any delicate tempera-
work could be executed. Absolute decision of design
was therefore necessary throughout ; hard linear sepa-
rations were unavoidable between the oil-colour and
the tempera, or between each and the gold or enamel.
General harmony of effect, aerial perspective, or de-

ceptive chiaroscuro, became totally impossible ; and the
dignity of the picture depended exclusively on the lines
of its design, the purity of its ornaments, and the
beauty of expression which could be attained in those
portions (the faces and hands) which, set off and
framed by this splendour of decoration, became the
cynosure of eyes. The painter's entire energy was
given to these portions ; and we can hardly imagine
any discipline more calculated to ensure a grand and
thoughtful school of art than the necessity of discrimi-
nated character and varied expression imposed by this
peculiarly separate and prominent treatment of the
features. The exquisite drawing of the hand also, at
least in outline, remained for this reason even to late
periods one of the crowning excellences of the religious
schools. It might be worthy the consideration of our
present painters whether some disadvantage may not
result from the exactly opposite treatment now frequently adopted, the finishing of the head before the
addition of its accessories. A flimsy and indolent
background is almost a necessary consequence, and
probably also a false flesh-colour, irrecoverable by any
after-opposition.

115. The reader is in possession of most of the
conclusions relating to the practice of oil-painting up
to about the year 1406.

"Its inconveniences were such that tempera was not

unreasonably preferred to it for works that required careful design, precision, and completeness. Hence the Van Eycks seem to have made it their first object to overcome the stigma that attached to oil-painting, as a process fit only for ordinary purposes and mechanical decorations. With an ambition partly explained by the previous coarse applications of the method, they sought to raise wonder by surpassing the finish of tempera with the very material that had long been considered intractable. Mere finish was, however, the least of the excellences of these reformers. The step was short which sufficed to remove the self-imposed difficulties of the art; but that effort would probably not have been so successful as it was, in overcoming long-established prejudices, had it not been accompanied by some of the best qualities which oil-painting, as a means of imitating nature, can command."—*Ib.* p. 88.

116. It has been a question to which of the two brothers, Hubert or John, the honour of the invention is to be attributed. Van Mander gives the date of the birth of Hubert 1366; and his interesting epitaph in the cathedral of St. Bavon, at Ghent, determines that of his death :—

"Take warning from me, ye who walk over me. I was as you are, but am now buried dead beneath you. Thus it appears that neither art nor medicine availed me. Art, honour, wisdom, power, affluence, are spared not when death comes. I was called Hubert Van Eyck; I am now food for worms. Formerly known and highly honoured in painting; this all was shortly after turned to nothing. It was in the year of the Lord one thousand four hundred and twenty-six, on the eighteenth day of September, that I rendered up my soul to God, in sufferings. Pray God for

me, ye who love art, that I may attain to His sight. Flee sin ;
turn to the best [objects] : for you must follow me at last."

John Van Eyck appears by sufficient evidence to
have been born between 1390 and 1395 ; and, as the
improved oil-painting was certainly introduced about
1410, the probability is greater that the system had been
discovered by the elder brother than by the youth of
15. What the improvement actually was is a far more
important question. Vasari's account, in the Life of
Antonello da Messina, is the first piece of evidence
here examined (p. 205); and it is examined at once
with more respect and more advantage than the half-
negligent, half-embarrassed wording of the passage
might appear either to deserve or to promise. Vasari
states that "*Giovanni* of Bruges," having finished a
tempera-picture on panel, and varnished it as usual,
placed it in the sun to dry—that the heat opened the
joinings—and that the artist, provoked at the destruction of his work—

" began to devise means for preparing a kind of varnish
which should dry in the shade, so as to avoid placing his
pictures in the sun. Having made experiments with many
things, both pure and mixed together, he at last found that
linseed-oil and nut-oil, among the many which he had
tested, were more drying than all the rest. These, therefore, boiled with *other mixtures of his*, made him the varnish
which he, nay, which all the painters of the world, had
long desired. Continuing his experiments with many
other things, he saw that the immixture of the colours

with these kinds of oils gave them a very firm consistence, which, when dry, was proof against wet; and, moreover, that the vehicle lit up the colours so powerfully, that it gave a gloss of itself without varnish; and that which appeared to him still more admirable was, that it allowed of blending [the colours] infinitely better than tempera. Giovanni, rejoicing in this invention, and being a person of discernment, began many works."

117. The reader must observe that this account is based upon and clumsily accommodated to the idea, prevalent in Vasari's time throughout Italy, that Van Eyck not merely improved, but first introduced, the art of oil-painting, and that no mixture of colour with linseed or nut oil had taken place before his time. We are only informed of the new and important part of the invention, under the pointedly specific and peculiarly Vasarian expression—"altre sue misture." But the real value of the passage is dependent on the one fact of which it puts us in possession, and with respect to which there is every reason to believe it trustworthy, that it was in search of a *Varnish* which would dry in the shade that Van Eyck discovered the new vehicle. The next point to be determined is the nature of the Varnish ordinarily employed, and spoken of by Cennini and many other writers under the familiar title of Vernice liquida. The derivation of the word Vernix bears materially on the question, and will not be devoid of interest for the general reader, who may perhaps be

surprised at finding himself carried by Mr. Eastlake's daring philology into regions poetical and planetary :—

"Eustathius, a writer of the twelfth century, in his commentary on Homer, states that the Greeks of his day called amber (ἤλεκτρον) Veronice (βερονίκη). Salmasius, quoting from a Greek medical MS. of the same period, writes it Verenice (βερενίκη). In the Lucca MS. (8th century) the word Veronica more than once occurs among the ingredients of varnishes, and it is remarkable that in the copies of the same recipes in the *Mappæ Clavicula* (12th century) the word is spelt, in the genitive, Verenicis and Vernicis. This is probably the earliest instance of the use of the Latinized word nearly in its modern form ; the original nominative Vernice being afterwards changed to Vernix.

"Veronice or Verenice, as a designation for amber, must have been common at an earlier period than the date of the Lucca MS., since it there occurs as a term in ordinary use. It is scarcely necessary to remark that the letter β was sounded v by the mediæval Greeks, as it is by their present descendants. Even during the classic ages of Greece β represented φ in certain dialects. The name Berenice or Beronice, borne by more than one daughter of the Ptolemies, would be more correctly written Pherenice or Pheronice. The literal coincidence of this name and its modifications with the Vernice of the middle ages, might almost warrant the supposition that amber, which by the best ancient authorities was considered a mineral, may, at an early period, have been distinguished by the name of a constellation, the constellation of Berenice's (golden) hair."—*Eastlake*, p. 230.

118. We are grieved to interrupt our reader's voyage among the constellations ; but the next page crys-

tallizes us again like ants in amber, or worse, in gum-sandarach. It appears, from conclusive and abundant evidence, that the greater cheapness of sandarach, and its easier solubility in oil rendered it the usual substitute for amber, and that the word Vernice, when it occurs alone, is the common synonym for dry sandarach resin. This, dissolved by heat in linseed oil, three parts oil to one of resin, was the Vernice liquida of the Italians, sold in Cennini's time ready prepared, and the customary varnish of tempera pictures. Concrete turpentine ("oyle of fir-tree," "Pece Greca," "Pegola"), previously prepared over a slow fire until it ceased to swell, was added to assist the liquefaction of the sandarach, first in Venice, where the material could easily be procured, and afterwards in Florence. The varnish so prepared, especially when it was long boiled to render it more drying, was of a dark colour, materially affecting the tints over which it was passed.*

"It is not impossible that the lighter style of colouring introduced by Giotto may have been intended by him to counteract the effects of this varnish, the appearance of which in the Greek pictures he could not fail to observe. Another peculiarity in the works of the painters of the

---

* "The mediæval painters were so accustomed to this appearance in varnishes, and considered it so indispensable, that they even supplied the tint when it did not exist. Thus Cardanus observes that when white of eggs was used as a varnish, it was customary to tinge it with red lead."—*Eastlake*, p. 270.

time referred to, particularly those of the Florentine and Sienese schools, is the greenish tone of their colouring in the flesh; produced by the mode in which they often prepared their works, viz. by a green underpainting. The appearance was neutralized by the red sandarac varnish, and pictures executed in the manner described must have looked better before it was removed."—*Ib.* p. 252.

Farther on, this remark is thus followed out :—

"The paleness or freshness of the tempera may have been sometimes calculated for this brown glazing (for such it was in effect), and when this was the case, the picture was, strictly speaking, unfinished without its varnish. It is, therefore, quite conceivable that a painter, averse to mere mechanical operations, would, in his final process, still have an eye to the harmony of his work, and, seeing that the tint of his varnish was more or less adapted to display the hues over which it was spread, would vary that tint, so as to heighten the effect of the picture. The practice of tinging varnishes was not even new, as the example given by Cardanus proves. The next step to this would be to treat the tempera picture still more as a preparation, and to calculate still further on the varnish, by modifying and adapting its colour to a greater extent. A work so completed must have nearly approached the appearance of an oil picture. This was perhaps the moment when the new method opened itself to the mind of Hubert Van Eyck. . . . The next change necessarily consisted in using opaque as well as transparent colours ; the former being applied over the light, the latter over the darker, portions of the picture ; while the work in tempera was now reduced to a light chiaroscuro preparation. . . . . It was now that the hue of the original varnish became an objection ; for, as a medium, it required to be itself colourless."—*Ib.* pp. 271—273.

119. Our author has perhaps somewhat embarrassed this part of the argument, by giving too much importance to the conjectural adaptation of the tints of the tempera picture to the brown varnish, and too little to the bold transition from transparent to opaque colour on the lights.   Up to this time, we must remember, the entire drawing of the flesh had been in tempera ; the varnish, however richly tinted, however delicately adjusted to the tints beneath, was still broadly applied over the whole surface, the design being seen through the transparent glaze.   But the mixture of opaque colour at once implies that portions of the design itself were executed with the varnish for a vehicle, and therefore that the varnish had been entirely changed both in colour and consistence.   If, as above stated, the improvement in the varnish had been made only after it had been mixed with opaque colour, it does not appear why the idea of so mixing it should have presented itself to Van Eyck more than to any other painter of the day, and Vasari's story of the split panel becomes nugatory.   But we apprehend, from a previous passage (p.   258), that Mr. Eastlake would not have us so interpret him. We rather suppose that we are expressing his real opinion in stating our own, that Van Eyck, seeking for a varnish which would dry in the shade, first perfected the methods of dissolving amber or copal

in oil, then sought for and added a good drier, and
thus obtained a varnish which, having been subjected
to no long process of boiling, was nearly colourless;
that in using this new varnish over tempera works he
might cautiously and gradually mix it with the opaque
colour, whose purity he now found unaffected by the
transparent vehicle; and, finally, as the thickness of
the varnish in its less perfect state was an obstacle to
precision of execution, increase the proportion of its
oil to the amber, or add a diluent, as occasion required.

120. Such, at all events, in the sum, whatever
might be the order or occasion of discovery, were
Van Eyck's improvements in the vehicle of colour,
and to these, applied by singular ingenuity and
affection to the imitation of nature, with a fidelity
hitherto unattempted, Mr. Eastlake attributes the
influence which his works obtained over his contemporaries :—

" If we ask in what the chief novelty of his practice
consisted, we shall at once recognise it in an amount of
general excellence before unknown. At all times, from
Van Eyck's day to the present, whenever nature has been
surprisingly well imitated in pictures, the first and last
question with the ignorant has been—What materials did
the artist use ? The superior mechanical secret is always
supposed to be in the hands of the greatest genius ; and an
early example of sudden perfection in art, like the fame of
the heroes of antiquity, was likely to monopolize and
represent the claims of many."—*Ib.* p. 266.

This is all true ; that Van Eyck saw nature more
truly than his predecessors is certain ; but it is disputable whether this rendering of nature recommended
his works to the imitation of the Italians.   On the
contrary, Mr. Eastlake himself observes in another
place (p. 220), that the character of delicate imitation common to the Flemish pictures militated
against the acceptance of their method :—

"The specimens of Van Eyck, Hugo van der Goes,
Memling, and others, which the Florentines had seen, may
have appeared, in the eyes of some severe judges (for
example, those who daily studied the frescoes of Masaccio),
to indicate a certain connection between oil painting and
minuteness, if not always of size, yet of style.   The
method, by its very finish and the possible completeness
of its gradations, must have seemed well calculated to
exhibit numerous objects on a small scale.   That this
was really the impression produced, at a later period,
on one who represented the highest style of design, has
been lately proved by means of an interesting document,
in which the opinions of Michael Angelo on the character of
Flemish pictures are recorded by a contemporary artist."*

121.   It was not, we apprehend, the resemblance to
nature, but the abstract power of colour, which inflamed with admiration and jealousy the artists of

---

* "Si je dis tant de mal de la peinture flamande, ce n'est pas
qu'elle soit entièrement mauvaise, mais elle veut *rendre avec perfection*
tant de choses, dont une seule suffirait par son importance, qu'elle
n'en fait aucune d'une manière satisfaisante." This opinion of M.
Angelo's is preserved by Francisco de Ollanda, quoted by Comte
Raczynski, "Les Arts en Portugal," Paris, 1846.

Italy; it was not the delicate touch nor the precise
verity of Van Eyck, but the "vivacita de' colori"
(says Vasari) which at the first glance induced
Antonello da Messina to "put aside every other
avocation and thought, and at once set out for
Flanders," assiduously to cultivate the friendship of
Giovanni, presenting to him many drawings and
other things, until *Giovanni*, finding himself already
old, was content that Antonello should see the
method of his colouring in oil, nor then to quit
Flanders until he had "thoroughly learned that
process." It was this *process*, separate, mysterious,
and admirable, whose communication the Venetian,
Domenico, thought the most acceptable kindness
which could repay his hospitality; and whose solitary possession Castagno thought cheaply purchased
by the guilt of the betrayer and murderer; it was in
this process, the deduction of watchful intelligence,
not by fortuitous discovery, that the first impulse
was given to European art. Many a plank had
yawned in the sun before Van Eyck's; but he alone
saw through the rent, as through an opening portal,
the lofty perspective of triumph widening its rapid
wedge;—many a spot of opaque colour had clouded
the transparent amber of earlier times; but the little
cloud that rose over Van Eyck's horizon was "like
unto a man's hand."

What this process was, and how far it differed from preceding practice, has hardly, perhaps, been pronounced by Mr. Eastlake with sufficient distinctness. One or two conclusions which he has not marked are, we think, deducible from his evidence. In one point, and that not an unimportant one, we believe that many careful students of colouring will be disposed to differ with him : our own intermediate opinion we will therefore venture to state, though with all diffidence.

122. We must not, however, pass entirely without notice the two chapters on the preparation of oils, and on the oleo-resinous vehicles, though to the general reader the recipes contained in them are of little interest ; and in the absence of all expression of opinion on the part of Mr. Eastlake as to their comparative excellence, even to the artist, their immediate utility appears somewhat doubtful. One circumstance, however, is remarkable in all, the care taken by the great painters, without exception, to avoid the yellowing of their oil. Perfect and stable clearness is the ultimate aim of all the processes described (many of them troublesome and tedious in the extreme) : and the effect of the altered oil is of course most dreaded on pale and cold colours. Thus Philippe Nunez tells us how to purify linseed oil " for white and blues ;" and Pacheco, "el de

linaza no me quele mal : aunque ai quien diga que
no a de ver el Azul ni el Blanco este Azeite."*   De
Mayerne recommends poppy oil "for painting white,
blue, and similar colours, so that they shall not
yellow;" and in another place, " for air-tints and
blue;"—while the inclination to green is noticed as
an imperfection in hempseed oil : so Vasari—speaking
of linseed-oil in contemporary practice—" benchè
il noce e meglio, perchè ingialla meno." The
Italians generally mixed an essential oil with their
delicate tints, including flesh tints (p. 431). Extraordinary methods were used by the Flemish painters
to protect their blues; they were sometimes painted
with size, and varnished; sometimes strewed in
powder on fresh white-lead (p. 456). Leonardo
gives a careful recipe for preventing the change of
colour in nut oil, supposing it to be owing to neglect
in removing the skin of the nut. His words, given
at p. 321, are incorrectly translated : "una certa
bucciolina," is not a husk or rind—but "a thin skin,"
meaning the white membranous covering of the nut
itself, of which it is almost impossible to detach all
the inner laminæ. This, "che tiene della natura del
mallo," Leonardo supposes to give the expressed oil
its property of forming a *skin* at the surface.

123. We think these passages interesting, because

* "Arte de Pintura." Sevilla, 1649.

they are entirely opposed to the modern ideas of the
desirableness of yellow lights and green blues, which
have been introduced chiefly by the study of altered
pictures. The anxiety of Rubens, expressed in various
letters, quoted at p. 516, lest any of his whites should
have become yellow, and his request that his pictures
might be exposed to the sun to remedy the defect, if
it occurred, are conclusive on this subject, as far as
regards the feeling of the Flemish painters : we shall
presently see that the *coolness* of their light was an
essential part of their scheme of colour.

The testing of the various processes given in these
two chapters must be a matter of time : many of them
have been superseded by recent discoveries. Copal
varnish is in modern practice no inefficient substitute
for amber, and we believe that most artists will agree
with us in thinking that the vehicles now in use are
sufficient for all purposes, if used rightly. We shall,
therefore, proceed in the first place to give a rapid
sketch of the entire process of the Flemish school as
it is stated by Mr. Eastlake in the 11th chapter, and
then examine the several steps of it one by one,
with the view at once of marking what seems disputable, and of deducing from what is certain some
considerations respecting the consequences of its
adoption in subsequent art.

124. The ground was with all the early masters

pure *white*, plaster of Paris, or washed chalk with
size ; a preparation which has been employed without
change from remote antiquity—witness the Egyptian
mummy-cases.   Such a ground, becoming brittle with
age, is evidently unsafe on canvas, unless exceedingly
thin ; and even on panel is liable to crack and detach
itself, unless it be carefully guarded against damp.   The
precautions of Van Eyck against this danger, as well
as against the warping of his panel, are remarkable
instances of his regard to points apparently trivial :—

"In large altar-pieces, necessarily composed of many
pieces, it may be often remarked that each separate plank
has become slightly convex in front : this is particularly
observable in the picture of the Transfiguration by Raphael.
The heat of candles on altars is supposed to have been
the cause of this not uncommon defect ; but heat, if
considerable, would rather produce the contrary appearance.   It would seem that the layer of paint, with its
substratum, slightly operates to prevent the wood from
contracting or becoming concave on that side ; it might
therefore be concluded that a similar protection at the back,
by equalizing the conditions, would tend to keep the wood
flat.   The oak panel on which the picture by Van Eyck in
the National Gallery is painted is protected at the back by
a composition of gesso, size, and tow, over which a coat of
black oil-paint was passed.   This, whether added when the
picture was executed   or   subsequently,   has   tended   to
preserve the wood (which is not at all worm-eaten), and
perhaps to prevent its warping."—*Ib*. pp. 373, 374.

On the white ground, scraped, when it was perfectly
dry, till it was "as white as milk and as smooth as

ivory " (Cennini), the outline of the picture was
drawn, and its light and shade expressed, usually
with the pen, with all possible care; and over this
outline a coating of size was applied in order to
render the gesso ground *non*-absorbent. The establishment of this fact is of the greatest importance,
for the whole question of the true function and use
of the gesso ground hangs upon it. That use has
been supposed by all previous writers on the technical
processes of painting to be, by absorbing the oil, to
remove in some degree the cause of yellowness in
the colours. Had this been so, the ground itself
would have lost its brilliancy, and it would have
followed that a dark ground, equally absorbent, would
have answered the purpose as well. But the
evidence adduced by Mr. Eastlake on this subject is
conclusive :—

" Pictures are sometimes transferred from panel to cloth.
The front being secured by smooth paper or linen, the
picture is laid on its face, and the wood is gradually planed
and scraped away. At last the ground appears; first, the
'gesso grosso,' then, next the painted surface, the 'gesso
sottile.' On scraping this it is found that it is whitest
immediately next the colours; for on the inner side it
may sometimes have received slight stains from the wood,
if the latter was not first sized. When a picture which
happens to be much cracked has been oiled or varnished,
the fluid will sometimes penetrate through the cracks into
the ground, which in such parts had become accessible.

In that case the white ground is stained in lines only,
corresponding in their direction with the cracks of the
picture.   This last circumstance also proves that the
ground was not sufficiently hard in itself to prevent the
absorption of oil.   Accordingly, it required to be rendered
non-absorbent by a coating of size ; and this was passed
over the outline, before the oil-priming was applied."—
Ib. pp. 383, 384.

The perfect whiteness of the ground being thus
secured, a transparent warm oil-priming, in early
practice flesh-coloured, was usually passed over the
entire picture.   This custom, says Mr. Eastlake, appears to have been "a remnant of the old habit of
covering tempera pictures with a warm varnish, and
was sometimes omitted."   When used it was permitted to dry thoroughly, and over it the shadows
were painted in with a rich transparent brown, mixed
with a somewhat thick oleo-resinous vehicle ; the
lighter colours were then added with a thinner
vehicle, taking care not to disturb the transparency
of the shadows by the unnecessary mixture of
opaque pigments, and leaving the ground bearing
bright *through the thin lights.* (?)   As the art advanced, the lights were more and more loaded, and
afterwards glazed, the shadows being still left in
untouched transparency.   This is the method of
Rubens.   The later Italian colourists appear to have
laid opaque local colour without fear even into the

shadows, and to have recovered transparency by ultimate glazing.

125. Such are the principal heads of the method of the early Flemish masters, as stated by Mr. Eastlake. We have marked as questionable the influence of the ground in supporting the lights: our reasons for doing so we will give, after we have stated what we suppose to be the advantages or disadvantages of the process in its earlier stages, guiding ourselves as far as possible by the passages in which any expression occurs of Mr. Eastlake's opinion.

The reader cannot but see that the *eminent* character of the whole system is its predeterminateness. From first to last its success depended on the decision and clearness of each successive step. The drawing and light and shade were secured without any interference of colour; but when over these the oil-priming was once laid, the design could neither be altered nor, if lost, recovered; a colour laid too opaquely in the shadow destroyed the inner organization of the picture, and remained an irremediable blemish; and it was necessary, in laying colour even on the lights, to follow the guidance of the drawing beneath with a caution and precision which rendered anything like freedom of handling, in the modern sense, totally impossible. Every quality which depends on rapidity, accident, or audacity was interdicted; no affectation of ease was suffered to disturb the humility of patient exertion. Let our readers consider in what temper such a work must be undertaken and carried through—a work in which error was irremediable, change impossible—which demanded the drudgery of a student, while it involved the deliberation of a master—in which the patience of a mechanic was to be united with the foresight of a magician—in which no licence could be indulged either to fitfulness of temper or felicity of invention—in which haste was forbidden, yet languor fatal, and consistency of conception no less incumbent than continuity of toil. Let them reflect what kind of men must have been called up and trained by work such as this, and then compare the tones of mind which are likely to be produced by our present practice,— a practice in which alteration is admitted to any extent in any stage—in which neither foundation is laid nor end foreseen—in which all is dared and nothing resolved, everything perilled, nothing provided for—in which men play the sycophant in the courts of their humours, and hunt wisps in the marshes of their wits—a practice which invokes accident, evades law, discredits application, despises system, and sets forth with chief exultation, contingent beauty, and extempore invention.

126. But it is not only the fixed nature of the

successive steps which influenced the character of these early painters. A peculiar *direction* was given to their efforts by the close attention to drawing which, as Mr. Eastlake has especially noticed, was involved in the preparation of the design on the white ground. That design was secured with a care and finish which in many instances might seem altogether supererogatory.* The preparation by John Bellini in the Florentine gallery is completed with exhaustless diligence into even the portions farthest removed from the light, where the thick brown of the shadows must necessarily have afterwards concealed the greater part of the work. It was the discipline undergone in producing this preparation which fixed the character of the school. The most important part of the picture was executed not with the brush, but with the point, and the refinements attainable by this instrument dictated the treatment of their subject. Hence the transition to etching and engraving, and the intense love of minute detail, accompanied by an imaginative communication of dignity and power to the smallest forms, in Albert Dürer and others. But this atten-

---

* The preparations of Hemling, at Bruges, we imagine to have been in water-colour, and perhaps the picture was carried to some degree of completion in this material. Van Mander observes that Van Eyck's dead colourings "were cleaner and sharper than the finished works of other painters."

tion to minutiæ was not the only result; the disposition of light and shade was also affected by the
method. Shade was not to be had at small cost;
its masses could not be dashed on in impetuous
generalization, fields for the future recovery of light.
They were measured out and wrought to their
depths only by expenditure of toil and time; and, as
future grounds for colour, they were necessarily restricted to the *natural* shadow of every object, white
being left for high lights of whatever hue. In consequence, the character of pervading daylight, almost
inevitably produced in the preparation, was afterwards assumed as a standard in the painting.
Effectism, accidental shadows, all obvious and
vulgar artistical treatment, were excluded, or introduced only as the lights became more loaded, and
were consequently imposed with more facility on
the dark ground. Where shade was required in large
mass, it was obtained by introducing an object of
locally dark colour. The Italian masters who followed
Van Eyck's system were in the constant habit of re-
lieving their principal figures by the darkness of some
object, foliage, throne, or drapery, introduced behind
the head, the open sky being left visible on each
side. A green drapery is thus used with great
quaintness by John Bellini in the noble picture of
the Brera Gallery; a black screen, with marbled

veins, behind the portraits of himself and his brother in the Louvre; a crimson velvet curtain behind the Madonna, in Francia's best picture at Bologna. Where the subject was sacred, and the painter great, this system of pervading light produced pictures of a peculiar and tranquil majesty; where the mind of the painter was irregularly or frivolously imaginative, its temptations to accumulative detail were too great to be resisted—the spectator was by the German masters overwhelmed with the copious inconsistency of a dream, or compelled to traverse the picture from corner to corner like a museum of curiosities.

127. The chalk or pen preparation being completed, and the oil-priming laid, we have seen that the shadows were laid in with a transparent *brown* in considerable body. The question next arises—What influence is this part of the process likely to have had upon the *colouring* of the school? It is to be remembered that the practice was continued to the latest times, and that when the thin light had been long abandoned, and a loaded body of colour had taken its place, the brown transparent shadow was still retained, and is retained often to this day, when asphaltum is used as its base, at the risk of the destruction of the picture. The utter loss of many of Reynolds' noblest works has been caused by the lavish use of this pigment. What the pigment

actually was in older times is left by Mr. Eastlake undecided :—

"A rich brown, which, whether an earth or mineral alone, or a substance of the kind enriched by the addition of a transparent yellow or orange, is not an unimportant element of the glowing colouring which is remarkable in examples of the school. Such a colour, by artificial combinations at least, is easily supplied ; and it is repeated, that, in general, the materials now in use are quite as good as those which the Flemish masters had at their command."—*Ib.* p. 488.

At p. 446 it is also asserted that the peculiar glow of the brown of Rubens is hardly to be accounted for by any accidental variety in the Cassel earths, but was obtained by the mixture of a transparent yellow. Evidence, however, exists of asphaltum having been used in Flemish pictures, and with safety, even though prepared in the modern manner :—

"It is not ground " (says De Mayerne), " but a drying oil is prepared with litharge, and the pulverized asphaltum mixed with this oil is placed in a glass vessel, suspended by a thread [in a water bath]. Thus exposed to the fire it melts like butter ; when it begins to boil it is instantly removed. It is an excellent colour for shadows, and may be glazed like lake ; it lasts well."—*Ib.* p. 463.

128. The great advantage of this primary laying in of the darks in brown was the obtaining an unity of shadow throughout the picture, which rendered variety of hue, where it occurred, an instantly accepted

evidence of light. It mattered not how vigorous or
how deep in tone the masses of local colour might
be, the eye could not confound them with true
shadow; it everywhere distinguished the transparent
browns as indicative of gloom, and became acutely
sensible of the presence and preciousness of light
wherever local tints rose out of their depths. But
however superior this method may be to the arbitrary
use of polychrome shadows, utterly unrelated to the
lights, which has been admitted in modern works;
and however beautiful or brilliant its results might be
in the hands of colourists as faithful as Van Eyck, or
as inventive as Rubens; the principle on which it is
based becomes dangerous whenever, in assuming that
the ultimate hue of every shadow is brown, it pre-
supposes a peculiar and conventional light. It is true,
that so long as the early practice of finishing the
under-drawing with the pen was continued, the grey
of that preparation might perhaps diminish the force
of the upper colour, which became in that case little
more than a glowing varnish—even thus sometimes
verging on too monotonous warmth, as the reader
may observe in the head of Dandolo, by John Bellini,
in the National Gallery. But when, by later and more
impetuous hands, the point tracing was dispensed
with, and the picture boldly thrown in with the brown
pigment, it became matter of great improbability that

the force of such a prevalent tint could afterwards be softened or melted into a pure harmony; the painter's feeling for truth was blunted; brilliancy and richness became his object rather than sincerity or solemnity; with the palled sense of colour departed the love of light, and the diffused sunshine of the early schools died away in the narrowed rays of Rembrandt. We think it a deficiency in the work before us that the extreme peril of such a principle, incautiously applied, has not been pointed out, and that the method of Rubens has been so highly extolled for its technical perfection, without the slightest notice of the gross mannerism into which its facile brilliancy too frequently betrayed the mighty master.

129. Yet it remains a question how far, under certain limitations and for certain effects, this system of pure brown shadow may be successfully followed. It is not a little singular that it has already been revived in water-colours by a painter who, in his realization of light and splendour of hue, stands without a rival among living schools—Mr. Hunt; his neutral shadows being, we believe, first thrown in frankly with sepia, the colour introduced upon the lights, and the central lights afterwards further raised by body colour, and glazed. But in this process the sepia shadows are admitted only on objects whose local colours are warm or neutral; wherever the tint

of the illumined portion is delicate or peculiar, a
relative hue of shade is at once laid on the white
paper; and the correspondence with the Flemish
school is in the use of brown as the ultimate representative of deep gloom, and in the careful preservation
of its transparency, not in the application of brown
universally as the shade of all colours. We apprehend
that this practice represents, in another medium, the
very best mode of applying the Flemish system ; and
that when the result proposed is an effect of vivid
colour under bright cool sunshine, it would be impossible to adopt any more perfect means. But a
system which in any stage prescribes the use of a
certain pigment, implies the adoption of a constant
aim, and becomes, in that degree, conventional.
Suppose that the effect desired be neither of sunlight
nor of bright colour, but of grave colour subdued by
atmosphere, and we believe that the use of brown
for an ultimate shadow would be highly inexpedient.
With Van Eyck and with Rubens the aim was always
consistent : clear daylight, diffused in the one case,
concentrated in the other, was yet the hope, the
necessity of both ; and any process which admitted
the slightest dimness, coldness, or opacity, would have
been considered an error in their system by either.
Alike, to Rubens, came subjects of tumult or tranquillity, of gaiety or terror ; the nether, earthly, and

upper world were to him animated with the same
feeling, lighted by the same sun; he dyed in the
same lake of fire the warp of the wedding-garment
or of the winding-sheet; swept into the same delirium
the recklessness of the sensualist, and rapture of the
anchorite; saw in tears only their glittering, and in
torture only its flush. To such a painter, regarding
every subject in the same temper, and all as mere
motives for the display of the power of his art, the
Flemish system, improved as it became in his hands,
was alike sufficient and habitual.   But among the
greater colourists of Italy the aim was not always
so simple nor the method so determinable.   We find
Tintoret passing like a fire-fly from light to darkness
in one oscillation, ranging from the fullest prism of
solar colour to the coldest greys of twilight, and from
the silver tinging of a morning cloud to the lava fire
of a volcano : one moment shutting himself into
obscure chambers of imagery, the next plunged into
the revolutionless day of heaven, and piercing space,
deeper than the mind can follow or the eye fathom ;
we find him by turns appalling, pensive, splendid,
profound, profuse ; and throughout sacrificing every
minor quality to the power of his prevalent mood.
By such an artist it might, perhaps, be presumed that
a different system of colour would be adopted in
almost every picture, and that if a chiaroscuro ground

were independently laid, it would be in a neutral grey,
susceptible afterwards of harmony with any tone he
might determine upon, and not in the vivid brown
which necessitated brilliancy of subsequent effect.
We believe, accordingly, that while some of the pieces
of this master's richer colour, such as the Adam and
Eve in the Gallery of Venice, and we suspect also
the miracle of St. Mark, may be executed on the pure
Flemish system, the greater number of his large
compositions will be found based on a grey shadow ;
and that this grey shadow was independently laid we
have more direct proof in the assertion of Boschini,
who received his information from the younger Palma :
"Quando haveva stabilita questa importante dis-
tribuzione, *abboggiava il quadro tutto di chiaroscuro ;*"
and we have, therefore, no doubt that Tintoret's well-
known reply to the question, "What were the most
beautiful colours ?" "*Il nero, e il bianco,*" is to be
received in a perfectly literal sense, beyond and above
its evident reference to abstract principle. Its main
and most valuable meaning was, of course, that the
design and light and shade of a picture were of greater
importance than its colour ; (and this Tintoret felt so
thoroughly that there is not one of his works which
would seriously lose in power if it were translated into
chiaroscuro) ; but it implied also that Tintoret's idea of
a shadowed preparation was in grey, and not in brown.

130. But there is a farther and more essential ground of difference in system of shadow between the Flemish and Italian colourists. It is a well-known optical fact that the colour of shadow is complemental to that of light : and that therefore, in general terms, warm light has cool shadow, and cool light hot shadow. The noblest masters of the northern and southern schools respectively adopted these contrary keys ; and while the Flemings raised their lights in frosty white and pearly greys out of a glowing shadow, the Italians opposed the deep and burning rays of their golden heaven to masses of solemn grey and majestic blue. Either, therefore, their preparation must have been different, or they were able, when they chose, to conquer the warmth of the ground by superimposed colour. We believe, accordingly, that Correggio will be found—as stated in the notes of Reynolds quoted at p. 495—to have habitually grounded with black, white, and ultramarine, then glazing with golden transparent colours ; while Titian used the most vigorous browns, and conquered them with cool colour in mass above. The remarkable sketch of Leonardo in the Uffizii of Florence is commenced in brown—over the brown is laid an olive green, on which the highest lights are struck with white.

Now it is well known to even the merely decorative painter that no colour can be brilliant which is laid

over one of a corresponding key, and that the best
ground for any given opaque colour will be a comparatively subdued tint of the complemental one ; of
green under red, of violet under yellow, and of
orange or *brown* therefore under *blue*. We apprehend accordingly that the real value of the brown
ground with Titian was far greater than even with
Rubens ; it was to support and give preciousness to
cool colour above, while it remained itself untouched
as the representative of warm reflexes and extreme
depth of transparent gloom. We believe this employment of the brown ground to be the only means
of uniting majesty of hue with profundity of shade·
But its value to the Fleming is connected with the
management of the lights, which we have next to
consider. As we here venture for the first time to
disagree in some measure with Mr. Eastlake, let us
be sure that we state his opinion fairly.   He says :—

"The light warm tint which Van Mander assumes to
have been generally used in the oil-priming was sometimes
omitted, as unfinished pictures prove.   Under such circumstances, the picture may have been executed at once on the
sized outline.   In the works of Lucas van Leyden, and
sometimes in those of Albert Durer, the thin yet brilliant
lights exhibit a still brighter ground underneath (p. 389).
. . . . It thus appears that the method proposed by the inventors of oil-painting, of preserving light within the
colours, involved a certain order of processes.   The
principal conditions were : first, that the outline should be

completed on the panel before the painting, properly so called, was begun. The object, in thus defining the forms, was to avoid alterations and repaintings, which might ultimately render the ground useless without supplying its place. Another condition was to avoid loading *the opaque* colours. *This limitation was not essential with regard to the transparent colours, as such could hardly exclude the bright ground* (p. 398). . . . . . The system of colouring adopted by the Van Eycks may have been influenced by the practice of glass-painting. They appear, in their first efforts at least, to have considered the white panel as representing light behind a coloured and transparent medium, and aimed at giving brilliancy to their tints by allowing the white ground to shine through them. If those painters and their followers erred, it was in sometimes too literally carrying out this principle. *Their lights are always transparent* (mere white excepted) and their shadows sometimes want depth. This is in accordance with the effect of glass-staining, in which transparency may cease with darkness, but never with light. The superior method of Rubens consisted in preserving transparency chiefly in his darks, and in contrasting their lucid depth with solid lights (p. 408). . . . . Among the technical improvements on the older process may be especially mentioned the preservation of transparency in the darker masses, the lights being loaded as required. The system of exhibiting the bright ground through the shadows still involved an adherence to the original method of defining the composition at first ; and the solid painting of the lights opened the door to that freedom of execution which the works of the early masters wanted." (p. 490.)

131. We think we cannot have erred in concluding from these scattered passages that Mr. Eastlake supposes the brilliancy of the high lights of the earlier

schools to be attributable to the under-power of the white ground. This we admit, so far as that ground gave value to the transparent flesh-coloured or brown preparation above it ; but we doubt the transparency of the highest lights, and the power of any white ground to add brilliancy to opaque colours. We have ourselves never seen an instance of a *painted brilliant* light that was not loaded to the exclusion of the ground. Secondary lights indeed are often perfectly transparent, a warm hatching over the under-white ; the highest light itself may be so— but then it is the white ground itself subdued by transparent *darker* colour, not supporting a light colour. In the Van Eyck in the National Gallery all the brilliant lights are loaded ; mere white, Mr. Eastlake himself admits, was always so ; and we believe that the flesh-colour and carnations are painted with colour as *opaque* as the white head-dress, but fail of brilliancy from not being *loaded enough;* the white ground beneath being utterly unable to add to the power of such tints, while its effect on more subdued tones depended in great measure on its receiving a transparent coat of warm colour first. This *may* have been sometimes omitted, as stated at p. 389 ; when it was so, we believe that an utter loss of brilliancy must have resulted ; but when it was used, the highest lights must have been

raised from it by opaque colour as distinctly by
Van Eyck as by Rubens. Rubens' Judgment of
Paris is quoted at p. 388 as an example of the best
use of the bright gesso ground :—and how in that
picture, how in all Rubens' best pictures, is it used ?
Over the ground is thrown a transparent glowing
brown tint, varied and deepened in the shadow;
boldly over that brown glaze, and into it, are struck
and painted the opaque grey middle tints, already
concealing the ground totally ; and above these are
loaded the high lights like gems—note the sparkling
strokes on the peacock's plumes. We believe that
Van Eyck's high lights were either, in proportion
to the scale of picture and breadth of handling, as
loaded as these, or, in the degree of their thinness,
less brilliant. Was then his system the same as
Rubens' ?   Not so ; but it differed more in the
management of middle tints than in the lights : the
main difference was, we believe, between the careful
preparation of the gradations of drawing in the one,
and the daring assumption of massy light in the
other.   There are theorists who would assert that
their system was the same—but they forget the
primal work, with the point underneath, and all that
it implied of transparency above. Van Eyck secured
his drawing in dark, then threw a pale transparent
middle tint over the whole, and recovered his *highest*

lights ; all was *transparent* except these. Rubens
threw a dark middle tint over the whole at first, and
then gave the *drawing* with opaque grey. All was
opaque except the shadows. No slight difference
this, when we reflect on the contrarieties of practice
ultimately connected with the opposing principles ;
above all on the eminent one that, as all Van Eyck's
colour, except the high lights, must have been
equivalent to a glaze, while the great body of *colour*
in Rubens was solid (ultimately glazed occasionally,
but not necessarily), it was possible for Van Eyck
to mix his tints to the local hues required, with far
less danger of heaviness in effect than would have
been incurred in the solid painting of Rubens. This
is especially noticed by Mr. Eastlake, with whom we
are delighted again to concur :—

" The practice of using compound tints has not been
approved by colourists ; the method, as introduced by the
early masters, was adapted to certain conditions, but, like
many of their processes, was afterwards misapplied.
Vasari informs us that Lorenzo di Credi, whose exaggerated nicety in technical details almost equalled that of
Gerard Dow, was in the habit of mixing about thirty
tints before he began to work. The opposite extreme
is perhaps no less objectionable. Much may depend on
the skilful use of the ground. The purest colour in an
opaque state and superficially light only, is less brilliant
than the foulest mixture through which light shines.
Hence, as long as the white ground was visible within

13

the tints, the habit of matching colours from nature (no matter by what complication of hues, provided the ingredients were not chemically injurious to each other) was likely to combine the truth of negative hues with clearness."—*Ib.* p. 400.

132. These passages open to us a series of questions far too intricate to be even cursorily treated within our limits. It is to be held in mind that one and the same quality of colour or kind of brilliancy is not always the best; the phases and phenomena of colour are innumerable in reality, and even the modes of imitating them become expedient or otherwise, according to the aim and scale of the picture. It is no question of mere authority whether the mixture of tints to a compound one, or their juxtaposition in a state of purity, be the better practice. There is not the slightest doubt that, the ground being the same, a stippled tint is more brilliant and rich than a mixed one; nor is there doubt on the other hand that in some subjects such a tint is impossible, and in others vulgar. We have above alluded to the power of Mr. Hunt in water-colour. The fruit-pieces of that artist are dependent for their splendour chiefly on the juxtaposition of pure colour for compound tints, and we may safely affirm that the method is for such purpose as exemplary as its results are admirable. Yet would you desire to see

the same means adopted in the execution of the fruit
in Rubens' Peace and War ? Or again, would the
lusciousness of tint obtained by Rubens himself,
adopting the same means on a grander scale in his
painting of flesh, have been conducive to the ends
or grateful to the feelings of the Bellinis or Albert
Dürer ? Each method is admirable as applied by its
master ; and Hemling and Van Eyck are as much to
be followed in the mingling of colour, as Rubens
and Rembrandt in its decomposition. If an award
is absolutely to be made of superiority to either
system, we apprehend that the palm of mechanical
skill must be rendered to the latter, and higher
dignity of moral purpose confessed in the former ; in
proportion to the nobleness of the subject and the
thoughtfulness of its treatment, simplicity of colour
will be found more desirable. Nor is the far higher
perfection of drawing attained by the earlier method
to be forgotten. Gradations which are expressed by
delicate execution of the *darks*, and then aided by a
few strokes of recovered light, must always be more
subtle and true than those which are struck violently
forth with opaque colour ; and it is to be remembered
that the handling of the brush, with the early Italian
masters, approached in its refinement to drawing
with the point—the more definitely, because the work
was executed, as we have just seen, with little change

or play of local colour. And—whatever discredit the looser and bolder practice of later masters may have thrown on the hatched and pencilled execution of earlier periods—we maintain that this method, necessary in fresco, and followed habitually in the first oil pictures, has produced the noblest renderings of human expression in the whole range of the examples of art : the best works of Raphael, all the glorious portraiture of Ghirlandajo and Masaccio, all the mightiest achievements of religious zeal in Francia, Perugino, Bellini, and such others. Take as an example in fresco Masaccio's hasty sketch of himself now in the Uffizii; and in oil, the two heads of monks by Perugino in the Academy of Florence ; and we shall search in vain for any work in portraiture, executed in opaque colours, which could contend with them in depth of expression or in fulness of *recorded* life—not mere imitative vitality, but chronicled action. And we have no hesitation in asserting that where the object of the painter is expression, and the picture is of a size admitting careful execution, the transparent system, developed as it is found in Bellini or Perugino, will attain the most profound and serene colour, while it will never betray into looseness or audacity. But if in the mind of the painter invention prevail over veneration,—if his eye be creative rather than penetrative, and his hand more powerful than patient

—let him not be confined to a system where light, once lost, is as irrecoverable as time, and where all success depends on husbandry of resource. Do not measure out to him his sunshine in inches of gesso; let him have the power of striking it even out of darkness and the deep.

133. If human life were endless, or human spirit could fit its compass to its will, it is possible a perfection might be reached which should unite the majesty of invention with the meekness of love. We might conceive that the thought, arrested by the readiest means, and at first represented by the boldest symbols, might afterwards be set forth with solemn and studied expression, and that the power might know no weariness in clothing which had known no restraint in creating. But dilation and contraction are for molluscs, not for men; we are not ringed into flexibility like worms, nor gifted with opposite sight and mutable colour like chameleons. The mind which moulds and summons cannot at will transmute itself into that which clings and contemplates; nor is it given to us at once to have the potter's power over the lump, the fire's upon the clay, and the gilder's upon the porcelain. Even the temper in which we behold these various displays of mind must be different; and it admits of more than doubt whether, if the bold work of rapid thought were afterwards in all its forms completed

with microscopic care, the result would be other than
painful. In the shadow at the foot of Tintoret's picture
of the Temptation, lies a broken rock-boulder. The
dark ground has been first laid in, of colour nearly
uniform; and over it a few, not more than fifteen or
twenty, strokes of the brush, loaded with a light grey,
have quarried the solid block of stone out of the
vacancy. Probably ten minutes are the utmost time
which those strokes have occupied, though the rock
is some four feet square. It may safely be affirmed
that no other method, however laborious, could have
reached the truth of form which results from the very
freedom with which the conception has been expressed;
but it is a truth of the simplest kind—the definition of
a stone, rather than the painting of one—and the lights
are in some degree dead and cold—the natural consequence of striking a mixed opaque pigment over a
dark ground. It would now be possible to treat this
skeleton of a stone, which could only have been knit
together by Tintoret's rough temper, with the care of a
Fleming; to leave its fiercely-stricken lights emanating
from a golden ground, to gradate with the pen its
ponderous shadows, and in its completion, to dwell
with endless and intricate precision upon fibres of
moss, bells of heath, blades of grass, and films of
lichen. Love like Van Eyck's would separate the
fibres as if they were stems of forest, twine the ribbed

grass into fanciful articulation, shadow forth capes and islands in the variegated film, and hang the purple bells in counted chiming. A year might pass away, and the work yet be incomplete ; yet would the purpose of the great picture have been better answered when all had been achieved ? or if so, is it to be wished that a year of the life of Tintoret (could such a thing be conceived possible) had been so devoted ?

134. We have put in as broad and extravagant a view as possible the difference of object in the two systems of loaded and transparent light ; but it is to be remembered that both are in a certain degree compatible, and that whatever exclusive arguments may be adduced in favour of the loaded system apply only to the ultimate stages of the work. The question is not whether the white ground be expedient in the commencement—but how far it must of necessity be preserved to the close ? There cannot be the slightest doubt that, whatever the object, whatever the power of the painter, the white ground, as intensely bright and perfect as it can be obtained, should be the base of his operations ; that it should be preserved as long as possible, shown wherever it is possible, and sacrificed only upon good cause. There are indeed many objects which do not admit of imitation unless the hand have power of superimposing and modelling the light ; but there are others which are equally unsus-

ceptible of every rendering except that of transparent colour over the pure ground.

It appears from the evidence now produced that there are at least three distinct systems traceable in the works of good colourists, each having its own merit and its peculiar application. First, the white ground, with careful chiaroscuro preparation, transparent colour in the middle tints, and opaque high lights only (Van Eyck). Secondly, white ground, transparent brown preparation, and solid painting of lights above (Rubens). Thirdly, white ground, brown preparation, and solid painting both of lights and shadows above (Titian); on which last method, indisputably the noblest, we have not insisted, as it has not yet been examined by Mr. Eastlake. But in all these methods the white ground was indispensable. It mattered not what transparent colour were put over it : red, frequently, we believe, by Titian, before the brown shadows— yellow sometimes by Rubens :—whatever warm tone might be chosen for the key of the composition, and for the support of its greys, depended for its own value upon the white gesso beneath ; nor can any system of colour be ultimately successful which excludes it. Noble arrangement, choice, and relation of colour, will indeed redeem and recommend the falsest system : our own Reynolds, and recently Turner, furnish magnificent examples of the power attainable by colourists of high calibre, after the light ground is lost—(we cannot agree with Mr. Eastlake in thinking the practice of painting first in white and black, with cool reds only, "equivalent to its preservation"):—but in the works of both, diminished splendour and sacrificed durability attest and punish the neglect of the best resources of their art.

135. We have stated, though briefly, the major part of the data which recent research has furnished respecting the early colourists; enough, certainly, to remove all theoretical obstacles to the attainment of a perfection equal to theirs.   A few carefully conducted experiments, with the efficient aids of modern chemistry, would probably put us in possession of an amber varnish, if indeed this be necessary, at least not inferior to that which they employed; the rest of their materials are already in our hands, soliciting only such care in their preparation as it ought, we think, to be no irksome duty to bestow.   Yet we are not sanguine of the immediate result.   Mr. Eastlake has done his duty excellently; but it is hardly to be expected that, after being long in possession of means which we could apply to no profit, the knowledge that the greatest men possessed no better, should at once urge to emulation and gift with strength.   We believe that some consciousness of their true position already existed in the minds of many living artists; example had at least been given by two of our Academicians,

Mr. Mulready and Mr. Etty, of a splendour based
on the Flemish system, and consistent, certainly, in
the first case, with a high degree of permanence;
while the main direction of artistic and public
sympathy to works of a character altogether opposed
to theirs, showed fatally how far more perceptible and
appreciable to our present instincts is the mechanism
of handling than the melody of hue.   Indeed we
firmly believe, that of all powers of enjoyment or of
judgment, that which is concerned with nobility of
colour is least communicable : it is also perhaps the
most rare.   The achievements of the draughtsman
are met by the curiosity of all mankind ; the appeals
of the dramatist answered by their sympathy; the
creatures of imagination acknowledged by their fear ;
but the voice of the colourist has but the adder's
listening, charm he never so wisely.   Men vie with
each other, untaught, in pursuit of smoothness and
smallness—of Carlo Dolci and Van Huysum ; their
domestic hearts may range them in faithful armies
round the throne of Raphael ; meditation and labour
may raise them to the level of the great mountain
pedestal of Buonarotti—"vestito gia de' raggi del
pianeta, che meno dritto altrui per ogni calle;" but
neither time nor teaching will bestow the sense, when
it is not innate, of that wherein consists the power
of Titian and the great Venetians.   There is proof

of this in the various degrees of cost and care devoted to the preservation of their works. The glass, the curtain, and the cabinet guard the preciousness of what is petty, guide curiosity to what is popular, invoke worship to what is mighty ;— Raphael has his palace—Michael his dome—respect protects and crowds traverse the sacristy and the saloon ; but the frescoes of Titian fade in the solitudes of Padua, and the gesso falls crumbled from the flapping canvas, as the sea-winds shake the Scuola di San Rocco.

136. But if, on the one hand, mere abstract excellence of colour be thus coldly regarded, it is equally certain that no work ever attains enduring celebrity which is eminently deficient in this great respect. Colour cannot be indifferent ; it is either beautiful and auxiliary to the purposes of the picture, or false, froward, and opposite to them. Even in the painting of Nature herself, this law is palpable ; chiefly glorious when colour is a predominant element in her working, she is in the next degree most impressive when it is withdrawn altogether : and forms and scenes become sublime in the neutral twilight, which were indifferent in the colours of noon. Much more is this the case in the feebleness of imitation ; all colour is bad which is less than beautiful ; all is gross and intrusive which is not attractive ; it repels where it cannot enthral, and destroys what it cannot assist.

It is besides the painter's peculiar craft; he who cannot colour is no painter. It is not painting to grind earths with oil and lay them smoothly on a surface. He only is a painter who can melodize and harmonize *hue*—if he fail in this, he is no member of the brotherhood. Let him etch, or draw, or carve: better the unerring graver than the unfaithful pencil— better the true sling and stone than the brightness of the unproved armour. And let not even those who deal in the deeper magic, and feel in themselves the loftier power, presume upon that power—nor believe in the reality of any success unless that which has been deserved by deliberate, resolute, successive operation. We would neither deny nor disguise the influences of sensibility or of imagination, upon this, as upon every other admirable quality of art;—we know that there is that in the very stroke and fall of the pencil in a master's hand, which creates colour with an unconscious enchantment—we know that there is a brilliancy which springs from the joy of the painter's heart—a gloom which sympathizes with its seriousness—a power correlative with its will; but these are all vain unless they be ruled by a seemly caution—a manly moderation—an indivertible foresight. This we think the one great conclusion to be received from the work we have been examining, that all power is vain—all invention vain—all enthusiasm

vain—all devotion even, and fidelity vain, unless these
are guided by such severe and exact law as we see
take place in the development of every great natural
glory ; and, even in the full glow of their bright and
burning operation, sealed by the cold, majestic, deep-
graven impress of the signet on the right hand of
Time.

SAMUEL PROUT.

137. THE first pages in the histories of artists, worthy
the name, are generally alike ; records of boyish resistance to every scheme, parental or tutorial, at variance
with the ruling desire and bent of the opening mind.
It is so rare an accident that the love of drawing
should be noticed and fostered in the child, that we are
hardly entitled to form any conclusions respecting the
probable result of an indulgent foresight ; it is enough
to admire the strength of will which usually accom-
panies every noble intellectual gift, and to believe that,
in early life, direct resistance is better than inefficient
guidance. Samuel Prout—with how many rich and
picturesque imaginations is the name now associated ?
—was born at Plymouth, September 17th, 1783, and
intended by his father for his own profession ; but
although the delicate health of the child might have
appeared likely to induce a languid acquiescence in his
parent's wish, the love of drawing occupied every

leisure hour, and at last trespassed upon every other occupation. Reproofs were affectionately repeated, and every effort made to dissuade the boy from what was considered an "idle amusement," but it was soon discovered that opposition was unavailing, and the attachment too strong to be checked. It might perhaps have been otherwise, but for some rays of encouragement received from the observant kindness of his first schoolmaster. To watch the direction of the little hand when it wandered from its task, to draw the culprit to him with a smile instead of a reproof, to set him on the high stool beside his desk, and stimulate him, by the loan of his own pen, to a more patient and elaborate study of the child's usual subject, his favourite cat, was a modification of preceptorial care as easy as it was wise ; but it perhaps had more influence on the mind and after-life of the boy than all the rest of his education together.

138. Such happy though rare interludes in school-hours, and occasional attempts at home, usually from the carts and horses which stopped at a public-house opposite, began the studentship of the young artist before he had quitted his pinafore. An unhappy accident which happened about the same time, and which farther enfeebled his health, rendered it still less advisable to interfere with his beloved occupation. We have heard the painter express, with a melancholy smile, the

distinct recollection remaining with him to this day, of a burning autumn morning, on which he had sallied forth alone, himself some four autumns old, armed with a hooked stick, to gather nuts. Unrestrainable alike with pencil or crook, he was found by a farmer, towards the close of the day, lying moaning under a hedge, prostrated by a sun-stroke, and was brought home insensible. From that day forward he was subject to attacks of violent pain in the head, recurring at short intervals; and until thirty years after marriage not a week passed without one or two days of absolute confinement to his room or to his bed. "Up to this hour," we may perhaps be permitted to use his own touching words, "I have to endure a great fight of afflictions; can I therefore be sufficiently thankful for the merciful gift of a buoyant spirit?"

139. That buoyancy of spirit—one of the brightest and most marked elements of his character—never failed to sustain him between the recurrences even of his most acute suffering; and the pursuit of his most beloved Art became every year more determined and independent. The first beginnings in landscape study were made in happy truant excursions, now fondly remembered, with the painter Haydon, then also a youth. This companionship was probably rather cemented by the energy than the delicacy of Haydon's sympathies. The two boys were directly opposed in their habits of application and

modes of study. Prout unremitting in diligence, patient in observation, devoted in copying what he loved in nature, never working except with his model before him ; Haydon restless, ambitious, and fiery ; exceedingly imaginative, never captivated with simple truth, nor using his pencil on the spot, but trusting always to his powers of memory. The fates of the two youths were inevitably fixed by their opposite characters. The humble student became the originator of a new School of Art, and one of the most popular painters of his age. The self-trust of the wanderer in the wilderness of his fancy betrayed him into the extravagances, and deserted him in the suffering, with which his name must remain sadly, but not unjustly, associated.

140. There was, however, little in the sketches made by Prout at this period to indicate the presence of dormant power. Common prints, at a period when engraving was in the lowest state of decline, were the only guides which the youth could obtain ; and his style, in endeavouring to copy these, became cramped and mannered ; but the unremitting sketching from nature saved him. Whole days, from dawn till night, were devoted to the study of the peculiar objects of his early interest, the ivy-mantled bridges, mossy water-mills, and rock-built cottages, which characterise the valley scenery of Devon. In spite of every disadvantage, the strong love of truth, and the instinctive perception of

14

the chief points of shade and characters of form on which his favourite effects mainly depended, enabled him not only to obtain an accumulated store of memoranda, afterwards valuable, but to publish several elementary works which obtained extensive and deserved circulation, and to which many artists, now high in reputation, have kindly and frankly confessed their early obligations.

141. At that period the art of water-colour drawing was little understood at Plymouth, and practised only by Payne, then an engineer in the citadel. Though mannered in the extreme, his works obtained reputation ; for the best drawings of the period were feeble both in colour and execution, with common-place light and shadow, a dark foreground being a *rule absolute*, as may be seen in several of Turner's first productions. But Turner was destined to annihilate such rules, breaking through and scattering them with an expansive force commensurate with the rigidity of former restraint. It happened "fortunately," as it is said,— naturally and deservedly, as it *should* be said,—that Prout was at this period removed from the narrow sphere of his first efforts to one in which he could share in, and take advantage of, every progressive movement.

142. The most respectable of the Plymouth amateurs was the Rev. Dr. Bidlake, who was ever kind in his

encouragement of the young painter, and with whom many delightful excursions were made. At his house, Mr. Britton, the antiquarian, happening to see some of the cottage sketches, and being pleased with them, proposed that Prout should accompany him into Cornwall, in order to aid him in collecting materials for his "Beauties of England and Wales." This was the painter's first recognised artistical employment, as well as the occasion of a friendship ever gratefully and fondly remembered. On Mr. Britton's return to London, after sending to him a portfolio of drawings, which were almost the first to create a sensation with lovers of Art, Mr. Prout received so many offers of encouragement, if he would consent to reside in London, as to induce him to take this important step—the first towards being established as an artist.

143. The immediate effect of this change of position was what might easily have been foretold, upon a mind naturally sensitive, diffident, and enthusiastic. It was a heavy discouragement. The youth felt that he had much to eradicate and more to learn, and hardly knew at first how to avail himself of the advantages presented by the study of the works of Turner, Girtin, Cousins, and others. But he had resolution and ambition as well as modesty; he knew that

"The noblest honours of the mind
On rigid terms descend."

He had every inducement to begin the race, in the clearer guidance and nobler ends which the very works that had disheartened him afforded and pointed out ; and the first firm and certain step was made. His range of subject was as yet undetermined, and was likely at one time to have been very different from that in which he has since obtained pre-eminence so confessed. Among the picturesque material of his native place, the forms of its shipping had not been neglected, though there was probably less in the order of Plymouth dockyard to catch the eye of the boy, always determined in its preference of purely pictur-esque arrangements, than might have been afforded by the meanest fishing hamlet. But a strong and lasting impression was made upon him by the wreck of the " Dutton " East Indiaman on the rocks under the citadel ; the crew were saved by the personal courage and devotion of Sir Edward Pellew, afterwards Lord Exmouth. The wreck held together for many hours under the cliff, rolling to and fro as the surges struck her. Haydon and Prout sat on the crags together and watched her vanish fragment by fragment into the gnashing foam. Both were equally awestruck at the·time ; both, on the morrow, resolved to paint their first pictures ; both failed ; but Haydon, always incapable of acknowledging and remaining loyal to the majesty of what he had seen, lost himself in vulgar thunder and

lightning. Prout struggled to some resemblance of the
actual scene, and the effect upon his mind was never
effaced.

144. At the time of his first residence in London, he
painted more marines than any thing else. But other
work was in store for him. About the year 1818, his
health, which as we have seen had never been vigorous,
showed signs of increasing weakness, and a short trial
of continental air was recommended. The route by
Havre to Rouen was chosen, and Prout found himself
for the first time, in the grotesque labyrinths of the
Norman streets. There are few minds so apathetic as
to receive no impulse of new delight from their first
acquaintance with continental scenery and architecture ;
and Rouen was, of all the cities of France, the richest
in those objects with which the painter's mind had the
profoundest sympathy. It was other then than it is
now ; revolutionary fury had indeed spent itself upon
many of its noblest monuments, but the interference of
modern restoration or improvement was unknown.
Better the unloosed rage of the fiend than the scrabble
of self-complacent idiocy. The façade of the cathedral
was as yet unencumbered by the blocks of new stone-
work, never to be carved, by which it is now defaced ;
the Church of St. Nicholas existed, (the last fragments
of the niches of its gateway were seen by the writer
dashed upon the pavement in 1840 to make room for

the new "Hotel St. Nicholas ";) the Gothic turret had
not vanished from the angle of the Place de la Pucelle, the
Palais de Justice remained in its grey antiquity, and the
Norman houses still lifted their fantastic ridges of gable
along the busy quay (now fronted by as formal a range
of hotels and offices as that of the West Cliff of
Brighton).   All was at unity with itself, and the city
lay under its guarding hills, one labyrinth of delight,
its grey and fretted towers, misty in their magnificence
of height, letting the sky like blue enamel through the
foiled spaces of their crowns of open work ; the walls
and gates of its countless churches wardered by saintly
groups of solemn statuary, clasped about by wandering
stems of sculptured leafage, and crowned by fretted
niche and fairy pediment—meshed like gossamer with
inextricable tracery : many a quaint monument of past
times standing to tell its far-off tale in the place from
which it has since perished—in the midst of the throng
and murmur of those shadowy streets—all grim with
jutting props of ebon woodwork, lightened only here
and there by a sunbeam glancing down from the scaly
backs, and points, and pyramids of the Norman roofs,
or carried out of its narrow range by the gay progress
of some snowy cap or scarlet camisole.   The painter's
vocation was fixed from that hour.   The first effect
upon his mind was irrepressible enthusiasm, with a
strong feeling of a new-born attachment to Art, in a

new world of exceeding interest. Previous impressions were presently obliterated, and the old embankments of fancy gave way to the force of overwhelming anticipations, forming another and a wider channel for its future course.

145. From this time excursions were continually made to the continent, and every corner of France, Germany, the Netherlands, and Italy ransacked for its fragments of carved stone. The enthusiasm of the painter was greater than his ambition, and the strict limitation of his aim to the rendering of architectural character permitted him to adopt a simple and consistent method of execution, from which he has rarely departed. It was adapted in the first instance to the necessities of the mouldering and mystic character of Northern Gothic; and though impressions received afterwards in Italy, more especially at Venice, have retained as strong a hold upon the painter's mind as those of his earlier excursions, his methods of drawing have always been influenced by the predilections first awakened. How far his love of the picturesque, already alluded to, was reconcilable with an entire appreciation of the highest characters of Italian architecture we do not pause to inquire; but this we may assert, without hesitation, that the picturesque *elements* of that architecture were unknown until he developed them, and that since Gentile Bellini, no one had regarded the palaces of

Venice with so affectionate an understanding of the
purpose and expression of their wealth of detail.   In
this respect the City of the Sea has been, and remains,
peculiarly his own.   There is, probably, no single
piazza nor sea-paved street from St. Georgio in Aliga
to the Arsenal, of which Prout has not in order drawn
every fragment of pictorial material.   Probably not
a pillar in Venice but occurs in some one of his innumerable studies ; while the peculiarly beautiful and
varied arrangements under which he has treated the
angle formed by St. Mark's Church with the Doge's
palace, have not only made every successful drawing of
those buildings by any other hand look like plagiarism,
but have added (and what is this but indeed to paint
the lily !) another charm to the spot itself.

146. This exquisite dexterity of arrangement has
always been one of his leading characteristics as an
artist.   Notwithstanding the deserved popularity of his
works, his greatness in composition remains altogether
unappreciated.   Many modern works exhibit greater
pretence at arrangement, and a more palpable system ;
masses of well-concentrated light or points of sudden
and dextrous colour are expedients in the works of our
second-rate artists as attractive as they are common-
place.   But the moving and natural crowd, the de-
composing composition, the frank and unforced, but
marvellously intricate grouping, the breadth of in-

artificial and unexaggerated shadow, these are merits
of an order only the more elevated because unobtrusive.
Nor is his system of colour less admirable. It is a
quality from which the character of his subjects
naturally withdraws much of his attention, and of
which sometimes that character precludes any high
attainment; but, nevertheless, the truest and happiest
association of hues in sun and shade to be found in
modern water-colour art,* (excepting only the studies
of Hunt and De Wint) will be found in portions of
Prout's more important works.

147. Of his *peculiar* powers we need hardly speak;
it would be difficult to conceive the circle of their
influence widened. There is not a landscape of recent
times in which the treatment of the architectural
features has not been affected, however unconsciously,
by principles which were first developed by Prout. Of
those principles the most original were his familiarisation
of the sentiment, while he elevated the subject, of the
picturesque. That character had been sought, before his
time, either in solitude or in rusticity; it was supposed
to belong only to the savageness of the desert or the
simplicity of the hamlet; it lurked beneath the brows
of rocks and the eaves of cottages; to seek it in a city
would have been deemed an extravagance, to raise it

---

* We do not mean under this term to include the drawings of
professed oil-painters, as of Stothard or Turner.

to the height of a cathedral, an heresy. Prout did
both, and both simultaneously ; he found and proved in
the busy shadows and sculptured gables of the Continental street sources of picturesque delight as rich
and as interesting as those which had been sought
amidst the darkness of thickets and the eminence of
rocks ; and he contrasted with the familiar circumstances of urban life, the majesty and the aërial
elevation of the most noble architecture, expressing
its details in more splendid accumulation, and with
a more patient love than ever had been reached or
manifested before his time by any artist who introduced such subjects as members of a general
composition.   He thus became the interpreter of a
great period of the world's history, of that in which
age and neglect had cast the interest of ruin over the
noblest ecclesiastical structures of Europe, and in which
there had been born at their feet a generation other
in its feelings and thoughts than that to which they
owed their existence, a generation which understood
not their meaning, and regarded not their beauty, and
which yet had a character of its own, full of vigour,
animation, and originality, which rendered the grotesque
association of the circumstances of its ordinary and
active life with the solemn memorialism of the elder
building, one which rather pleased by the strangeness
than pained by the violence of its contrast.

148. That generation is passing away, and another dynasty is putting forth its character and its laws. Care and observance, more mischievous in their mis-direction than indifference or scorn, have in many places given the mediæval relics the aspect and associations of a kind of cabinet preservation, instead of that air of majestic independence, or patient and stern endurance, with which they frowned down the insult of the regardless crowd. Nominal restoration has done tenfold worse, and has hopelessly destroyed what time, and storm, and anarchy, and impiety had spared. The picturesque material of a lower kind is fast departing—and for ever. There is not, so far as we know, one city scene in central Europe which has not suffered from some jarring point of modernisa-tion. The railroad and the iron wheel have done their work, and the characters of Venice, Florence, and Rouen are yielding day by day to a lifeless extension of those of Paris and Birmingham. A few lustres more, and the modernisation will be complete : the archæologist may still find work among the wrecks of beauty, and here and there a solitary fragment of the old cities may exist by toleration, or rise strangely before the workmen who dig the new foundations, left like some isolated and tottering rock in the midst of sweeping sea. But the life of the middle ages is dying from their embers, and the warm mingling of the past

and present will soon be for ever dissolved. The works of Prout, and of those who have followed in his footsteps, will become memorials the most precious of the things that have been ; to their technical value, however great, will be added the far higher interest of faithful and fond records of a strange and unreturning era of history. May he long be spared to us, and enabled to continue the noble series, conscious of a purpose and function worthy of being followed with all the zeal of even his most ardent and affectionate mind. A time will come when that zeal will be understood, and his works will be cherished with a melancholy gratitude when the pillars of Venice shall lie mouldering in the salt shallows of her sea, and the stones of the goodly towers of Rouen have become ballast for the barges of the Seine.

SIR JOSHUA AND HOLBEIN.*

149. LONG ago discarded from our National Gallery, with the contempt logically due to national or English pictures,—lost to sight and memory for many a year in the Ogygian seclusions of Marlborough House—there have reappeared at last, in more honourable exile at Kensington, two great pictures by Sir Joshua Reynolds. Two, with others; but these alone worth many an entanglement among the cross-roads of the West, to see for half-an-hour by spring sunshine :— the *Holy Family*, and the *Graces*, side by side now in the principal room. Great, as ever was work wrought by man. In placid strength, and subtlest science, unsurpassed ;—in sweet felicity, incomparable.

150. If you truly want to know what good work of painter's hand is, study those two pictures from side to side, and miss no inch of them (you will hardly, eventually, be inclined to miss one): in some respects there is no execution like it; none so open in the magic. For the work of other great

* *Cornhill Magazine*, March, 1860.—ED.

men is hidden in its wonderfulness—you cannot see
how it was done. But in Sir Joshua's there is no
mystery: it is all amazement. No question but that
the touch was so laid; only that it *could* have been
so laid, is a marvel for ever. So also there is no
painting so majestic in sweetness. He is lily-
sceptred: his power blossoms, but burdens not.
All other men of equal dignity paint more slowly;
all others of equal force paint less lightly. Tintoret
lays his line like a king marking the boundaries of
conquered lands; but Sir Joshua leaves it as a
summer wind its trace on a lake; he could have
painted on a silken veil, where it fell free, and not
bent it.

151. Such at least is his touch when it is life
that he paints: for things lifeless he has a severer
hand. If you examine that picture of the *Graces*
you will find it reverses all the ordinary ideas of
expedient treatment. By other men flesh is firmly
painted, but accessories lightly. Sir Joshua paints
accessories firmly,* flesh lightly;—nay, flesh not at
all, but spirit. The wreath of flowers he feels to be
material; and gleam by gleam strikes fearlessly the
silver and violet leaves out of the darkness. But the

* As showing gigantic power of hand, joined with utmost accuracy
and rapidity, the folds of drapery under the breast of the Virgin are,
perhaps, as marvellous a piece of work as could be found in any
picture, of whatever time or master.

three maidens are less substantial than rose petals. No flushed nor frosted tissue that ever faded in night wind is so tender as they; no hue may reach, no line measure, what is in them so gracious and so fair. Let the hand move softly—itself as a spirit; for this is Life, of which it touches the imagery.

152. "And yet——"

Yes : you do well to pause. There is a "yet" to be thought of. I did not bring you to these pictures to see wonderful work merely, or womanly beauty merely. I brought you chiefly to look at that Madonna, believing that you might remember other Madonnas, unlike her; and might think it desirable to consider wherein the difference lay :—other Madonnas not by Sir Joshua, who painted Madonnas but seldom. Who perhaps, if truth must be told, painted them never : for surely this dearest pet of an English girl, with the little curl of lovely hair under her ear, is *not* one.

153. Why did not Sir Joshua—or could not—or would not Sir Joshua—paint Madonnas ? neither he, nor his great rival-friend Gainsborough ? Both of them painters of women, such as since Giorgione and Correggio had not been ; both painters of men, such as had not been since Titian. How is it that these English friends can so brightly paint that particular order of humanity which we call "gentlemen and

ladies," but neither heroes, nor saints, nor angels?
Can it be because they were both country-bred boys,
and for ever after strangely sensitive to courtliness?
Why, Giotto also was a country-bred boy. Allegri's
native Correggio, Titian's Cadore, were but hill
villages; yet these men painted, not the court, nor
the drawing-room, but the Earth: and not a little of
Heaven besides: while our good Sir Joshua never
trusts himself outside the park palings. He could
not even have drawn the strawberry girl, unless she
had got through a gap in them—or rather, I think,
she must have been let in at the porter's lodge, for
her strawberries are in a pottle, ready for the ladies
at the Hall. Giorgione would have set them, wild
and fragrant, among their leaves, in her hand.
Between his fairness, and Sir Joshua's May-fairness,
there is a strange, impassable limit—as of the white
reef that in Pacific isles encircles their inner lakelets,
and shuts them from the surf and sound of sea.
Clear and calm they rest, reflecting fringed shadows
of the palm-trees, and the passing of fretted clouds
across their own sweet circle of blue sky. But
beyond, and round and round their coral bar, lies
the blue of sea and heaven together—blue of eternal
deep.

154. You will find it a pregnant question, if you
follow it forth, and leading to many others, not

trivial, Why it is, that in Sir Joshua's girl, or Gainsborough's, we always think first of the Ladyhood ;
but in Giotto's, of the Womanhood ? Why, in Sir
Joshua's hero, or Vandyck's, it is always the Prince
or the Sir whom we see first ; but in Titian's, the
man.

Not that Titian's gentlemen are less finished than
Sir Joshua's ; but their gentlemanliness* is not the
principal thing about them ; their manhood absorbs,
conquers, wears it as a despised thing. Nor—and
this is another stern ground of separation—will
Titian make a gentleman of every one he paints.
He will make him so if he is so, not otherwise ;
and this not merely in general servitude to truth, but
because in his sympathy with deeper humanity, the
courtier is not more interesting to him than any
one else. "You have learned to dance and fence ;
you can speak with clearness, and think with precision ; your hands are small, your senses acute, and
your features well-shaped. Yes : I see all this in
you, and will do it justice. You shall stand as

---

* The reader must observe that I use the word here in a limited
sense, as meaning only the effect of careful education, good society,
and refined habits of life, on average temper and character.   Of
deep and true gentlemanliness—based as it is on intense sensibility
and sincerity, perfected by courage, and other qualities of race ; as
well as of that union of insensibility with cunning, which is the
essence of vulgarity, I shall have to speak at length in another
place.

15

none but a well-bred man could stand; and your fingers shall fall on the sword-hilt as no fingers could but those that knew the grasp of it. But for the rest, this grisly fisherman, with rusty cheek and rope-frayed hand, is a man as well as you, and might possibly make several of you, if souls were divisible. His bronze colour is quite as interesting to me, Titian, as your paleness, and his hoary spray of stormy hair takes the light as well as your waving curls. Him also I will paint, with such picturesqueness as he may have; yet not putting the picturesqueness first in him, as in you I have not put the gentlemanliness first. In him I see a strong human creature, contending with all hardship : in you also a human creature, uncontending, and possibly not strong. Contention or strength, weakness or picturesqueness, and all other such accidents in either, shall have due place. But the immortality and miracle of you—this clay that burns, this colour that changes—are in truth the awful things in both : these shall be first painted—and last."

155. With which question respecting treatment of character we have to connect also this further one : How is it that the attempts of so great painters as Reynolds and Gainsborough are, beyond portraiture, limited almost like children's ? No domestic drama— no history—no noble natural scenes, far less any

religious subject:—only market carts; girls with pigs; woodmen going home to supper; watering-places; grey cart-horses in fields, and such like. Reynolds, indeed, once or twice touched higher themes,—"among the chords his fingers laid," and recoiled: wisely; for, strange to say, his very sensibility deserts him when he leaves his courtly quiet. The horror of the subjects he chose (Cardinal Beaufort and Ugolino) showed inherent apathy: had he felt deeply, he would not have sought for this strongest possible excitement of feeling,—would not willingly have dwelt on the worst conditions of despair—the despair of the ignoble. His religious subjects are conceived even with less care than these. Beautiful as it is, this Holy Family by which we stand has neither dignity nor sacredness, other than those which attach to every group of gentle mother and ruddy babe; while his Faiths, Charities, or other well-ordered and emblem-fitted virtues are even less lovely than his ordinary portraits of women.

It was a faultful temper, which, having so mighty a power of realization at command, never became so much interested in any fact of human history as to spend one touch of heartfelt skill upon it;—which, yielding momentarily to indolent imagination, ended, at best, in a Puck, or a Thais; a Mercury as Thief, or a Cupid as Linkboy. How wide the

interval between this gently trivial humour, guided by
the wave of a feather, or arrested by the enchantment
of a smile,—and the habitual dwelling of the thoughts
of the great Greeks and Florentines among the beings
and the interests of the eternal world !

156. In some degree it may indeed be true that
the modesty and sense of the English painters are the
causes of their simple practice.   All that they did, they
did well, and attempted nothing over which conquest
was doubtful.   They knew they could paint men
and women : it did not follow that they could paint
angels   Their own gifts never appeared to them so
great as to call for serious question as to the use to be
made of them.   "They could mix colours and catch
likeness—yes ; but were they therefore able to teach
religion, or reform the world ?   To support themselves
honourably, pass the hours of life happily, please their
friends, and leave no enemies, was not this all that
duty could require, or prudence recommend ?   Their
own art was, it seemed, difficult enough to employ all
their genius : was it reasonable to hope also to be
poets or theologians ?   Such men had, indeed, existed ;
but the age of miracles and prophets was long past ;
nor, because they could seize the trick of an expression,
or the turn of a head, had they any right to think
themselves able to conceive heroes with Homer, or
gods with Michael Angelo."

157. Such was, in the main, their feeling: wise, modest, unenvious, and unambitious. Meaner men, their contemporaries or successors, raved of high art with incoherent passion; arrogated to themselves an equality with the masters of elder time, and declaimed against the degenerate tastes of a public which acknow-ledged not the return of the Heraclidæ. But the two great—the two only painters of their age—happy in a reputation founded as deeply in the heart as in the judgment of mankind, demanded no higher function than that of soothing the domestic affections; and achieved for themselves at last an immortality not the less noble, because in their lifetime they had concerned themselves less to claim it than to bestow.

158. Yet, while we acknowledge the discretion and simple-heartedness of these men, honouring them for both : and the more when we compare their tranquil powers with the hot egotism and hollow ambition of their inferiors : we have to remember, on the other hand, that the measure they thus set to their aims was, if a just, yet a narrow one ; that amiable discretion is not the highest virtue, nor to please the frivolous, the best success. There is probably some strange weak-ness in the painter, and some fatal error in the age, when in thinking over the examples of their greatest work, for some type of culminating loveliness or vera-city, we remember no expression either of religion or

heroism, and instead of reverently naming a Madonna di San Sisto, can only whisper, modestly, " Mrs. Pelham feeding chickens."

159. The nature of the fault, so far as it exists in the painters themselves, may perhaps best be discerned by comparing them with a man who went not far beyond them in his general range of effort, but who did all his work in a wholly different temper—Hans Holbein.

The first great difference between them is of course in completeness of execution. Sir Joshua's and Gainsborough's work, at its best, is only magnificent sketching; giving indeed, in places, a perfection of result unattainable by other methods, and possessing always a charm of grace and power exclusively its own ; yet, in its slightness addressing itself, purposefully, to the casual glance, and common thought—eager to arrest the passer-by, but careless to detain him ; or detaining him, if at all, by an unexplained enchantment, not by continuance of teaching, or development of idea. But the work of Holbein is true and thorough ; accomplished, in the highest as the most literal sense, with a calm entireness of unaffected resolution, which sacrifices nothing, forgets nothing, and fears nothing.

160. In the portrait of the Hausmann George Gyzen,* every accessory is perfect with a fine perfection : the

* Museum of Berlin.

carnations in the glass vase by his side—the ball of
gold, chased with blue enamel, suspended on the wall
—the books—the steelyard—the papers on the table,
the seal-ring, with its quartered bearings,—all intensely
there, and there in beauty of which no one could have
dreamed that even flowers or gold were capable, far
less parchment or steel.   But every change of shade is
felt, every rich and rubied line of petal followed ; every
subdued gleam in the soft blue of the enamel and
bending of the gold touched with a hand whose
patience of regard creates rather than paints.   The
jewel itself was not so precious as the rays of enduring
light which form it, and flash from it, beneath that
errorless hand.   The man himself, what he was—not
more ; but to all conceivable proof of sight—in all
aspect of life or thought—not less.   He sits alone in
his accustomed room, his common work laid out before
him ; he is conscious of no presence, assumes no
dignity, bears no sudden or superficial look of care or
interest, lives only as he lived—but for ever.

161. The time occupied in painting this portrait was
probably twenty times greater than Sir Joshua ever
spent on a single picture, however large.   The result
is, to the general spectator, less attractive.   In some
qualities of force and grace it is absolutely inferior.
But it is inexhaustible.   Every detail of it wins, retains,
rewards the attention with a continually increasing

sense of wonderfulness. It is also wholly true. So far as it reaches, it contains the absolute facts of colour, form, and character, rendered with an unaccusable faithfulness. There is no question respecting things which it is best worth while to know, or things which it is unnecessary to state, or which might be overlooked with advantage. What of this man and his house were visible to Holbein, are visible to us : we may despise if we will ; deny or doubt, we shall not ; if we care to know anything concerning them, great or small, so much as may by the eye be known is for ever knowable, reliable, indisputable.

162. Respecting the advantage, or the contrary, of so great earnestness in drawing a portrait of an uncelebrated person, we raise at present no debate : I only wish the reader to note this quality of earnestness, as entirely separating Holbein from Sir Joshua,—raising him into another sphere of intellect. For here is no question of mere difference in style or in power, none of minuteness or largeness. It is a question of Entireness. Holbein is *complete* in intellect : what he sees, he sees with his whole soul : what he paints, he paints with his whole might. Sir Joshua sees partially, slightly, tenderly—catches the flying lights of things, the momentary glooms : paints also partially, tenderly, never with half his strength ; content with uncertain visions, insecure delights ; the

truth not precious nor significant to him, only pleasing; falsehood also pleasurable, even useful on occasion—must, however, be discreetly touched, just enough to make all men noble, all women lovely: "we do not need this flattery often, most of those we know being such; and it is a pleasant world, and with diligence—for nothing can be done without diligence—every day till four" (says Sir Joshua) —"a painter's is a happy life."

Yes: and the Isis, with her swans, and shadows of Windsor Forest, is a sweet stream, touching her shores softly. The Rhine at Basle is of another temper, stern and deep, as strong, however bright its face: winding far through the solemn plain, beneath the slopes of Jura, tufted and steep: sweeping away into its regardless calm of current the waves of that little brook of St. Jakob, that bathe the Swiss Thermopylæ;* the low village nestling beneath a little bank of sloping fields—its spire seen white against the deep blue shadows of the Jura pines.

163. Gazing on that scene day by day, Holbein went his own way, with the earnestness and silent

---

* Of 1,200 Swiss, who fought by that brookside, ten only returned. The battle checked the attack of the French, led by Louis XI. (then Dauphin) in 1444; and was the first of the great series of efforts and victories which were closed at Nancy by the death of Charles of Burgundy.

swell of the strong river—not unconscious of the
awe, nor of the sanctities of his life. The snows of
the eternal Alps giving forth their strength to it; the
blood of the St. Jakob brook poured into it as it
passes by—not in vain. He also could feel his
strength coming from white snows far off in heaven.
He also bore upon him the purple stain of the earth
sorrow. A grave man, knowing what steps of men
keep truest time to the chanting of Death. Having
grave friends also;—the same singing heard far off,
it seems to me, or, perhaps, even low in the room,
by that family of Sir Thomas More; or mingling
with the hum of bees in the meadows outside the
towered wall of Basle; or making the words of the
book more tuneable, which meditative Erasmus looks
upon. Nay, that same soft Death-music is on the
lips even of Holbein's Madonna. Who, among many,
is the Virgin you had best compare with the one
before whose image we have stood so long.

Holbein's is at Dresden, companioned by the Madonna di San Sisto; but both are visible enough to
you here, for, by a strange coincidence, they are (at
least so far as I know) the only two great pictures
in the world which have been faultlessly engraved.

164. The received tradition respecting the Holbein
Madonna is beautiful; and I believe the interpretation to be true. A father and mother have prayed

to her for the life of their sick child. She appears
to them, her own Christ in her arms. She puts
down her Christ beside them—takes their child into
her arms instead. It lies down upon her bosom,
and stretches its hand to its father and mother,
saying farewell.

This interpretation of the picture has been doubted,
as nearly all the most precious truths of pictures
have been doubted, and forgotten. But even supposing it erroneous, the design is not less characteristic of Holbein. For that there are signs of
suffering on the features of the child in the arms
of the Virgin, is beyond question ; and if this child
be intended for the Christ, it would not be doubtful
to my mind, that, of the two—Raphael and Holbein
—the latter had given the truest aspect and deepest
reading of the early life of the Redeemer. Raphael
sought to express His power only ; but Holbein His
labour and sorrow.

165. There are two other pictures which you
should remember together with this (attributed, indeed, but with no semblance of probability, to the
elder Holbein, none of whose work, preserved at
Basle, or elsewhere, approaches in the slightest
degree to their power), the St. Barbara and St.
Elizabeth.* I do not know among the pictures of

* Pinacothek of Munich.

the great sacred schools any at once so powerful, so
simple, so pathetically expressive of the need of the
heart that conceived them.   Not ascetic, nor quaint,
nor feverishly or fondly passionate, nor wrapt in
withdrawn solemnities of thought.   Only entirely
true—entirely pure.   No depth of glowing heaven
beyond them—but the clear sharp sweetness of the
northern air : no splendour of rich colour, striving
to adorn them with better brightness than of the
day : a grey glory, as of moonlight without mist,
dwelling on face and fold of dress ;—all faultless-
fair.   Creatures they are, humble by nature, not by
self-condemnation ; merciful by habit, not by tearful
impulse ; lofty without consciousness ; gentle without
weakness ; wholly in this present world, doing its
work calmly ; beautiful with all that holiest life can
reach—yet already freed from all that holiest death
can cast away.

ART.

II.

PRE-RAPHAELITISM.

ITS PRINCIPLES, AND TURNER.

(*Pamphlet*, 1851.)

ITS THREE COLOURS.

(*Nineteenth Century, Nov.—Dec.* 1878.)

PREFACE.

Eight years ago, in the close of the first volume of "Modern Painters," I ventured to give the following advice to the young artists of England :—

"They should go to nature in all singleness of heart, and walk with her laboriously and trustingly, having no other thought but how best to penetrate her meaning; rejecting nothing, selecting nothing, and scorning nothing." Advice which, whether bad or good, involved infinite labour and humiliation in the following it, and was therefore, for the most part, rejected.

It has, however, at last been carried out, to the very letter, by a group of men who, for their reward, have been assailed with the most scurrilous abuse which I ever recollect seeing issue from the public press. I have, therefore, thought it due to them to contradict the directly false statements which have been made respecting their works ; and to point out the kind of merit which, however deficient in some respects, those works possess beyond the possibility of dispute.

Denmark Hill, August, 1851.

166. IT may be proved, with much certainty, that God intends no man to live in this world without working : but it seems to me no less evident that He intends every man to be happy in his work. It is written, "in the sweat of thy brow," but it was never written, "in the breaking of thine heart," thou shalt eat bread : and I find that, as on the one hand, infinite misery is caused by idle people, who both fail in doing what was appointed for them to do, and set in motion various springs of mischief in matters in which they should have had no concern, so on the other hand, no small misery is caused by over-worked and unhappy people, in the dark views which they necessarily take up themselves, and force upon

* This Essay was first published in 1851 as a separate pamphlet entitled "Pre-Raphaelitism," by the author of "Modern Painters." (8vo, pp. 68. London : Smith, Elder, & Co.) It was afterwards reprinted in 1862, without alteration, except that the later issue bore the author's name, and omitted a dedication which in the first edition ran as follows :—"To Francis Hawkesworth Fawkes, Esq., of Farnley, These pages, Which owe their present form to advantages granted By his kindness, Are affectionately inscribed, By his obliged friend, John Ruskin.—ED.

others, of work itself. Were it not so, I believe
the fact of their being unhappy is in itself a violation
of divine law, and a sign of some kind of folly or
sin in their way of life.   Now in order that people
may be happy in their work, these three things are
needed: They must be fit for it: They must not do
too much of it: and they must have a sense of
success in it—not a doubtful sense, such as needs
some testimony of other people for its confirmation,
but a sure sense, or rather knowledge, that so much
work has been done well, and fruitfully done, whatever the world may say or think about it. So that
in order that a man may be happy, it is necessary
that he should not only be capable of his work, but
a good judge of his work.

167. The first thing then that he has to do, if
unhappily his parents or masters have not done it
for him, is to find out what he is fit for. In which
inquiry a man may be safely guided by his likings,
if he be not also guided by his pride. People
usually reason in some such fashion as this: "I
don't seem quite fit for a head-manager in the firm
of ——— & Co., therefore, in all probability, I am
fit to be Chancellor of the Exchequer." Whereas,
they ought rather to reason thus: "I don't seem
quite fit to be head-manager in the firm of ———
& Co., but I dare say I might do something in a

small greengrocery business ; I used to be a good
judge of pease ; " that is to say, always trying lower
instead of trying higher, until they find bottom : once
well set on the ground, a man may build up by
degrees, safely, instead of disturbing everyone in his
neighbourhood by perpetual catastrophes. But this
kind of humility is rendered especially difficult in
these days, by the contumely thrown on men in
humble employments. The very removal of the
massy bars which once separated one class of society
from another, has rendered it tenfold more shameful
in foolish people's, *i.e.*, in most people's eyes, to
remain in the lower grades of it, than ever it was
before. When a man born of an artisan was looked
upon as an entirely different species of animal from
a man born of a noble, it made him no more
uncomfortable or ashamed to remain that different
species of animal, than it makes a horse ashamed to
remain a horse, and not to become a giraffe. But
now that a man may make money, and rise in the
world, and associate himself, unreproached, with
people once far above him, not only is the natural
discontentedness of humanity developed to an unheard-of extent, whatever a man's position, but it
becomes a veritable shame to him to remain in the
state he was born in, and everybody thinks it his
duty to try to be a " gentleman." Persons who have

16

any influence in the management of public institutions for charitable education know how common this feeling has become. Hardly a day passes but they receive letters from mothers who want all their six or eight sons to go to college, and make the grand tour in the long vacation, and who think there is something wrong in the foundations of society because this is not possible. Out of every ten letters of this kind, nine will allege, as the reason of the writers' importunity, their desire to keep their families in such and such a "station of life."* There is no real desire for the safety, the discipline, or the moral good of the children, only a panic horror of the inexpressibly pitiable calamity of their living a ledge or two lower on the molehill of the world—a calamity to be averted at any cost whatever, of struggle, anxiety, and shortening of life itself. I do not believe that any greater good could be achieved for the country, than the change in public feeling on this head, which might be brought about by a few benevolent men, undeniably in the class of "gentlemen," who would, on principle, enter into some of our commonest trades, ·and make them honourable; showing that it was possible for a man to retain his dignity, and remain, in the best sense, a gentleman, though part of his time was every day occupied

* Compare 'Sesame and Lilies,' pp. 2, 3, § 2.—ED.

in manual labour, or even in serving customers over a counter. I do not in the least see why courtesy, and gravity, and sympathy with the feelings of others, and courage, and truth, and piety, and what else goes to make up a gentleman's character, should not be found behind a counter as well as elsewhere, if they were demanded, or even hoped for, there.

168. Let us suppose, then, that the man's way of life and manner of work have been discreetly chosen; then the next thing to be required is, that he do not over-work himself therein. I am not going to say anything here about the various errors in our systems of society and commerce, which appear (I am not sure if they ever do more than appear) to force us to over-work ourselves merely that we may live; nor about the still more fruitful cause of unhealthy toil—the incapability, in many men, of being content with the little that is indeed necessary to their happiness. I have only a word or two to say about one special cause of over-work—the ambitious desire of doing great or clever things, and the hope of accomplishing them by immense efforts: hope as vain as it is pernicious; not only making men over-work themselves, but rendering all the work they do unwholesome to them. I say it is a vain hope, and let the reader be assured of this (it is a truth all-important to the best interests of humanity). *No*

great intellectual thing was ever done by great effort;
a great thing can only be done by a great man, and
he does it *without* effort. Nothing is, at present, less
understood by us than this—nothing is more necessary to be understood. Let me try to say it as clearly,
and explain it as fully as I may.

169. I have said no great *intellectual* thing: for
I do not mean the assertion to extend to things
moral. On the contrary, it seems to me that just
because we are intended, as long as we live, to be
in a state of intense moral effort, we are *not* intended
to be in intense physical or intellectual effort. Our
full energies are to be given to the soul's work—to
the great fight with the Dragon—the taking the
kingdom of heaven by force. But the body's work
and head's work are to be done quietly, and comparatively without effort. Neither limbs nor brain
are ever to be strained to their utmost; that is not
the way in which the greatest quantity of work
is to be got out of them: they are never to be
worked furiously, but with tranquillity and constancy.
We are to follow the plough from sunrise to sunset,
but not to pull in race-boats at the twilight: we shall
get no fruit of that kind of work, only disease of
the heart.

170. How many pangs would be spared to thousands,
if this great truth and law were but once sincerely,

humbly understood—that if a great thing can be done at all, it can be done easily ; that, when it is needed to be done, there is perhaps only one man in the world who can do it ; but *he* can do it without any trouble—without more trouble, that is, than it costs small people to do small things ; nay, perhaps, with less. And yet what truth lies more openly on the surface of all human phenomena ? Is not the evidence of Ease on the very front of all the greatest works in existence ? Do they not say plainly to us, not, "there has been a great *effort* here," but, "there has been a great *power* here" ? It is not the weariness of mortality, but the strength of divinity, which we have to recognise in all mighty things ; and that is just what we now *never* recognize, but think that we are to do great things, by help of iron bars and perspiration :— alas ! we shall do nothing that way but lose some pounds of our own weight.

171. Yet let me not be misunderstood, nor this great truth be supposed anywise resolvable into the favourite dogma of young men, that they need not work if they have genius. The fact is that a man of genius is always far more ready to work than other people, and gets so much more good from the work that he does, and is often so little conscious of the inherent divinity in himself, that he is very apt to ascribe all his capacity to his work, and to tell those

who ask how he came to be what he is: "If I *am* anything, which I much doubt, I made myself so merely by labour." This was Newton's way of talking, and I suppose it would be the general tone of men whose genius had been devoted to the physical sciences. Genius in the Arts must commonly be more self-conscious, but in whatever field, it will always be distinguished by its perpetual, steady, well-directed, happy, and faithful labour in accumulating and disciplining its powers, as well as by its gigantic, incommunicable facility in exercising them. Therefore, literally, it is no man's business whether he has genius or not : work he must, whatever he is, but quietly and steadily; and the natural and unforced results of such work will be always the things that God meant him to do, and will be his best. No agonies nor heart-rendings will enable him to do any better. If he be a great man, they will be great things; if a small man, small things; but always, if thus peacefully done, good and right; always, if restlessly and ambitiously done, false, hollow, and despicable.

172. Then the third thing needed was, I said, that a man should be a good judge of his work; and this chiefly that he may not be dependent upon popular opinion for the manner of doing it, but also that he may have the just encouragement of the sense of

progress, and an honest consciousness of victory; how else can he become

"That awful independent on to-morrow,
  Whose yesterdays look backwards with a smile "?

I am persuaded that the real nourishment and help of such a feeling as this is nearly unknown to half the workmen of the present day. For whatever appearance of self-complacency there may be in their outward bearing, it is visible enough, by their feverish jealousy of each other, how little confidence they have in the sterling value of their several doings. Conceit may puff a man up, but never prop him up; and there is too visible distress and hopelessness in men's aspects to admit of the supposition that they have any stable support of faith in themselves.

173. I have stated these principles generally, because there is no branch of labour to which they do not apply: but there is one in which our ignorance or forgetfulness of them has caused an incalculable amount of suffering ; and I would endeavour now to reconsider them with special reference to it—the branch of the Arts.

In general, the men who are employed in the Arts have freely chosen their profession, and suppose themselves to have special faculty for it; yet, as a body, they are not happy men. For which this seems to me the reason— that they are expected, and themselves expect, to make their bread *by being clever*—not by steady or quiet work; and are therefore, for the most part, trying to be clever, and so living in an utterly false state of mind and action.

174. This is the case, to the same extent, in no other profession or employment. A lawyer may indeed suspect that, unless he has more wit than those around him, he is not likely to advance in his profession; but he will not be always thinking how he is to display his wit. He will generally understand, early in his career, that wit must be left to take care of itself, and that it is hard knowledge of law and vigorous examination and collation of the facts of every case entrusted to him, which his clients will mainly demand: this it is which he is to be paid for; and this is healthy and measurable labour, payable by the hour. If he happen to have keen natural perception and quick wit, these will come into play in their due time and place, but he will not think of them as his chief power; and if he have them not, he may still hope that industry and conscientiousness may enable him to rise in his profession without them. Again in the case of clergymen: that they are sorely tempted to display their eloquence or wit, none who know their own hearts will deny, but then they *know* this to *be* a temptation: they never would suppose that cleverness was all that was to be expected from them, or would sit down

deliberately to write a clever sermon : even the dullest
or vainest of them would throw some veil over their
vanity, and pretend to some profitableness of purpose
in what they did. They would not openly ask of
their hearers—Did you think my sermon ingenious,
or my language poetical ? They would early understand that they were not paid for being ingenious,
nor called to be so, but to preach truth ; that if they
happened to possess wit, eloquence, or originality,
these would appear and be of service in due time, but
were not to be continually sought after or exhibited ;
and if it should happen that they had them not, they
might still be serviceable pastors without them.

175. Not so with the unhappy artist. No one
expects any honest or useful work of him ; but every
one expects him to be ingenious. Originality, dexterity, invention, imagination, everything is asked of
him except what alone is to be had for asking—
honesty and sound work, and the due discharge of
his function as a painter. What function ? asks the
reader in some surprise. He may well ask ; for I
suppose few painters have any idea what their function
is, or even that they have any at all.

176. And yet surely it is not so difficult to discover.
The faculties, which when a man finds in himself, he
resolves to be a painter, are, I suppose, intenseness
of observation and facility of imitation. The man is

created an observer and an imitator; and his function
is to convey knowledge to his fellow-men, of such
things as cannot be taught otherwise than ocularly.
For a long time this function remained a religious one :
it was to impress upon the popular mind the reality
of the objects of faith, and the truth of the histories
of Scripture, by giving visible form to both. That
function has now passed away, and none has as yet
taken its place. The painter has no profession, no
purpose. He is an idler on the earth, chasing the
shadows of his own fancies.

177. But he was never meant to be this. The
sudden and universal Naturalism, or inclination to
copy ordinary natural objects, which manifested itself
among the painters of Europe, at the moment when
the invention of printing superseded their legendary
labours, was no false instinct. It was misunderstood
and misapplied, but it came at the right time, and has
maintained itself through all kinds of abuse ; presenting, in the recent schools of landscape, perhaps
only the first fruits of its power. That instinct was
urging every painter in Europe at the same moment
to his true duty—*the faithful representation of all objects
of historical interest, or of natural beauty existent at the
period;* representation such as might at once aid the
advance of the sciences, and keep faithful record of
every monument of past ages which was likely to be

swept away in the approaching eras of revolutionary change.

178. The instinct came, as I said, exactly at the right moment; and let the reader consider what amount and kind of general knowledge might by this time have been possessed by the nations of Europe, had their painters understood and obeyed it. Suppose that, after disciplining themselves so as to be able to draw, with unerring precision, each the particular kind of subject in which he most delighted, they had separated into two great armies of historians and naturalists;—that the first had painted with absolute faithfulness every edifice, every city, every battlefield, every scene of the slightest historical interest, precisely and completely rendering their aspect at the time; and that their companions, according to their several powers, had painted with like fidelity the plants and animals, the natural scenery, and the atmospheric phenomena of every country on the earth—suppose that a faithful and complete record were now in our museums of every building destroyed by war, or time, or innovation, during these last 200 years—suppose that each recess of every mountain chain of Europe had been penetrated, and its rocks drawn with such accuracy that the geologist's diagram was no longer necessary—suppose that every tree of the forest had been drawn in its noblest aspect, every beast of the

field in its savage life—that all these gatherings were
already in our national galleries, and that the painters
of the present day were labouring, happily and
earnestly, to multiply them, and put such means of
knowledge more and more within reach of the common
people—would not that be a more honourable life for
them, than gaining precarious bread by " bright
effects"? They think not, perhaps. They think it
easy, and therefore contemptible, to be truthful; they
have been taught so all their lives. But it is not so,
whoever taught it them. It is most difficult, and
worthy of the greatest men's greatest effort, to render,
as it should be rendered, the simplest of the natural
features of the earth; but also be it remembered, no
man is confined to the simplest; each may look out
work for himself where he chooses, and it will be
strange if he cannot find something hard enough for
him. The excuse is, however, one of the lips only;
for every painter knows, that when he draws back
from the attempt to render nature as she is, it is
oftener in cowardice than in disdain.

179. I must leave the reader to pursue this subject
for himself; I have not space to suggest to him the
tenth part of the advantages which would follow, both
to the painter from such an understanding of his mission,
and to the whole people, in the results of his labour.
Consider how the man himself would be elevated; how

content he would become, how earnest, how full of all accurate and noble knowledge, how free from envy —knowing creation to be infinite, feeling at once the value of what he did, and yet the nothingness. Consider the advantage to the people : the immeasurably larger interest given to art itself; the easy, pleasurable, and perfect knowledge conveyed by it, in every subject; the far greater number of men who might be healthily and profitably occupied with it as a means of livelihood ; the useful direction of myriads of inferior talents now left fading away in misery. Conceive all this, and then look around at our exhibitions, and behold the "cattle pieces," and "sea pieces," and "fruit pieces," and "family pieces ;" the eternal brown cows in ditches, and white sails in squalls, and sliced lemons in saucers, and foolish faces in simpers ; —and try to feel what we are, and what we might have been.

180. Take a single instance in one branch of archæology. Let those who are interested in the history of Religion consider what a treasure we should now have possessed, if, instead of painting pots, and vegetables, and drunken peasantry, the most accurate painters of the seventeenth and eighteenth centuries had been set to copy, line for line, the religious and domestic sculpture on the German, Flemish, and French cathedrals and castles ; and if every building

destroyed in the French or in any other subsequent
revolution, had thus been drawn in all its parts with
the same precision with which Gerard Dow or Mieris
paint bas-reliefs of Cupids. Consider, even now, what
incalculable treasure is still left in ancient bas-reliefs,
full of every kind of legendary interest, of subtle
expression, of priceless evidence as to the character,
feelings, habits, histories, of past generations, in
neglected and shattered churches and domestic buildings, rapidly disappearing over the whole of Europe—
treasure which, once lost, the labour of all men living
cannot bring back again; and then look at the myriads
of men, with skill enough, if they had but the
commonest schooling, to record all this faithfully, who
are making their bread by drawing dances of naked
women from academy models, or idealities of chivalry
fitted out with Wardour Street armour, or eternal
scenes from Gil Blas, Don Quixote, and the Vicar
of Wakefield, or mountain sceneries with young idiots
of Londoners wearing Highland bonnets and brandish-
ing rifles in the foregrounds. Do but think of these
things in the breadth of their inexpressible imbecility,
and then go and stand before that broken basrelief in
the southern gate of Lincoln Cathedral, and see if
there is no fibre of the heart in you that will break
too.

181. But is there to be no place left, it will be

indignantly asked, for imagination and invention, for poetical power, or love of ideal beauty? Yes, the highest, the noblest place—that which these only can attain when they are all used in the cause, and with the aid of truth. Wherever imagination and sentiment are, they will either show themselves without forcing, or, if capable of artificial development, the kind of training which such a school of art would give them would be the best they could receive. The infinite absurdity and failure of our present training consists mainly in this, that we do not rank imagination and invention high enough, and suppose that they *can* be taught. Throughout every sentence that I ever have written, the reader will find the same rank attributed to these powers—the rank of a purely divine gift, not to be attained, increased, or in anywise modified by teaching, only in various ways capable of being concealed or quenched. Understand this thoroughly; know once for all, that a poet on canvas is exactly the same species of creature as a poet in song, and nearly every error in our methods of teaching will be done away with. For who among us now thinks of bringing men up to be poets?—of producing poets by any kind of general recipe or method of cultivation? Suppose even that we see in a youth that which we hope may, in its development, become a power of this kind, should we instantly, supposing that we wanted to make a poet of him, and nothing else, forbid him all quiet, steady, rational labour? Should we force him to perpetual spinning of new crudities out of his boyish brain, and set before him, as the only objects of his study, the laws of versification which criticism has supposed itself to discover in the works of previous writers? Whatever gifts the boy had, would much be likely to come of them so treated? unless, indeed, they were so great as to break through all such snares of falsehood and vanity, and build their own foundation in spite of us; whereas if, as in cases numbering millions against units, the natural gifts were too weak to do this, could anything come of such training but utter inanity and spuriousness of the whole man? But if we had sense, should we not rather restrain and bridle the first flame of invention in early youth, heaping material on it as one would on the first sparks and tongues of a fire which we desired to feed into greatness? Should we not educate the whole intellect into general strength, and all the affections into warmth and honesty, and look to heaven for the rest? This, I say, we should have sense enough to do, in order to produce a poet in words: but, it being required to produce a poet on canvas, what is our way of setting to work? We begin, in all probability, by telling the youth of fifteen or sixteen, that Nature is full of faults, and that he is to improve her ; but that Raphael is perfection, and that the more he copies Raphael the better ; that after much copying of Raphael, he is to try what he can do himself in a Raphaelesque, but yet original manner : that is to say, he is to try to do something very clever, all out of his own head, but yet this clever something is to be properly subjected to Raphaelesque rules, is to have a principal light occupying one-seventh of its space, and a principal shadow occupying one-third of the same ; that no two people's heads in the picture are to be turned the same way, and that all the personages represented are to possess ideal beauty of the highest order, which ideal beauty consists partly in a Greek outline of nose, partly in proportions expressible in decimal fractions between the lips and chin ; but mostly in that degree of improvement which the youth of sixteen is to bestow upon God's work in general. This I say is the kind of teaching which through various channels, Royal Academy lecturings, press criticisms, public enthusiasm, and not least by solid weight of gold, we give to our young men. And we wonder we have no painters !

182. But we do worse than this. Within the last few years some sense of the real tendency of such teaching has appeared in some of our younger painters. It only *could* appear in the younger ones, our older men having become familiarised with the

17

false system, or else having passed through it and forgotten it, not well knowing the degree of harm they had sustained. This sense appeared, among our youths,—increased,—matured into resolute action. Necessarily, to exist at all, it needed the support both of strong instincts and of considerable self-confidence, otherwise it must at once have been borne down by the weight of general authority and received canon law. Strong instincts are apt to make men strange and rude; self-confidence, however well founded, to give much of what they do or say the appearance of impertinence. Look at the self-confidence of Wordsworth, stiffening every other sentence of his prefaces into defiance; there is no more of it than was needed to enable him to do his work, yet it is not a little ungraceful here and there. Suppose this stubbornness and self-trust in a youth, labouring in an art of which the executive part is confessedly to be best learnt from masters, and we shall hardly wonder that much of his work has a certain awkwardness and stiffness in it, or that he should be regarded with disfavour by many, even the most temperate, of the judges trained in the system he was breaking through, and with utter contempt and reprobation by the envious and the dull. Consider, further, that the particular system to be overthrown was, in the present case, one of which the main characteristic was the pursuit of beauty at the

expense of manliness and truth ; and it will seem likely
à priori, that the men intended successfully to resist
the influence of such a system should be endowed with
little natural sense of beauty, and thus rendered dead
to the temptation it presented. Summing up these
conditions, there is surely little cause for surprise that
pictures painted, in a temper of resistance, by exceedingly young men, of stubborn instincts and positive
self-trust, and with little natural perception of beauty,
should not be calculated, at the first glance, to win us
from works enriched by plagiarism, polished by con-
vention, invested with all the attractiveness of artificial
grace, and recommended to our respect by established
authority.

183. We should, however, on the other hand, have
anticipated, that in proportion to the strength of character required for the effort, and to the absence of
distracting sentiments, whether respect for precedent, or
affection for ideal beauty, would be the energy exhibited
in the pursuit of the special objects which the youths proposed to themselves, and their success in attaining them.

All this has actually been the case, but in a degree
which it would have been impossible to anticipate.
That two youths, of the respective ages of eighteen
and twenty, should have conceived for themselves a
totally independent and sincere method of study, and
enthusiastically persevered in it against every kind of

dissuasion and opposition, is strange enough ; that in the third or fourth year of their efforts they should have produced works in many parts not inferior to the best of Albert Durer, this is perhaps not less strange. But the loudness and universality of the howl which the common critics of the press have raised against them, the utter absence of all generous help or encouragement from those who can both measure their toil and appreciate their success, and the shrill, shallow laughter of those who can do neither the one nor the other—these are strangest of all—unimaginable unless they had been experienced.

184. And as if these were not enough, private malice is at work against them, in its own small, slimy way. The very day after I had written my second letter to the Times in the defence of the Pre-Raphaelites,[*] I received an anonymous letter respecting one of them, from some person apparently hardly capable of spelling, and about as vile a specimen of petty malignity as ever blotted paper. I think it well that the public should know this, and so get some insight into the sources of the spirit which is at work against these men : how first roused it is difficult to say, for one would hardly have thought that mere eccentricity in young artists could have excited an hostility so deter-

* See "Arrows of the Chace," vol. i., p. 92, together with the other letters there collected under the head of Pre-Raphaelitism (Ibid. pp. 85—114).—ED.

mined and so cruel ; hostility which hesitated at no assertion, however impudent. That of the "absence of perspective" was one of the most curious pieces of the hue and cry which began with the Times, and died away in feeble maundering in the Art Union ; I contradicted it in the Times—I here contradict it directly for the second time. There was not a single error in perspective in three out of the four pictures in question. But if otherwise, would it have been anything remarkable in them ? I doubt if, with the exception of the pictures of David Roberts, there were one architectural drawing in perspective on the walls of the Academy ; I never met but with two men in my life who knew enough of perspective to draw a Gothic arch in a retiring plane, so that its lateral dimensions and curvatures might be calculated to scale from the drawing. Our architects certainly do not, and it was but the other day that, talking to one of the most distinguished among them, the author of several most valuable works, I found he actually did not know how to draw a circle in perspective. And in this state of general science our writers for the press take it upon them to tell us, that the forest-trees in Mr. Hunt's *Sylvia*, and the bunches of lilies in Mr. Collins's *Convent Thoughts*, are out of perspective.*

* It was not a little curious, that in the very number of the Art Union which repeated this direct falsehood about the Pre-Raphaelite

185. It might not, I think, in such circumstances, have been ungraceful or unwise in the Academicians themselves to have defended their young pupils, at least by the contradiction of statements directly false respecting them,* and the direction of the mind and sight of the public to such real merit as they possess. If Sir Charles Eastlake, Mulready, Edwin and Charles Landseer, Cope, and Dyce would each of them simply state their own private opinion respecting their paintings, sign it, and publish it, I believe the act would be of more service to English art than anything the Academy has done since it was founded. But as I cannot hope for this, I can only ask the public to give

rejection of "linear perspective" (by-the-bye, the next time J. B. takes upon him to speak of any one connected with the Universities, he may as well first ascertain the difference between a Graduate and an Under-Graduate), the second plate given should have been of a picture of Bonington's—a professional landscape painter, observe— for the want of *aerial* perspective in which the Art Union itself was obliged to apologise, and in which the artist has committed nearly as many blunders in *linear* perspective as there are lines in the picture.

* These false statements may be reduced to three principal heads, and directly contradicted in succession.

The first, the current fallacy of society as well as of the press, was, that the Pre-Raphaelites imitated the *errors* of early painters.

A falsehood of this kind could not have obtained credence anywhere but in England, few English people, comparatively, having ever seen a picture of early Italian Masters. If they had they would have known that the Pre-Raphaelite pictures are just as superior to the early Italian in skill of manipulation, power of drawing, and knowledge of effect, as inferior to them in grace of design; and that in a word, there is not a shadow of resemblance between the two styles. The Pre-Raphaelites imitate no pictures : they paint from nature only. But they have opposed themselves as a body, to that kind of teaching their pictures careful examination, and to look at them at once with the indulgence and the respect which I have endeavoured to show they deserve.

Yet let me not be misunderstood. I have adduced them only as examples of the kind of study which I would desire to see substituted for that of our modern schools, and of singular success in certain characters, finish of detail, and brilliancy of colour. What faculties, higher than imitative, may be in these men, I do not yet venture to say ; but I do say, that if they exist, such faculties will manifest themselves in due time all the more forcibly because they have received training so severe.

above described, which only began after Raphael's time : and they have opposed themselves as sternly to the entire feeling of the Renaissance schools ; a feeling compounded of indolence, infidelity, sensuality, and shallow pride. Therefore they have called themselves Pre-Raphaelite. If they adhere to their principles, and paint nature as it is around them, with the help of modern science, with the earnestness of the men of the thirteenth and fourteenth centuries, they will, as I said, found a new and noble school in England. If their sympathies with the early artists lead them into mediævalism or Romanism, they will of course come to nothing. But I believe there is no danger of this, at least for the strongest among them. There may be some weak ones, whom the Tractarian heresies may touch ; but if so, they will drop off like decayed branches from a strong stem. I hope all things from the school.

The second falsehood was, that the Pre-Raphaelites did not draw well. This was asserted, and could have been asserted only by persons who had never looked at the pictures.

The third falsehood was, that they had no system of light and shade. To which it may be simply replied that their system of light and shade is exactly the same as the Sun's ; which is, I believe, likely to outlast that of the Renaissance, however brilliant.

186. For it is always to be remembered that no one mind is like another, either in its powers or perceptions ; and while the main principles of training must be the same for all, the result in each will be as various as the kinds of truth which each will apprehend ; therefore, also, the modes of effort, even in men whose inner principles and final aims are exactly the same. Suppose, for instance, two men, equally honest, equally industrious, equally impressed with a humble desire to render some part of what they saw in nature faithfully ; and, otherwise, trained in convictions such as I have above endeavoured to induce. But one of them is quiet in temperament, has a feeble memory, no invention, and excessively keen sight. The other is impatient in temperament, has a memory which nothing escapes, an invention which never rests, and is comparatively near-sighted.

187. Set them both free in the same field in a mountain valley. One sees everything, small and large, with almost the same clearness ; mountains and grass-hoppers alike ; the leaves on the branches, the veins in the pebbles, the bubbles in the stream ; but he can remember nothing, and invent nothing. Patiently he sets himself to his mighty task ; abandoning at once all thoughts of seizing transient effects, or giving general impressions of that which his eyes present to him in microscopical dissection, he chooses some small

portion out of the infinite scene, and calculates with courage the number of weeks which must elapse before he can do justice to the intensity of his perceptions, or the fulness of matter in his subject.

188. Meantime, the other has been watching the change of the clouds, and the march of the light along the mountain sides; he beholds the entire scene in broad, soft masses of true gradation, and the very feebleness of his sight is in some sort an advantage to him, in making him more sensible of the aerial mystery of distance, and hiding from him the multitudes of circumstances which it would have been impossible for him to represent. But there is not one change in the casting of the jagged shadows along the hollows of the hills, but it is fixed on his mind for ever; not a flake of spray has broken from the sea of cloud about their bases, but he has watched it as it melts away, and could recall it to its lost place in heaven by the slightest effort of his thoughts. Not only so, but thousands and thousands of such images, of older scenes, remain congregated in his mind, each mingling in new associations with those now visibly passing before him, and these again confused with other images of his own ceaseless, sleepless imagination, flashing by in sudden troops. Fancy how his paper will be covered with stray symbols and blots, and undecipherable shorthand :—as for his sitting down to " draw from Nature,"

there was not one of the things which he wished to represent, that stayed for so much as five seconds together : but none of them escaped for all that : they are scaled up in that strange storehouse of his; he may take one of them out perhaps, this day twenty years, and paint it in his dark room, far away. Now, observe, you may tell both of these men, when they are young, that they are to be honest, that they have an important function, and that they are not to care what Raphael did. This you may wholesomely impress on them both. But fancy the exquisite absurdity of expecting either of them to possess any of the qualities of the other.

189. I have supposed the feebleness of sight in the last, and of invention in the first painter, that the contrast between them might be more striking ; but, with very slight modification, both the characters are real. Grant to the first considerable inventive power, with exquisite sense of colour ; and give to the second, in addition to all his other faculties, the eye of an eagle ; and the first is John Everett Millais, the second Joseph Mallard William Turner.

They are among the few men who have defied all false teaching, and have therefore, in great measure, done justice to the gifts with which they were intrusted. They stand at opposite poles, marking culminating points of art in both directions ; between them, or in various relations to them, we may class five or six more living artists who, in like manner, have done justice to their powers. I trust that I may be pardoned for naming them, in order that the reader may know how the strong innate genius in each has been invariably accompanied with the same humility, earnestness, and industry in study.

190. It is hardly necessary to point out the earnestness or humility in the works of William Hunt; but it may be so to suggest the high value they possess as records of English rural life, and *still* life. Who is there who for a moment could contend with him in the unaffected, yet humorous truth with which he has painted our peasant children? Who is there who does not sympathise with him in the simple love with which he dwells on the brightness and bloom of our summer fruit and flowers? And yet there is something to be regretted concerning him: why should he be allowed continually to paint the same bunches of hot-house grapes, and supply to the Water Colour Society a succession of pineapples with the regularity of a Covent Garden fruiterer? He has of late discovered that primrose banks are lovely, but there are other things grow wild besides primroses: what undreamt-of loveliness might he not bring back to us, if he would lose himself for a summer in Highland foregrounds; if he would

paint the heather as it grows, and the foxglove and the harebell as they nestle in the clefts of the rocks, and the mosses and bright lichens of the rocks themselves. And then, cross to the Jura, and bring back a piece of Jura pasture in spring; with the gentians in their earliest blue, and a soldanelle beside the fading snow! And return again, and paint a gray wall of alpine crag, with budding roses crowning it like a wreath of rubies. That is what he was meant to do in this world; not to paint bouquets in china vases.

191. I have in various other places expressed my sincere respect for the works of Samuel Prout: his shortness of sight has necessarily prevented their possessing delicacy of finish or fulness of minor detail; but I think that those of no other living artist furnish an example so striking of innate and special instinct, sent to do a particular work at the exact and only period when it was possible. At the instant when peace had been established all over Europe, but when neither national character nor national architecture had as yet been seriously changed by promiscuous intercourse or modern "improvement"; when, however, nearly every ancient and beautiful building had been long left in a state of comparative neglect, so that its aspect of partial ruinousness, and of separation from recent active life, gave to every

edifice a peculiar interest—half sorrowful, half sublime;—at that moment Prout was trained among the
rough rocks and simple cottages of Cornwall, until
his eye was accustomed to follow with delight the
rents and breaks, and irregularities which, to another
man, would have been offensive; and then, gifted
with infinite readiness in composition, but also with
infinite affection for the kind of subjects he had to
portray, he was sent to preserve, in an almost innumerable series of drawings, *every one made on the
spot*, the aspect borne, at the beginning of the nineteenth century, by cities which, in a few years more,
re-kindled wars, or unexpected prosperities, were to
ravage, or renovate, into nothingness.*

192. It seems strange to pass from Prout to John
Lewis; but there is this fellowship between them,
that both seem to have been intended to appreciate
the characters of foreign countries more than of their
own, nay, to have been born in England chiefly that
the excitement of strangeness might enhance to them
the interest of the scenes they had to represent. I
believe John Lewis to have done more entire justice
to all his powers (and they are magnificent ones),
than any other man amongst us. His mission was
evidently to portray the comparatively animal life of
the southern and eastern families of mankind. For

* See ante, pp. 206-220.—ED.

this he was prepared in a somewhat singular way—
by being led to study, and endowed with altogether
peculiar apprehension of, the most sublime characters
of animals themselves.   Rubens, Rembrandt, Snyders,
Tintoret, and Titian, have all, in various ways, drawn
wild beasts magnificently ; but they have in some sort
humanised or demonised them, making them either
ravenous fiends, or educated beasts, that would draw
cars, and had respect for hermits.   The sullen
isolation of the brutal nature; the dignity and quietness of the mighty limbs ; the shaggy mountainous
power, mingled with grace as of a flowing stream ;
the stealthy restraint of strength and wrath in every
soundless motion of the gigantic frame ;   all this
seems never to have been seen, much less drawn,
until Lewis drew and himself engraved a series of
animal subjects, now many years ago.   Since then,
he has devoted himself to the portraiture of those
European and Asiatic races, among whom the refinements of civilization exist without its laws or its
energies, and in whom the fierceness, indolence, and
subtlety of animal nature are associated with brilliant
imagination and strong affections.   To this task he
has brought not only intense perception of the kind
of character, but powers of artistical composition
like those of the great Venetians, displaying, at
the same time, a refinement of drawing almost

miraculous, and appreciable only, as the minutiæ of nature itself are appreciable, by the help of the microscope. The value, therefore, of his works, as records of the aspect of the scenery and inhabitants of the south of Spain and of the East, in the earlier part of the nineteenth century, is quite above all estimate.

193. I hardly know how to speak of Mulready: in delicacy and completion of drawing, and splendour of colour, he takes place beside John Lewis and the pre-Raphaelites; but he has, throughout his career, displayed no definiteness in choice of subject. He must be named among the painters who have studied with industry, and have made themselves great by doing so; but, having obtained a consummate method of execution, he has thrown it away on subjects either altogether uninteresting, or above his powers, or unfit for pictorial representation. "The Cherry Woman," exhibited in 1850, may be named as an example of the first kind; the "Burchell and Sophia" of the second (the character of Sir William Thornhill being utterly missed); the "Seven Ages" of the third; for this subject cannot be painted. In the written passage, the thoughts are progressive and connected; in the picture they must be co-existent, and yet separate; nor can all the characters of the ages be rendered in painting at all. One

may represent the soldier at the cannon's mouth, but one cannot paint the "bubble reputation" which he seeks. Mulready, therefore, while he has always produced exquisite pieces of painting, has failed in doing anything which can be of true or extensive use. He has, indeed, understood how to discipline his genius, but never how to direct it.

194. Edwin Landseer is the last painter but one whom I shall name : I need not point out to any one acquainted with his earlier works, the labour, or watchfulness of nature which they involve, nor need I do more than allude to the peculiar faculties of his mind. It will at once be granted that the highest merits of his pictures are throughout found in those parts of them which are least like what had before been accomplished; and that it was not by the study of Raphael that he attained his eminent success, but by a healthy love of Scotch terriers.

None of these painters, however, it will be answered, afford examples of the rise of the highest imaginative power out of close study of matters of fact. Be it remembered, however, that the imaginative power, in its magnificence, is not to be found every day. Lewis has it in no mean degree, but we cannot hope to find it at its highest more than once in an age. We *have* had it once, and must be content.

195. Towards the close of the last century, among the various drawings executed, according to the quiet manner of the time, in greyish blue, with brown foregrounds, some began to be noticed as exhibiting rather more than ordinary diligence and delicacy, signed W. Turner.* There was nothing, however, in them at all indicative of genius, or even of more than ordinary talent, unless in some of the subjects a large perception of space, and excessive clearness and decision in the arrangement of masses. Gradually and cautiously the blues became mingled with delicate green, and then with gold; the browns in the foreground became first more positive, and then were slightly mingled with other local colours ; while the touch, which had at first been heavy and broken, like that of the ordinary drawing masters of the time, grew more and more refined and expressive, until it lost itself in a method of execution often too delicate for the eye to follow, rendering, with a precision before unexampled, both the texture and the form of every object. The style may be considered as perfectly formed about the year 1800, and it remained unchanged for twenty years.

During that period the painter had attempted, and with more or less success had rendered, every order

* He did not use his full signature, " J. M. W.," until about the year 1800.

of landscape subject, but always on the same principle, subduing the colours of nature into a harmony
of which the key-notes are greyish green and
brown ; pure blues, and delicate golden yellows being
admitted in small quantity as the lowest and highest
limits of shade and light : and bright local colours
in extremely small quantity in figures or other minor
accessories.

196. Pictures executed on such a system are not,
properly speaking, works in *colour* at all ; they are
studies of light and shade, in which both the shade
and the distance are rendered in the general hue
which best expresses their attributes of coolness and
transparency ; and the lights and the foreground are
executed in that which best expresses their warmth
and solidity. This advantage may just as well be
taken as not, in studies of light and shadow to be
executed with the hand ; but the use of two, three,
or four colours, always in the same relations and
places, does not in the least constitute the work a
study of colour, any more than the brown engravings
of the Liber Studiorum ; nor would the idea of colour
be in general more present to the artist's mind when
he was at work on one of these drawings, than when
he was using pure brown in the mezzotint engraving.
But the idea of space, warmth, and freshness being
not successfully expressible in a single tint, and

perfectly expressible by the admission of three or four, he allows himself this advantage when it is possible, without in the least embarrassing himself with the actual colour of the objects to be represented. A stone in the foreground might in nature have been cold grey, but it will be drawn nevertheless of a rich brown, because it is in the foreground; a hill in the distance might in nature be purple with heath, or golden with furze; but it will be drawn, nevertheless, of a cool grey, because it is in the distance.

197. This at least was the general theory,—carried out with great severity in many, both of the drawings and pictures executed by him during the period : in others more or less modified by the cautious introduction of colour, as the painter felt his liberty increasing ; for the system was evidently never considered as final, or as anything more than a means of progress : the conventional, easily manageable colour, was visibly adopted, only that his mind might be at perfect liberty to address itself to the acquirement of the first and most necessary knowledge in all art—that of form. But as form, in landscape, implies vast bulk and space, the use of the tints which enabled him best to express them, was actually auxiliary to the mere drawing ; and, therefore, not only permissible, but even necessary,

while more brilliant or varied tints were never indulged in, except when they might be introduced without the slightest danger of diverting his mind for an instant from his principal object. And, therefore, it will be generally found in the works of this period, that exactly in proportion to the importance and general toil of the composition, is the severity of the tint; and that the play of colour begins to show itself first in slight and small drawings, where he felt that he could easily secure all that he wanted in form.

198. Thus the "Crossing the Brook," and such other elaborate and large compositions, are actually painted in nothing but grey, brown, and blue, with a point or two of severe local colour in the figures; but in the minor drawings, tender passages of complicated colour occur not unfrequently in easy places; and even before the year 1800 he begins to introduce it with evident joyfulness and longing in his rude and simple studies, just as a child, if it could be supposed to govern itself by a fully developed intellect, would cautiously, but with infinite pleasure, add now and then a tiny dish of fruit or other dangerous luxury to the simple order of its daily fare. Thus, in the foregrounds of his most severe drawings, we not unfrequently find him indulging in the luxury of a peacock; and it is im-

possible to express the joyfulness with which he seems to design its graceful form, and deepen with soft pencilling the bloom of its blue, after he has worked through the stern detail of his almost colourless drawing. A rainbow is another of his most frequently permitted indulgences ; and we find him very early allowing the edges of his evening clouds to be touched with soft rose-colour or gold ; while, whenever the hues of nature in anywise fall into his system, and can be caught without a dangerous departure from it, he instantly throws his whole soul into the faithful rendering of them. Thus the usual brown tones of his foreground become warmed into sudden vigour, and are varied and enhanced with indescribable delight, when he finds himself by the shore of a moorland stream, where they truly express the stain of its golden rocks, and the darkness of its clear, Cairngorm-like pools, and the usual serenity of his aerial blue is enriched into the softness and depth of the sapphire, when it can deepen the distant slumber of some Highland lake, or temper the gloomy shadows of the evening upon its hills.

199. The system of his colour being thus simplified, he could address all the strength of his mind to the accumulation of facts of form ; his choice of subject, and his methods of treatment, are therefore as various

as his colour is simple; and it is not a little difficult
to give the reader who is unacquainted with his works,
an idea either of their infinitude of aims, on the one
hand, or of the kind of feeling which pervades them
all, on the other. No subject was too low or too
high for him; we find him one day hard at work on
a cock and hen, with their family of chickens in a
farm-yard; and bringing all the refinement of his
execution into play to express the texture of the
plumage; next day he is drawing the Dragon of
Colchis. One hour he is much interested in a gust
of wind blowing away an old woman's cap; the next,
he is painting the fifth plague of Egypt. Every landscape painter before him had acquired distinction by
confining his efforts to one class of subject. Hobbima
painted oaks; Ruysdael, waterfalls and copses; Cuyp,
river or meadow scenes in quiet afternoons; Salvator
and Poussin, such kind of mountain scenery as people
could conceive, who lived in towns in the seventeenth
century. But I am well persuaded that if all the
works of Turner, up to the year 1820, were divided
into classes (as he has himself divided them in the Liber
Studiorum), no preponderance could be assigned to
one class over another. There is architecture, including a large number of formal "gentlemen's seats,"
I suppose drawings commissioned by the owners;
then lowland pastoral scenery of every kind, including

nearly all farming operations—ploughing, harrowing,
hedging and ditching, felling trees, sheep-washing, and
I know not what else; then all kinds of town life—
courtyards of inns, starting of mail coaches, interiors
of shops, house-buildings, fairs, elections, etc.; then
all kinds of inner domestic life—interiors of rooms,
studies of costumes, of still life, and heraldry, including multitudes of symbolical vignettes; then marine
scenery of every kind, full of local incident; every
kind of boat and method of fishing for particular fish,
being specifically drawn, round the whole coast of
England—pilchard fishing at St. Ives, whiting fishing
at Margate, herring at Loch Fyne; and all kinds of
shipping, including studies of every separate part of
the vessels, and many marine battle pieces, two in
particular of Trafalgar, both of high importance—one
of the Victory after the battle, now in Greenwich
Hospital; another of the death of Nelson, in his own
gallery; then all kinds of mountain scenery, some
idealized into compositions, others of definite localities;
together with classical compositions, Romes, and
Carthages, and such others, by the myriad, with
mythological, historical, or allegorical figures—nymphs,
monsters, and spectres; heroes and divinities.*

200. What general feeling, it may be asked incredu-

---

* I shall give a *catalogue raisonnée* of all this in the third volume of
Modern Painters.

lously, can possibly pervade all this? This, the greatest of all feelings—an utter forgetfulness of self. Throughout the whole period with which we are at present concerned, Turner appears as a man of sympathy absolutely infinite—a sympathy so all-embracing, that I know nothing but that of Shakspeare comparable with it. A soldier's wife resting by the roadside is not beneath it; Rizpah, the daughter of Aiah, watching the dead bodies of her sons, not above it. Nothing can possibly be so mean as that it will not interest his whole mind, and carry away his whole heart; nothing so great or solemn but that he can raise himself into harmony with it; and it is impossible to prophesy of him at any moment, whether, the next, he will be in laughter or in tears.

201. This is the root of the man's greatness; and it follows as a matter of course that this sympathy must give him a subtle power of expression, even of the characters of mere material things, such as no other painter ever possessed. The man who can best feel the difference between rudeness and tenderness in humanity, perceives also more difference between the branches of an oak and a willow than any one else would; and, therefore, necessarily the most striking character of the drawings themselves is the speciality of whatever they represent—the thorough stiffness of what is stiff, and grace of what is grace-

ful, and vastness of what is vast; but through and beyond all this, the condition of the mind of the painter himself is easily enough discoverable by comparison of a large number of the drawings. It is singularly serene and peaceful: in itself quite passionless, though entering with ease into the external passion which it contemplates. By the effort of its will it sympathises with tumult or distress, even in their extremes, but there is no tumult, no sorrow in itself, only a chastened and exquisitely peaceful cheerfulness, deeply meditative; touched, without loss of its own perfect balance, by sadness on the one side, and stooping to playfulness upon the other. I shall never cease to regret the destruction, by fire, now several years ago, of a drawing which always seemed to me to be the perfect image of the painter's mind at this period,—the drawing of Brignal Church near Rokeby, of which a feeble idea may still be gathered from the engraving (in the Yorkshire series). The spectator stands on the "Brignal banks," looking down into the glen at twilight; the sky is still full of soft rays, though the sun is gone, and the Greta glances brightly in the valley, singing its even-song; two white clouds, following each other, move without wind through the hollows of the ravine, and others lie couched on the far away moorlands; every leaf of the woods is still in the delicate air; a boy's kite, incapable of rising, has become entangled in their branches, he is climbing to recover it ; and just behind it in the picture, almost indicated by it, the lowly church is seen in its secluded field between the rocks and the stream; and around it the low churchyard wall, and the few white stones which mark the resting places of those who can climb the rocks no more, nor hear the river sing as it passes.

There are many other existing drawings which indicate the same character of mind, though I think none so touching or so beautiful: yet they are not, as I said above, more numerous than those which express his sympathy with sublimer or more active scenes ; but they are almost always marked by a tenderness of execution, and have a look of being beloved in every part of them, which shows them to be the truest expression of his own feelings.

202. One other characteristic of his mind at this period remains to be noticed—its reverence for talent in others. Not the reverence which acts upon the practices of men as if they were the laws of nature, but that which is ready to appreciate the power, and receive the assistance, of every mind which has been previously employed in the same direction, so far as its teaching .seems to be consistent with the great text-book of nature itself. Turner thus studied almost every preceding landscape painter, chiefly Claude,

Poussin, Vandevelde, Loutherbourg, and Wilson. It was probably by the Sir George Beaumonts and other feeble conventionalists of the period, that he was persuaded to devote his attention to the works of these men ; and his having done so will be thought, a few scores of years hence, evidence of perhaps the greatest modesty ever shown by a man of original power. Modesty at once admirable and unfortunate, for the study of the works of Vandevelde and Claude was productive of unmixed mischief to him : he spoiled many of his marine pictures, as for instance Lord Ellesmere's, by imitation of the former ; and from the latter learned a false ideal, which, confirmed by the notions of Greek art prevalent in London in the beginning of this century, has manifested itself in many vulgarities in his composition pictures, vulgarities which may perhaps be best expressed by the general term " Twickenham Classicism," as consisting principally in conceptions of ancient or of rural life such as have influenced the erection of most of our suburban villas. From Nicolo Poussin and Loutherbourg he seems to have derived advantage ; perhaps also from Wilson ; and much in his subsequent travels from far higher men, especially Tintoret and Paul Veronese. I have myself heard him speaking with singular delight of the putting in of the beech leaves in the upper right-hand corner of Titian's Peter Martyr. I cannot in any of his works trace the slightest influence of Salvator; and I am not surprised at it, for though Salvator was a man of far higher powers than either Vandevelde or Claude, he was a wilful and gross caricaturist. Turner would condescend to be helped by feeble men, but could not be corrupted by false men. Besides, he had never himself seen classical life, and Claude was represented to him as competent authority for it. But he *had* seen mountains and torrents, and knew therefore that Salvator could not paint them.

203. One of the most characteristic drawings of this period fortunately bears a date, 1818, and brings us within two years of another dated drawing, no less characteristic of what I shall henceforward call Turner's Second period. It is in the possession of Mr. Hawkesworth Fawkes of Farnley, one of Turner's earliest and truest friends; and bears the inscription, unusually conspicuous, heaving itself up and down over the eminences of the foreground—" PASSAGE OF MONT CENIS. J. M. W. TURNER, January 15th, 1820."

The scene is on the summit of the pass close to the hospice, or what seems to have been a hospice at that time,—I do not remember any such at present,—a small square-built house, built as if partly for a fortress, with a detached flight of stone steps in front of it, and a kind of drawbridge to the door. This building, about 400 or 500 yards off, is seen in a

dim, ashy grey against the light, which by help of
a violent blast of mountain wind has broken through
the depth of clouds which hangs upon the crags.
There is no sky, properly so called, nothing but this
roof of drifting cloud ; but neither is there any weight
of darkness—the high air is too thin for it,—all savage,
howling, and luminous with cold, the massy bases of
the granite hills jutting out here and there grimly
through the snow wreaths. There is a desolate-
looking refuge on the left, with its number 16, marked
on it in long ghastly figures, and the wind is drifting
the snow off the roof and through its window in a
frantic whirl ; the near ground is all wan with half-
thawed, half-trampled snow ; a diligence in front,
whose horses, unable to face the wind, have turned
right round with fright, its passengers struggling to
escape, jammed in the window ; a little farther on is
another carriage off the road, some figures pushing
at its wheels, and its driver at the horses' heads,
pulling and lashing with all his strength, his lifted arm
stretched out against the light of the distance, though
too far off for the whip to be seen.

204. Now I am perfectly certain that any one
thoroughly accustomed to the earlier works of the
painter, and shown this picture for the first time, would
be struck by two altogether new characters in it.

The first, a seeming enjoyment of the excitement

of the scene, totally different from the contemplative philosophy with which it would formerly have been regarded. Every incident of motion and of energy is seized upon with indescribable delight, and every line of the composition animated with a force and fury which are now no longer the mere expression of a contemplated external truth, but have origin in some inherent feeling in the painter's mind.

The second, that although the subject is one in itself almost incapable of colour, and although, in order to increase the wildness of the impression, all brilliant local colour has been refused even where it might easily have been introduced, as in the figures ; yet in the low minor key which has been chosen, the melodies of colour have been elaborated to the utmost possible pitch, so as to become a leading, instead of a subordinate, element in the composition ; the subdued warm hues of the granite promontories, the dull stone colour of the walls of the buildings, clearly opposed, even in shade, to the grey of the snow wreaths heaped against them, and the faint greens and ghastly blues of the glacier ice, being all expressed with delicacies of transition utterly unexampled in any previous drawings.

205. These, accordingly, are the chief characteristics of the works of Turner's second period, as distinguished from the first,—a new energy inherent in the mind of the painter, diminishing the repose

and exalting the force and fire of his conceptions, and the presence of Colour, as at least an essential, and often a principal, element of design.

Not that it is impossible, or even unusual, to find drawings of serene subject, and perfectly quiet feeling, among the compositions of this period; but the repose is in them, just as the energy and tumult were in the earlier period, an external quality, which the painter images by an effort of the will: it is no longer a character inherent in himself. The "Ulleswater," in the England series, is one of those which are in most perfect peace; in the "Cowes," the silence is only broken by the dash of the boat's oars, and in the "Alnwick" by a stag drinking; but in at least nine drawings out of ten, either sky, water, or figures are in rapid motion, and the grandest drawings are almost always those which have even violent action in one or other, or in all; e. g. high force of Tees, Coventry, Llanthony, Salisbury, Llanberis, and such others.

206. The colour is, however, a more absolute distinction; and we must return to Mr. Fawkes's collection in order to see how the change in it was effected. That such a change would take place at one time or other was of course to be securely anticipated, the conventional system of the first period being, as above stated, merely a means of study. But the

immediate cause was the journey of the year 1820. As might be guessed from the legend on the drawing above described, "Passage of Mont Cenis, January 15th, 1820," that drawing represents what happened on the day in question to the painter himself. He passed the Alps then in the winter of 1820; and either in the previous or subsequent summer, but on the same journey, he made a series of sketches on the Rhine, in body colour, now in Mr. Fawkes's collection. Every one of those sketches is the almost instantaneous record of an *effect* of colour or atmosphere, taken strictly from nature, the drawing and the details of every subject being comparatively subordinate, and the colour nearly as principal as the light and shade had been before,—certainly the leading feature, though the light and shade are always exquisitely harmonized with it. And naturally, as the colour becomes the leading object, those times of day are chosen in which it is most lovely; and whereas before, at least five out of six of Turner's drawings represented ordinary daylight, we now find his attention directed constantly to the evening: and, for the first time, we have those rosy lights upon the hills, those gorgeous falls of sun through flaming heavens, those solemn twilights, with the blue moon rising as the western sky grows dim, which have ever since been the themes of his mightiest thoughts.

207. I have no doubt, that the *immediate* reason of this change was the impression made upon him by the colours of the continental skies. When he first travelled on the Continent (1800), he was comparatively a young student ; not yet able to draw form as he wanted, he was forced to give all his thoughts and strength to this primary object. But now he was free to receive other impressions ; the time was come for perfecting his art, and the first sunset which he saw on the Rhine taught him that all previous landscape art was vain and value-less, that in comparison with natural colour, the things that had been called paintings were mere ink and charcoal, and that all precedent and all authority must be cast away at once, and trodden under foot. He cast them away : the memories of Vandevelde and Claude were at once weeded out of the great mind they had encumbered ; they and all the rubbish of the schools together with them ; the waves of the Rhine swept them away for ever : and a new dawn rose over the rocks of the Siebengebirge.

208. There was another motive at work, which rendered the change still more complete. His fellow artists were already conscious enough of his superior power in drawing, and their best hope was that he might not be able to colour. They had begun to express this hope loudly enough for it to reach his

19

cars. The engraver of one of his most important
marine pictures told me, not long ago, that one day
about the period in question, Turner came into his
room to examine the progress of the plate, not having
seen his own picture for several months. It was
one of his dark early pictures, but in the foreground
was a little piece of luxury, a pearly fish wrought
into hues like those of an opal. He stood before
the picture for some moments ; then laughed, and
pointed joyously to the fish :—" They say that Turner
can't colour ! " and turned away.

209. Under the force of these various impulses
the change was total. *Every subject thenceforward
was primarily conceived in colour ;* and no engraving
ever gave the slightest idea of any drawing of this
period.

The artists who had any perception of the truth
were in despair ; the Beaumontites, classicalists, and
"owl species" in general, in as much indignation as
their dulness was capable of. They had deliberately
closed their eyes to all nature, and had gone on
inquiring, " Where do you put your brown 'tree' ? "
A vast revelation was made to them at once, enough
to have dazzled any one ; but to *them*, light unen-
durable as incomprehensible. They "did to the
moon complain," in one vociferous, unanimous, continuous "Tu whoo." Shrieking rose from all dark

places at the same instant, just the same kind
of shrieking that is now raised against the Pre-
Raphaelites. Those glorious old Arabian Nights,
how true they are! Mocking and whispering, and
abuse loud and low by turns, from all the black
stones beside the road, when one living soul is toiling
up the hill to get the golden water. Mocking and
whispering, that he may look back, and become a
black stone like themselves.

210. Turner looked not back, but he went on in such
a temper as a strong man must be in, when he is forced
to walk with his fingers in his ears. He retired into
himself; he could look no longer for help, or counsel,
or sympathy from any one ; and the spirit of defiance
in which he was forced to labour led him sometimes
into violences, from which the slightest expression of
sympathy would have saved him. The new energy
that was upon him, and the utter isolation into which
he was driven, were both alike dangerous, and many
drawings of the time show the evil effects of both ;
some of them being hasty, wild, or experimental, and
others little more than magnificent expressions of
defiance of public opinion.

But all have this noble virtue—they are in everything his own : there are no more reminiscences of
dead masters, no more trials of skill in the manner
of Claude or Poussin ; every faculty of his soul is

fixed upon nature only, as he saw her, or as he remembered her.

211. I have spoken above of his gigantic memory: it is especially necessary to notice this, in order that we may understand the kind of grasp which a man of real imagination takes of all things that are once brought within his reach—grasp thenceforth not to be relaxed for ever.

On looking over any catalogues of his works, or of particular series of them, we shall notice the recurrence of the same subject two, three, or even many times. In any other artist this would be nothing remarkable. Probably, most modern landscape painters multiply a favourite subject twenty, thirty, or sixty fold, putting the shadows and the clouds in different places, and "inventing," as they are pleased to call it, a new "effect" every time. But if we examine the successions of Turner's subjects, we shall find them either the records of a succession of impressions actually received by him at some favourite locality, or else repetitions of one impression received in early youth, and again and again realised as his increasing powers enabled him to do better justice to it. In either case we shall find them records of *seen facts; never* compositions in his room to fill up a favourite outline.

212. For instance, every traveller—at least, every tra-

veller of thirty years' standing—must love Calais, the
place where he first felt himself in a strange world.
Turner evidently loved it excessively. I have never
catalogued his studies of Calais, but I remember, at
this moment, five : there is first the "Pas de Calais,"
a very large oil painting, which is what he saw in
broad daylight as he crossed over, when he got near
the French side. It is a careful study of French
fishing boats running for the shore before the wind,
with the picturesque old city in the distance. Then
there is the "Calais Harbour" in the Liber Studiorum : that is what he saw just as he was going
into the harbour—a heavy brig warping out, and
very likely to get in his way or run against the pier,
and bad weather coming on. Then there is the
"Calais Pier," a large painting, engraved some years
ago by Mr. Lupton : * that is what he saw when he
had landed, and ran back directly to the pier to see
what had become of the brig. The weather had got
still worse, the fishwomen were being blown about
in a distressful manner on the pier head, and some
more fishing-boats were running in with all speed.
Then there is the "Fortrouge," Calais : that is what
he saw after he had been home to Dessein's, and
dined, and went out again in the evening to walk on
the sands, the tide being down. He had never seen

* The plate was, however, never published.

such a waste of sands before, and it made an impression on him. The shrimp girls were all scattered over them too, and moved about in white spots on the wild shore ; and the storm had lulled a little, and there was a sunset—such a sunset !—and the bars of Fortrouge seen against it, skeleton-wise. He did not paint that directly ; thought over it—painted it a long while afterwards.

213. Then there is the vignette in the illustrations to Scott. That is what he saw as he was going home, meditatively ; and the revolving lighthouse came blazing out upon him suddenly, and disturbed him. He did not like that so much ; made a vignette of it, however, when he was asked to do a bit of Calais, twenty or thirty years afterwards, having already done all the rest.

Turner never told me all this, but any one may see it if he will compare the pictures. They might, possibly, not be impressions of a single day, but of two days or three ; though, in all human probability, they were seen just as I have stated them ;* but they *are* records of successive impressions, as plainly written as ever traveller's diary. All of them pure veracities. Therefore immortal.

214. I could multiply these series almost indefinitely

* And the more probably because Turner was never fond of staying long at any place, and was least of all likely to make a pause of two or three days at the beginning of his journey.

from the rest of his works. What is curious, some of them have a kind of private mark running through all the subjects. Thus, I know three drawings of Scarborough, and all of them have a starfish in the foreground: I do not remember any others of his marine subjects which have a starfish.

The other kind of repetition—the recurrence to one early impression—is, however, still more remarkable. In the collection of F. H. Bale, Esq., there is a small drawing of Llanthony Abbey. It is in his boyish manner, its date probably about 1795; evidently a sketch from nature, finished at home. It had been a showery day; the hills were partially concealed by the rain, and gleams of sunshine breaking out at intervals. A man was fishing in the mountain stream. The young Turner sought a place of some shelter under the bushes; made his sketch; took great pains when he got home to imitate the rain, as he best could; added his child's luxury of a rainbow; put in the very bush under which he had taken shelter, and the fisherman, a somewhat ill-jointed and long-legged fisherman, in the courtly short breeches which were the fashion of the time.

215. Some thirty years afterwards, with all his powers in their strongest training, and after the total change in his feelings and principles, which I have

endeavoured to describe, he undertook the series of "England and Wales," and in that series introduced the subject of Llanthony Abbey. And behold, he went back to his boy's sketch and boy's thought. He kept the very bushes in their places, but brought the fisherman to the other side of the river, and put him, in somewhat less courtly dress, under their shelter, instead of himself. And then he set all his gained strength and new knowledge at work on the well-remembered shower of rain, that had fallen thirty years before, to do it better. The resultant drawing * is one of the very noblest of his second period.

216. Another of the drawings of the England series, Ulleswater, is the repetition of one in Mr. Fawkes's collection, which, by the method of its execution, I should conjecture to have been executed about the year 1808 or 1810: at all events, it is a very quiet drawing of the first period. The lake is quite calm; the western hills in grey shadow, the eastern massed in light. Helvellyn rising like a mist between them, all being mirrored in the calm water. Some thin and slightly evanescent cows are standing in the shallow water in front; a boat floats motionless about a hundred yards from the shore; the foreground is of broken rocks, with some lovely pieces of copse on the right and left.

* *Vide* Modern Painters, Part II. Sect. III. Chap. IV. § 14.

This was evidently Turner's record of a quiet evening by the shore of Ulleswater, but it was a feeble
one. He could not at that time render the sunset colours : he went back to it, therefore, in the
England series, and painted it again with his new
power. The same hills are there, the same shadows,
the same cows,—they had stood in his mind, on
the same spot, for twenty years,—the same boat, the
same rocks, only the copse is cut away—it interfered
with the masses of his colour. Some figures are
introduced bathing ; and what was grey, and feeble
gold in the first drawing, becomes purple and burning rose-colour in the last.

217. But perhaps one of the most curious examples
is in the series of subjects from Winchelsea. That in
the Liber Studiorum, "Winchelsea, Sussex," bears
date 1812, and its figures consist of a soldier speaking to a woman, who is resting on the bank beside the
road. There is another small subject, with Winchelsea in the distance, of which the engraving bears date
1817. It has *two* women with bundles, and *two*
soldiers toiling along the embankment in the plain,
and a baggage waggon in the distance. Neither of
these seems to have satisfied him, and at last he
did another for the England series, of which the
engraving bears date 1830. There is now a regiment
on the march ; the baggage waggon is there, having

got no farther on in the thirteen years, but one of the
women is tired, and has fainted on the bank; another
is supporting her against her bundle, and giving her
drink; a third sympathetic woman is added, and the
two soldiers have stopped, and one is drinking from
his canteen.

218. Nor is it merely of entire scenes, or of particular
incidents that Turner's memory is thus tenacious.
The slightest passages of colour or arrangement that
have pleased him—the fork of a bough, the casting of
a shadow, the fracture of a stone—will be taken up
again and again, and strangely worked into new relations with other thoughts. There is a single sketch
from nature in one of the portfolios at Farnley, of a
common wood-walk on the estate, which has furnished
passages to no fewer than three of the most elaborate
compositions in the Liber Studiorum.

219. I am thus tedious in dwelling on Turner's
powers of memory, because I wish it to be thoroughly
seen how all his greatness, all his infinite luxuriance of
invention, depends on his taking possession of everything that he sees,—on his grasping all, and losing
hold of nothing,—on his forgetting himself, and
forgetting nothing else. I wish it to be understood
how every great man paints what he sees or did see,
his greatness being indeed little else than his intense
sense of fact. And thus Pre-Raphaelitism and Raphael-

itism, and Turnerism, are all one and the same, so far as education can influence them. They are different in their choice, different in their faculties, but all the same in this, that Raphael himself, so far as he was great, and all who preceded or followed him who ever were great, became so by painting the truths around them as they appeared to each man's own mind, not as he had been taught to see them, except by the God who made both him and them.

220. There is, however, one more characteristic of Turner's second period, on which I have still to dwell, especially with reference to what has been above advanced respecting the fallacy of overtoil; namely, the magnificent ease with which all is done when it is *successfully* done. For there are one or two drawings of this time which are *not* done easily. Turner had in these set himself to do a fine thing to exhibit his powers; in the common phrase, to excel himself; so sure as he does this, the work is a failure. The worst drawings that have ever come from his hands are some of this second period, on which he has spent much time and laborious thought; drawings filled with incident from one side to the other, with skies stippled into morbid blue, and warm lights set against them in violent contrast; one of Bamborough Castle, a large water-colour, may be named as an example. But the truly noble works are those in which, without effort, he

has expressed his thoughts as they came, and forgotten himself; and in these the outpouring of invention is not less miraculous than the swiftness and obedience of the mighty hand that expresses it. Any one who examines the drawings may see the evidence of this facility, in the strange freshness and sharpness of every touch of colour ; but when the multitude of delicate touches, with which all the aërial tones are worked, is taken into consideration, it would still appear impossible that the drawing could have been completed with *ease*, unless we had direct evidence on the matter : fortunately, it is not wanting. There is a drawing in Mr. Fawkes's collection of a man-of-war taking in stores : it is of the usual size of those of the England series, about sixteen inches by eleven : it does not appear one of the most highly finished, but it is still farther removed from slightness. The hull of a first-rate occupies nearly one-half of the picture on the right, her bows towards the spectator, seen in sharp perspective from stem to stern, with all her port-holes, guns, anchors, and lower rigging elaborately detailed ; there are two other ships of the line in the middle distance, drawn with equal precision ; a noble breezy sea dancing against their broad bows, full of delicate drawing in its waves ; a store-ship beneath the hull of the larger vessel, and several other boats, and a complicated cloudy sky. It might appear no small exertion of mind to draw the detail of all this shipping down to the smallest ropes, from memory, in the drawing-room of a mansion in the middle of Yorkshire, even if considerable time had been given for the effort. But Mr. Fawkes sat beside the painter from the first stroke to the last. Turner took a piece of blank paper one morning after breakfast, outlined his ships, finished the drawing in three hours, and went out to shoot.

221. Let this single fact be quietly meditated upon by our ordinary painters, and they will see the truth of what was above asserted,—that if a great thing can be done at all, it can be done easily; and let them not torment themselves with twisting of compositions this way and that, and repeating, and experimenting, and scene-shifting. If a man can compose at all, he can compose at once, or rather he must compose in spite of himself. And this is the reason of that silence which I have kept in most of my works, on the subject of Composition. Many critics, especially the architects, have found fault with me for not " teaching people how to arrange masses ; " for not "attributing sufficient importance to composition." Alas ! I attribute far more importance to it than they do ;—so much importance, that I should just as soon think of sitting down to teach a man how to write a Divina Commedia, or King Lear, as how to "compose," in the true sense, a single building or picture. The marvellous stupidity

of this age of lecturers is, that they do not see that what they call, " principles of composition," are mere principles of common sense in everything, as well as in pictures and buildings ;—A picture is to have a principal light ? Yes ; and so a dinner is to have a principal dish, and an oration a principal point, and an air of music a principal note, and every man a principal object. A picture is to have harmony of relation among its parts ? Yes ; and so is a speech well uttered, and an action well ordered, and a company well chosen, and a ragout well mixed. Composition ! As if a man were not composing every moment of his life, well or ill, and would not do it instinctively in his picture as well as elsewhere, if he could. Composition of this lower or common kind is of exactly the same importance in a picture that it is in anything else,—no more. It is well that a man should say what he has to say in good order and sequence, but the main thing is to say it truly. And yet we go on preaching to our pupils as if to have a principal light was everything, and so cover our academy walls with Shacabac feasts, wherein the courses are indeed well ordered, but the dishes empty.

222. It is not, however, only in invention that men overwork themselves, but in execution also ; and here I have a word to say to the Pre-Raphaelites specially. They are working too hard. There is evidence in failing portions of their pictures, showing that they

have wrought so long upon them that their very sight has failed for weariness, and that the hand refused any more to obey the heart. And, besides this, there are certain qualities of drawing which they miss from over-carefulness. For, let them be assured, there is a great truth lurking in that common desire of men to see things done in what they call a "masterly," or " bold," or " broad," manner: a truth oppressed and abused, like almost every other in this world, but an eternal one nevertheless; and whatever mischief may have followed from men's looking for nothing else but this facility of execution, and supposing that a picture was assuredly all right if only it were done with broad dashes of the brush, still the truth remains the same :— that because it is not intended that men shall torment or weary themselves with any earthly labour, it is appointed that the noblest results should only be attainable by a certain ease and decision of manipulation. I only wish people understood this much of sculpture, as well as of painting, and could see that the finely-finished statue is, in ninety-nine cases out of a hundred, a far more vulgar work than that which shows rough signs of the right hand laid to the workman's hammer : but at all events, in painting it is felt by all men, and justly felt. The freedom of the lines of nature can only be represented by a similar freedom in the hand that follows them ; there are curves in the flow of the hair, and in the form of the features, and in the muscular outline of the body, which can in no wise be caught but by a sympathetic freedom in the stroke of the pencil. I do not care what example is taken, be it the most subtle and careful work of Leonardo himself, there will be found a play and power and ease in the outlines, which no *slow* effort could ever imitate. And if the Pre-Raphaelites do not understand how this kind of power, in its highest perfection, may be united with the most severe rendering of all other orders of truth, and especially of those with which they themselves have most sympathy, let them look at the drawings of John Lewis.

223. These then are the principal lessons which we have to learn from Turner, in his second or central period of labour. There is one more, however, to be received; and that is a warning; for towards the close of it, what with doing small conventional vignettes for publishers, making showy drawings from sketches taken by other people of places he had never seen, and touching up the bad engravings from his works submitted to him almost every day,— engravings utterly destitute of animation, and which had to be raised into a specious brilliancy by scratching them over with white, spotty lights, he gradually got inured to many conventionalities, and even falsities; and, having trusted for ten or twelve

years almost entirely to his memory and invention, living, I believe, mostly in London, and receiving a new sensation only from the burning of the Houses of Parliament, he painted many pictures between 1830 and 1840 altogether unworthy of him. But he was not thus to close his career.

224. In the summer either of 1840 or 1841, he undertook another journey into Switzerland. It was then at least forty years since he had first seen the Alps; (the source of the Arveron, in Mr. Fawkes's collection, which could not have been painted till he had seen the thing itself, bears date 1800,) and the direction of his journey in 1840 marks his fond memory of that earliest one; for, if we look over the Swiss studies and drawings executed in his first period, we shall be struck by his fondness for the pass of the St. Gothard; the most elaborate drawing in the Farnley collection is one of the Lake of Lucerne from Fluelen; and, counting the Liber Studiorum subjects, there are, to my knowledge, six compositions taken at the same period from the pass of St. Gothard, and, probably, several others are in existence. The valleys of Sallenche and Chamouni, and Lake of Geneva, are the only other Swiss scenes which seem to have made very profound impressions on him.

He returned in 1841 to Lucerne; walked up

Mont Pilate on foot, crossed the St. Gothard, and returned by Lausanne and Geneva. He made a large number of coloured sketches on this journey, and realised several of them on his return. The drawings thus produced are different from all that had preceded them, and are the first which belong definitely to what I shall henceforward call his Third period.

The perfect repose of his youth had returned to his mind, while the faculties of imagination and execution appeared in renewed strength; all conventionality being done away by the force of the impression which he had received from the Alps, after his long separation from them. The drawings are marked by a peculiar largeness and simplicity of thought : most of them by deep serenity, passing into melancholy; all by a richness of colour, such as he had never before conceived. They, and the works done in following years, bear the same relation to those of the rest of his life that the colours of sunset do to those of the day; and will be recognized, in a few years more, as the noblest landscapes ever yet conceived by human intellect.

225. Such has been the career of the greatest painter of this century. Many a century may pass away before there rises such another; but what greatness any among us may be capable of, will, at

least, be best attained by following in his path;—by
beginning in all quietness and hopefulness to use
whatever powers we may possess to represent the
things around us as we see and feel them; trusting
to the close of life to give the perfect crown to the
course of its labours, and knowing assuredly that the
determination of the degree in which watchfulness is
to be exalted into invention, rests with a higher will
than our own. And, if not greatness, at least a
certain good, is thus to be achieved; for though I
have above spoken of the mission of the more humble
artist, as if it were merely to be subservient to that
of the antiquarian or the man of science, there is an
ulterior aspect, in which it is not subservient, but
superior. Every archæologist, every natural philosopher, knows that there is a peculiar rigidity of
mind brought on by long devotion to logical and
analytical inquiries. Weak men, giving themselves
to such studies, are utterly hardened by them, and
become incapable of understanding anything nobler,
or even of feeling the value of the results to which
they lead. But even the best men are in a sort
injured by them, and pay a definite price, as in most
other matters, for definite advantages. They gain a
peculiar strength, but lose in tenderness, elasticity,
and impressibility. The man who has gone, hammer
in hand, over the surface of a romantic country, feels no

longer, in the mountain ranges he has so laboriously explored, the sublimity or mystery with which they were veiled when he first beheld them, and with which they are adorned in the mind of the passing traveller. In his more informed conception, they arrange themselves like a dissected model : where another man would be awe-struck by the magnificence of the precipice, he sees nothing but the emergence of a fossiliferous rock, familiarized already to his imagination as extending in a shallow stratum, over a perhaps uninteresting district ; where the unlearned spectator would be touched with strong emotion by the aspect of the snowy summits which rise in the distance, he sees only the culminating points of a metamorphic formation, with an uncomfortable web of fan-like fissures radiating, in his imagination, through their centres.* That in the grasp he has obtained of the inner relations of all these things to the universe, and to man, that in the views which have been

---

* This state of mind appears to have been the only one which Wordsworth had been able to discern in men of science ; and in disdain of which, he wrote that short-sighted passage in the Excursion, Book III. l. 165—190, which is, I think, the only one in the whole range of his works which his true friends would have desired to see blotted out. What else has been found fault with as feeble or superfluous, is not so in the intense distinctive relief which it gives to his character. But these lines are written in mere ignorance of the matter they treat ; in mere want of sympathy with the men they describe : for, observe, though the passage is put into the mouth of the Solitary, it is fully confirmed, and even rendered more scornful, by the speech which follows.

opened to him of natural energies such as no human mind would have ventured to conceive, and of past states of being, each in some new way bearing witness to the unity of purpose and everlastingly consistent providence of the Maker of all things, he has received reward well worthy the sacrifice, I would not for an instant deny; but the sense of the loss is not less painful to him if his mind be rightly constituted; and it would be with infinite gratitude that he would regard the man, who, retaining in his delineation of natural scenery a fidelity to the facts of science so rigid as to make his work at once acceptable and credible to the most sternly critical intellect, should yet invest its features again with the sweet veil of their daily aspect; should make them dazzling with the splendour of wandering light, and involve them in the unsearchableness of stormy obscurity; should restore to the divided anatomy its visible vitality of operation, clothe the naked crags with soft forests, enrich the mountain ruins with bright pastures, and lead the thoughts from the monotonous recurrence of the phenomena of the physical world, to the sweet interests and sorrows of human life and death.

THE THREE COLOURS OF
PRE-RAPHAELITISM.*

I.

226. I WAS lately staying in a country house, in which, opposite each other at the sides of the drawing-room window, were two pictures, belonging to what in the nineteenth century must be called old times, namely Rossetti's "Annunciation," and Millais' " Blind Girl " ; while, at the corner of the chimney-piece in the same room, there was a little drawing of a Marriage-dance, by Edward Burne Jones. And in my bedroom, at one side of my bed, there was a photograph of the tomb of Ilaria di Caretto at Lucca, and on the other, an engraving, in long since superannuated manner, from Raphael's " Transfiguration." Also over the looking-glass in my bedroom, there was this large illuminated text, fairly well written, but with more vermilion in it than was needful : " Lord, teach us to pray."

And for many reasons I would fain endeavour to tell my Oxford pupils some facts which seem to me worth memory about these six works of art ; which, if they will reflect upon, being, in the present state

* *Nineteenth Century,* Nov.-Dec. 1878.—ED.

of my health, the best I can do for them in the way of autumn lecturing, it will be kind to me. And as I cannot speak what I would say, and believe my pupils are more likely to read it if printed in the *Nineteenth Century* than in a separate pamphlet, I have asked, and obtained of the editor, space in columns which ought, nevertheless, I think, usually to be occupied with sterner subjects, as the Fates are now driving the nineteenth century on its missionary path.

227. The first picture I named, Rossetti's "Annunciation," was, I believe, among the earliest that drew some public attention to the so-called "Pre-Raphaelite" school. The one opposite to it,—Millais' "Blind Girl," is among those chiefly characteristic of that school in its determined manner. And the third, though small and unimportant, is no less characteristic, in its essential qualities, of the mind of the greatest master whom that school has yet produced.

I believe most readers will start at the application of the term "master," to any English painter. For the hope of the nineteenth century is more and more distinctly every day, to teach all men how to live without mastership either in art or morals (primarily, of course, substituting for the words of Christ, "Ye say well, for so I am,"—the probable emendation, "Ye say ill, for so I am not"); and to limit the idea of magistracy altogether, no less than the functions of the magistrate, to the suppression of disturbance in the manufacturing districts.

Nor would I myself use the word " Master " in any but the most qualified sense, of any " modern painter "; scarcely even of Turner, and not at all, except for convenience and as a matter of courtesy, of any work-man of the pre-Raphaelite school, as yet. In such courtesy, only, let the masterless reader permit it me.

228. I must endeavour first to give, as well as I can by description, some general notion of the subjects and treatment of the three pictures.

Rossetti's "Annunciation" differs from every pre-vious conception of the scene known to me, in repre-senting the angel as waking the Virgin from sleep to give her his message. The Messenger himself also differs from angels as they are commonly represented, in not depending, for recognition of his supernatural character, on the insertion of bird's wings at his shoulders. If we are to know him for an angel at all, it must be by his face, which is that simply of youthful, but grave, manhood. He is neither transparent in body, luminous in presence, nor auri-ferous in apparel ;—wears a plain, long, white robe, —casts a natural and undiminished shadow,—and, although there are flames beneath his feet, which upbear him, so that he does not touch the earth, these are unseen by the Virgin.

She herself is an English, not a Jewish girl, of about sixteen or seventeen, of such pale and thought-ful beauty as Rossetti could best imagine for her; concerning which effort, and its degree of success, we will inquire farther presently.

She has risen half up, not *started* up, in being awakened; and is not looking at the angel, but only thinking, it seems, with eyes cast down, as if supposing herself in a strange dream. The morning light fills the room, and shows at the foot of her little pallet-bed, her embroidery work, left off the evening before,— an upright lily.

Upright, and very accurately upright, as also the edges of the piece of cloth in its frame,—as also the gliding form of the angel,—as also, in severe fore-shortening, that of the Virgin herself. It has been studied, so far as it has been studied at all, from a very thin model; and the disturbed coverlid is thrown into confused angular folds, which admit no suggestion whatever of ordinary girlish grace. So that, to any spectator little inclined towards the praise of barren " uprightnesse," and accustomed on the contrary to expect radiance in archangels, and grace in Madonnas, the first effect of the design must be extremely dis-pleasing, and the first is perhaps, with most art-amateurs of modern days, likely to be the last.

229. The background of the second picture (Millais'

"Blind Girl"), is an open English common, skirted by the tidy houses of a well-to-do village in the cockney rural districts. I have no doubt the scene is a real one within some twenty miles from London, and painted mostly on the spot. The houses are entirely uninteresting, but decent, trim, as human dwellings should be, and on the whole inoffensive—not "cottages," mind you, in any sense, but respectable brick-walled and slated constructions, old-fashioned in the sense of 'old' at, suppose, Bromley or Sevenoaks, and with a pretty little church belonging to them, its window traceries freshly whitewashed by order of the careful warden.

The common is a fairly spacious bit of ragged pasture, with a couple of donkeys feeding on it, and a cow or two, and at the side of the public road passing over it, the blind girl has sat down to rest awhile. She is a simple beggar, not a poetical or vicious one ;—being peripatetic with musical instrument, she will, I suppose, come under the general term of tramp ; a girl of eighteen or twenty, extremely plain-featured, but healthy, and just now resting, as any one of us would rest, not because she is much tired, but because the sun has but this moment come out after a shower, and the smell of the grass is pleasant.

The shower has been heavy, and is so still in the

distance, where an intensely bright double rainbow
is relieved against the departing thunder-cloud. The
freshly wet grass is all radiant through and through
with the new sunshine ; full noon at its purest, the
very donkeys bathed in the raindew, and prismatic
with it under their rough breasts as they graze ; the
weeds at the girl's side as bright as a Byzantine
enamel, and inlaid with blue veronica ; her upturned
face all aglow with the light that seeks its way through
her wet eyelashes (wet only with the rain). Very
quiet she is,—so quiet that a radiant butterfly has
settled on her shoulder, and basks there in the warm
sun. Against her knee, on which her poor instrument
of musical beggary rests (harmonium), leans another
child, half her age—her guide ;—indifferent, this one,
either to sun or rain, only a little tired of waiting.
No more than a half profile of her face is seen ; and
that is quite expressionless, and not the least pretty.

230. Both of these pictures are oil-paintings. The
third, Mr. Burne Jones' " Bridal," is a small water-
colour drawing, scarcely more than a sketch ; but full
and deep in such colour as it admits. Any careful
readers of my recent lectures at Oxford know that
I entirely ignore the difference of material between
oil and water as diluents of colour, when I am examining any grave art question : nor shall I hereafter,
throughout this paper, take notice of it. Nor do I

think it needful to ask the pardon of any of the three
artists for confining the reader's attention at present
to comparatively minor and elementary examples of
their works. If I can succeed in explaining the
principles involved in them, their application by the
reader will be easily extended to the enjoyment of
better examples.

This drawing of Mr. Jones's, however, is far less
representative of his scale of power than either of the
two pieces already described, which have both cost
their artists much care and time ; while this little
water-colour has been perhaps done in the course
of a summer afternoon. It is only about seven inches
by nine : the figures of the average size of Angelico's
on any altar predella ; and the heads, of those on an
average Corinthian or Syracusan coin. The bride
and bridegroom sit on a slightly raised throne at the
side of the picture, the bride nearest us ; her head seen
in profile, a little bowed. Before them, the three
bridesmaids and their groomsmen dance in circle,
holding each other's hands, barefooted, and dressed
in long dark blue robes. Their figures are scarcely
detached from the dark background, which is a wilful
mingling of shadow and light, as the artist chose to
put them, representing, as far as I remember, nothing
in particular. The deep tone of the picture leaves
several of the faces in obscurity, and none are drawn

with much care, not even the bride's ; but with enough to show that her features are at least as beautiful as those of an ordinary Greek goddess, while the depth of the distant background throws out her pale head in an almost lunar, yet unexaggerated, light ; and the white and blue flowers of her narrow coronal, though *merely* white and blue, shine, one knows not how, like gems. Her bridegroom stoops forward a little to look at her, so that we see his front face, and can see also that he loves her.

231. Such being the respective effort and design of the three pictures, although I put by, for the moment, any question of their mechanical skill or manner, it must yet, I believe, be felt by the reader that, as works of young men, they contained, and even nailed to the Academy gates, a kind of Lutheran challenge to the then accepted teachers in all European schools of Art : perhaps a little too shrill and petulant in the tone of it, but yet curiously resolute and steady in its triple Fraternity, as of William of Burglen with his Melchthal and Stauffacher, in the Grutli meadow, not wholly to be scorned by even the knightliest powers of the Past.

We have indeed, since these pictures were first exhibited, become accustomed to many forms both of pleasing and revolting innovation : but consider, in those early times, how the pious persons who had always been accustomed to see their Madonnas dressed in scrupulously folded and exquisitely falling robes of blue, with edges embroidered in gold,—to find them also, sitting under arcades of exquisitest architecture by Bernini,—and reverently to observe them receive the angel's message with their hands folded on their breasts in the most graceful positions, and the missals they had been previously studying laid open on their knees, (see my own outline from Angelico of the "Ancilla Domini," the first plate of the fifth volume of *Modern Painters*) ;—consider, I repeat, the shock to the feelings of all these delicately minded persons, on being asked to conceive a Virgin waking from her sleep on a pallet bed, in a plain room, startled by sudden words and ghostly presence which she does not comprehend, and casting in her mind what manner of Salutation this should be.

232. Again, consider, with respect to the second picture, how the learned possessors of works of established reputation by the ancient masters, classically catalogued as "landscapes with figures"; and who held it for eternal, artistic law that such pictures should either consist of a rock, with a Spanish chestnut growing out of the side of it, and three banditti in helmets and big feathers on the top, or else of a Corinthian temple, built beside an arm of the sea, with the Queen of Sheba beneath, preparing for

embarkation to visit Solomon,—the whole properly toned down with amber varnish :—imagine the first consternation, and final wrath, of these *cognoscenti,* at being asked to contemplate, deliberately, and to the last rent of her ragged gown, and for principal object in a finished picture, a vagrant who ought at once to have been sent to the workhouse; and some really green grass and blue flowers, as they actually may any day be seen on an English common-side.

And finally, let us imagine, if imagination fail us not, the far more wide and weighty indignation of the public, accustomed always to see its paintings of marriages elaborated in Christian propriety and splendour; with a bishop officiating, assisted by a dean and an archdeacon; the modesty of the bride expressed by a veil of the most expensive Valenciennes, and the robes of the bridesmaids designed by the perfectest of Parisian artists, and looped up with stuffed robins or other such tender rarities;— think with what sense of hitherto unheard-of impropriety, the British public must have received a picture of a marriage, in which the bride was only crowned with flowers,—at which the bridesmaids danced barefoot,—and in which nothing was known, or even conjecturable, respecting the bridegroom, but his love !

233. Such being the manifestly opponent and agonistic temper of these three pictures (and admitting, which I will crave the reader to do for the nonce, their real worth and power to be considerable), it surely becomes a matter of no little interest to see what spirit it is that they have in common, which, recognized as revolutionary in the minds of the young artists themselves, caused them, with more or less of firmness, to constitute themselves into a society, partly monastic, partly predicatory, called " Pre-Raphaelite ": and also recognized as such, with indignation, by the public, caused the youthfully didactic society to be regarded with various degrees of contempt, passing into anger (as of offended personal dignity), and embittered farther, among certain classes of persons, even into a kind of instinctive abhorrence.

234. I believe the reader will discover, on reflection, that there is really only one quite common and sympathetic impulse shown in these three works, otherwise so distinct in aim and execution. And this fraternal link he will, if careful in reflection, discover to be an effort to represent, so far as in these youths lay either the choice or the power, things as they are, or were, or may be, instead of, according to the practice of their instructors and the wishes of their public, things as they are *not*,

never were, and never can be: this effort being
founded deeply on a conviction that it is at first
better, and finally more pleasing, for human minds
to contemplate things as they are, than as they are
not.

Thus, Mr. Rossetti, in this and subsequent works
of the kind, thought it better for himself and his
public to make some effort towards a real notion of
what actually did happen in the carpenter's cottage
at Nazareth, giving rise to the subsequent traditions
delivered in the Gospels, than merely to produce a
variety in the pattern of Virgin, pattern of Virgin's
gown, and pattern of Virgin's house, which. had
been set by the jewellers of the fifteenth century.

Similarly, Mr. Millais, in this and other works of
the kind, thought it desirable rather to paint such
grass and foliage as he saw in Kent, Surrey, and
other solidly accessible English counties, than to
imitate even the most Elysian fields enamelled by
Claude, or the gloomiest branches of Hades forest
rent by Salvator: and yet more, to manifest his own
strong personal feeling that the humanity, no less
than the herbage, near us and around, was that
which it was the painter's duty first to portray;
and that, if Wordsworth were indeed right in feeling that the meanest flower that blows can give,—
much more, for any kindly heart it should be true

that the meanest tramp that walks can give—"thoughts that do often lie too deep for tears."

235. And if at first—or even always to careless sight—the third of these pictures seem opposite to the two others in the very point of choice, between what is and what is not; insomuch that while *they* with all their strength avouch realities, *this* with simplest confession dwells upon a dream,—yet in this very separation from them it sums their power and seals their brotherhood ; reaching beyond them to the more perfect truth of things, not only that once were,—not only that now are,—but which are the same yesterday, to-day, and for ever;—the love by whose ordaining the world itself, and all that dwell therein, live, and move, and have their being ; by which the Morning stars rejoice in their courses —in which the virgins of deathless Israel rejoice in the dance—and in whose constancy the Giver of light to stars, and love to men, Himself is glad in the creatures of His hand,—day by new day proclaiming to His Church of all the ages, "As the bridegroom rejoiceth over the bride, so shall thy Lord rejoice over thee."

Such, the reader will find, if he cares to learn it, is indeed the purport and effort of these three designs —so far as, by youthful hands and in a time of trouble and rebuke, such effort could be brought to good end. Of their visible weaknesses, with the best justice I may,—of their veritable merits with the best insight I may, and of the farther history of the school which these masters founded, I hope to be permitted to speak more under the branches that do not " remember their green felicity " ; adding a corollary or two respecting the other pieces of art above named* as having taken part in the tenor of my country hours of idleness.

* May I in the meantime recommend any reader interested in these matters to obtain for himself such photographic representation as may be easily acquirable of the tomb of Ilaria ?   It is in the north transept of the Cathedral of Lucca ; and is certainly the most beautiful work existing by the master who wrought it,—Jacopo della Quercia.

THE THREE COLOURS OF PRE-RAPHAELITISM.

II.

230. THE feeling which, in the foregoing notes on the pictures that entertained my vacation, I endeavoured to illustrate as dominant over early Pre-Raphaelite work, is very far from being new in the world. Demonstrations in support of fact against fancy have been periodical motives of earthquake and heartquake, under the too rigidly incumbent burdens of drifted tradition, which, throughout the history of humanity, during phases of languid thought, cover the vaults of searching fire that must at last try every man's work, what it is.

But the movement under present question derived unusual force, and in some directions a morbid and mischievous force, from the vulgarly called * "scientific" modes of investigation which had destroyed in the minds of the public it appealed to, all possi-

---

* "Vulgarly "; the use of the word "scientia," as if it differed from "knowledge," being a modern barbarism ; enhanced usually by the assumption that the knowledge of the difference between acids and alkalies is a more respectable one than that of the difference between vice and virtue.

bility, or even conception, of reverence for anything,
past, present, or future, invisible to the eyes of a
mob, and inexpressible by popular vociferation. It
was indeed, and had long been, too true, as the
wisest of us felt, that the mystery of the domain
between things that are universally visible, and are
only occasionally so to some persons,—no less than
the myths or words in which those who had entered
that kingdom related what they had seen, had become, the one uninviting, and the other useless, to
men dealing with the immediate business of our
day ; so that the historian of the last of European
kings might most reasonably mourn that "the Berlin
Galleries, which are made up, like other galleries, of
goat-footed Pan, Europa's Bull, Romulus's She-wolf,
and the Coreggiosity of Coreggio, contain, for instance, no portrait of Friedrich the Great; no likeness
at all, or next to none at all, of the noble series of
human realities, or of any part of them, who have
sprung not from the idle brains of dreaming dilet-
tanti, but from the Head of God Almighty, to make
this poor authentic earth a little memorable for us,
and to do a little work that may be eternal there."

237. But we must surely, in fairness to modernism,
remember that although no portraits of great Frederick,
of a trustworthy character, may be found at Berlin,
portraits of the English squire, be he great or small,

may usually be seen at his country house. And Edinburgh, as I lately saw,—if she boasts of no Venetian perfectness of art in the portraiture of her Bruce or James, her Douglas or Knox, at Holyrood, has at least a charming portrait of a Scottish beauty in the Attic Institution, whose majesty, together with that of the more extensive glass roofs of the railway station, and the tall chimney of the gasworks, inflates the Caledonian mind, contemplative around the spot where the last of its minstrels appears to be awaiting eternal extinction under his special extinguisher;—and pronouncing of all its works and ways that they are very good.

And are there not also sufficiently resembling portraits of all the mouthpieces of constituents in British Parliament—as their vocal powers advance them into that worshipful society—presented to the people, with due felicitation on the new pipe it has got to its organ, in the *Illustrated* or other graphic *News*? Surely, therefore, it cannot be portraiture of merely human greatness of mind that we are any way short of; but another manner of greatness altogether? And may we not regret that as great Frederick is dead, so also great Pan is dead, and only the goat-footed Pan, or rather the goat's feet of him without the Pan, left for portraiture?

238. I chanced to walk, to-day, 9th of November, through the gallery of the Liverpool Museum, in

which the good zeal and sense of Mr. Gatty have already, in beautiful order, arranged the Egyptian antiquities, but have not yet prevailed far enough to group, in like manner, the scattered Byzantine and Italian ivories above. Out of which collection, every way valuable, two primarily important pieces, it seems to me, may be recommended for accurate juxtaposition, bringing then for us into briefest compass an extensive story of the Arts of Mankind.

The first is an image of St. John the Baptist, carved in the eleventh century ; being then conceived by the image-maker as decently covered by his raiment of camel's hair ; bearing a gentle aspect, because the herald of a gentle Lord ; and pointing to his quite legibly written message concerning the Lamb which is that gentle Lord's heraldic symbol.

The other carving is also of St. John the Baptist, Italian work of the sixteenth century. He is represented thereby as bearing no aspect, for he is without his head ;—wearing no camel's hair, for he is without his raiment ;—and indicative of no message, for he has none to bring.

239. Now if these two carvings are ever put in due relative position, they will constitute a precise and permanent art-lecture to the museum-visitants of Liverpool-burg ; exhibiting to them instantly, and in sum, the conditions of the change in the aims of art

which, beginning in the thirteenth century under
Niccolo Pisano, consummated itself three hundred
years afterwards in Raphael and his scholars. Niccolo,
first among Italians, thought mainly in carving the
Crucifixion, not how heavy Christ's head was when
He bowed it;—but how heavy His body was when
people came to take it down. And the apotheosis of
flesh, or, in modern scientific terms, the molecular
development of flesh, went steadily on, until at last,
as we see in the instance before us, it became really
of small consequence to the artists of the Renaissance
Incarnadine, whether a man had his head on or not,
so only that his legs were handsome: and the de-
capitation, whether of St. John or St. Cecilia; the
massacre of any quantity of Innocents; the flaying,
whether of Marsyas or St. Bartholomew, and the
deaths, it might be of Laocoon by his vipers, it might
be of Adonis by his pig, or it might be of Christ
by His people, became, one and all, simply subjects
for analysis of muscular mortification; and the vast
body of artists accurately, therefore, little more than
a chirurgically useless sect of medical students.

Of course there were many reactionary tendencies
among the men who had been trained in the pure
Tuscan schools, which partly concealed, or adorned, the
materialism of their advance; and Raphael himself,
after profoundly studying the arabesques of Pompeii

and of the palace of the Cæsars, beguiled the tedium, and illustrated the spirituality of the converse of Moses and Elias with Christ concerning His decease which He should accomplish at Jerusalem, by placing them, above the Mount of Transfiguration, in the attitudes of two humming-birds on the top of a honeysuckle.

240. But the best of these ornamental arrangements were insufficient to sustain the vivacity, while they conclusively undermined the sincerity, of the Christian faith, and "the real consequences of the acceptance of this kind (Roman Bath and Sarcophagus kind)" of religious idealism were instant and manifold.*

So far as it was received and trusted in by thoughtful persons, it only served to chill all the conceptions of sacred history which they might otherwise have obtained. Whatever they could have fancied for themselves about the wild, strange, infinitely stern, infinitely tender, infinitely varied veracities of the life of Christ, was blotted out by the vapid fineries of Raphael : the rough Galilean pilot, the orderly custom receiver, and all the questioning wonder and fire of uneducated apostleship, were obscured under an antique mask of philosophical faces and long robes. The feeble, subtle, suffering, ceaseless energy and humiliation of St. Paul were confused with an idea of a meditative Hercules leaning on a sweeping sword ; and the mighty presences of Moses and Elias were softened by introductions of delicate grace, adopted from dancing nymphs and rising Auroras.

* *Modern Painters*, vol. iii. p. 55. I proceed in my old words, of which I cannot better the substance, though—with all deference to the taste of those who call that book my best— I could, the expression.

Now no vigorously minded religious person could possibly receive pleasure or help from such art as this ; and the necessary result was the instant rejection of it by the healthy religion of the world. Raphael ministered, with applause, to the impious luxury of the Vatican, but was trampled under foot at once by every believing and advancing Christian of his own and subsequent times; and thenceforward pure Christianity and "high art" took separate roads, and fared on, as best they might, independently of each other.

But although Calvin, and Knox, and Luther, and their flocks, with all the hardest-headed and truest-hearted faithful left in Christendom, thus spurned away the spurious art, and all art with it (not without harm to themselves, such as a man must needs sustain in cutting off a decayed limb), certain conditions of weaker Christianity suffered the false system to retain influence over them ; and to this day the clear and tasteless poison of the art of Raphael infects with sleep of infidelity the hearts of millions of Christians. It is the first cause of all that pre-eminent *dulness* which characterises what Protestants call sacred art; a dulness not merely baneful in making religion distasteful to the young, but in sickening, as we have seen, all vital belief of religion in the old. A dim sense of impossibility attaches itself always to the graceful emptiness of the representation ; we feel instinctively that the painted Christ and painted apostle are not beings that ever did of could exist; and this fatal sense of fair fabulousness, and well-composed impossibility, steals gradually from the picture into the history, until we find ourselves reading St. Mark or St. Luke with the same admiring, but uninterested, incredulity, with which we contemplate Raphael.

241. Without claiming,—nay, so far as my knowledge can reach, utterly disclaiming—any personal

influence over, or any originality of suggestion to, the men who founded our presently realistic schools, I may yet be permitted to point out the sympathy which I had as an outstanding spectator with their effort; and the more or less active fellowship with it, which, unrecognised, I had held from the beginning. The passage I have just quoted (with many others enforcing similar truths) is in the third volume of *Modern Painters*; but if the reader can refer to the close of the preface to the second edition * of the first, he will find this very principle of realism asserted for the groundwork of all I had to teach in that volume. The lesson so far pleased the public of that day, that ever since, they have refused to listen to any corollaries or conclusions from it, assuring me, year by year, continually, that the older I grew, the less I knew, and the worse I wrote. Nevertheless, that first volume of *Modern Painters* did by no means contain all that even then I knew; and in the third, nominally treating of " Many Things," will be found the full expression of what I knew best; namely, that all " things," many or few, which we ought to paint, must be first distinguished boldly from the nothings which we ought not; and that a faithful realist, before he could question whether his art was representing

* The *third* edition was published in 1846, while the Pre-Raphaelite School was still in swaddling clothes.

anything truly, had first to ask whether it meant
seriously to represent anything at all !

242. And such definition has in these days become
more needful than ever before, in this solid, or spectral
—whichever the reader pleases to consider it—world
of ours.   For some of us, who have no perception but
of solidity, are agreed to consider all that is not solid,
or weighably liquid, nothing.   And others of us, who
have also perception of the spectral, are sometimes too
much inclined to call what is no more than solid, or
weighably liquid, nothing.   But the general reader
may be at least assured that it is not at all possible
for the student to enter into useful discussion concerning the qualities of art which takes on itself to
represent things as they are, unless he include in its
subjects the spectral, no less than the substantial,
reality ; and understand what difference must be between the powers of veritable representation, for the
men whose models are of ponderable flesh, as for
instance, the "Sculptor's model," lately under debate
in Liverpool,—and the men whose models pause perhaps
only for an instant—painted on the immeasurable air,
—forms which they themselves can but discern darkly,
and remember uncertainly, saying: "A vision passed
before me, but I could not discern the form thereof."

243. And the most curious, yet the most common,
deficiency in the modern contemplative mind, is its

inability to comprehend that these phenomena of true imagination are yet no less real, and often more vivid than phenomena of matter. We continually hear artists blamed or praised for having painted this or that (either of material or spectral kind), without the slightest implied inquiry whether they *saw* this, or that. Whereas the quite primal difference between the first and second order of artists, is that the first is indeed painting what he has seen ; and the second only what he would like to see ! But as the one that can paint what he would like, has therefore the power, if he chooses, of painting more or less what also his public likes, he has a chance of being received with sympathetic applause, on all hands, while the first, it may be, meets only reproach for not having painted something more agreeable. Thus Mr. Millais, going out at Tunbridge or Sevenoaks, sees a blind vagrant led by an ugly child ; and paints that highly objectionable group, as they appeared to him. But your pliably minded painter gives you a beautiful young lady guiding a sightless Belisarius (see the gift by one of our most tasteful modistes to our National Gallery), and the gratified public never troubles itself to ask whether these ethereal mendicants were ever indeed apparent in this world, or any other. Much more, if, in deeper vistas of his imagination, some presently graphic Zechariah paint—(let us say) four carpenters, the public will most likely declare that he ought to have painted persons in a higher class of life, without ever inquiring whether the Lord had shown him four carpenters or not. And the worst of the business is that the public impatience, in such sort, is not wholly unreasonable. For truly, a painter who has eyes can, for the most part, see what he "likes" with them; and is, by divine law, answerable for his liking. And, even at this late hour of the day, it is still conceivable that such of them as would *verily* prefer to see, suppose, instead of a tramp with a harmonium, Orpheus with his lute, or Arion on his dolphin, pleased Proteus rising beside him from the sea,—might, standing on the "pleasant lea" of Margate or Brighton, have sight of those personages.

Orpheus with his lute,—Jubal with his harp and horn,—Harmonia, bride of the warrior seed-sower,—Musica herself, lady of all timely thought and sweetly ordered things, — Cantatrice and Incantatrice to all but the museless adder; these the Amphion of Fésole saw, as he shaped the marble of his tower; these, Memmi of Siena, fair-figured on the shadows of his vault;—but for us, here is the only manifestation granted to our best practical painter—a vagrant with harmonium — and yonder blackbirds and iridescent jackasses, to be harmonised thereby.

244. Our best *painter* (among the living) I say;—no

question has ever been of that. Since Van Eyck
and Durer there has nothing been seen so well done in
laying of clear oil-colour within definite line. And what
he might have painted for us, if *we* had only known
what we would have of him ! Heaven only knows.
But we none of us knew,—nor he neither; and on the
whole the perfectest of his works, and the representative
picture of that generation—was no Annunciate Maria
bowing herself; but only a Newsless Mariana stretching
herself: which is indeed the best symbol of the mud-
moated Nineteenth century ; in *its* Grange, Stable—
Stye, or whatever name of dwelling may best befit the
things it calls Houses and Cities : imprisoned therein
by the unassailablest of walls, and blackest of ditches
—by the pride of Babel, and the filthiness of Aholah
and Aholibamah ; and their worse younger sister ;—
craving for any manner of News from any world—
and getting none trustworthy even of its own.

245. I said that in this second paper I would try
to give some brief history of the rise, and the issue,
of that Pre-Raphaelite school : but, as I look over
two of the essays* that were printed with mine in
that last number of the *Nineteenth Century*—the first—
in laud of the Science which accepts for practical
spirits, inside of men, only Avarice and Indolence ;

---

* These essays were, " Recent Attacks on Political Economy," by
Robert Lowe, and " Virchow and Evolution," by Prof. Tyndall.—ED.

and the other,—in laud of the Science which "rejects the Worker" outside of Men, I am less and less confident in offering to the readers of the *Nineteenth Century* any History relating to such despised things as unavaricious industry,—or incorporeal vision. I will be as brief as I can.

246. The central branch of the school, represented by the central picture above described:—"The Blind Girl"—was essentially and vitally an uneducated one. It was headed, in literary power, by Wordsworth; but the first pure example of its mind and manner of Art, as opposed to the erudite and *artificial* schools, will be found, so far as I know, in Molière's song: *j'aime mieux ma mie.*

Its mental power consisted in discerning what was lovely in present nature, and in pure moral emotion concerning it.

Its physical power, in an intense veracity of direct realisation to the eye.

So far as Mr. Millais saw what was beautiful in vagrants, or commons, or crows, or donkeys, or the straw under children's feet in the Ark (Noah's or anybody else's does not matter),—in the Huguenot and his mistress, or the ivy behind them,—in the face of Ophelia, or in the flowers floating over it as it sank;—much more, so far as he saw what instantly comprehensible nobleness of passion might be in the binding of a handkerchief,—in the utterance of two words, "Trust me" or the like : he prevailed, and rightly prevailed, over all prejudice and opposition ; to that extent he will in what he has done, or may yet do, take, as a standard-bearer, an honourable place among the reformers of our day.

So far as he could not see what was beautiful, but what was essentially and for ever common (in that God had not cleansed it), and so far as he did not see truly what he thought he saw ; (as for instance, in this picture, under immediate consideration, when he paints the spark of light in a crow's eye a hundred yards off, as if he were only painting a miniature of a crow close by,)—he failed of his purpose and hope ; but how far I have neither the power nor the disposition to consider.

247. The school represented by Mr. Rossetti's picture and adopted for his own by Mr. Holman Hunt, professed, necessarily, to be a learned one ; and to represent things which had happened long ago, in a manner credible to any moderns who were interested in them. The value to us of such a school necessarily depends on the things it chooses to represent, out of the infinite history of mankind. For instance, David, of the first Republican Academe, was a true master of this school ; and, painting the Horatii receiving their swords, foretold the triumph of that

Republican Power. Gerome, of the latest Republican Academe, paints the dying Polichinelle, and the *mori-turi* gladiators : foretelling, in like manner, the shame and virtual ruin of modern Republicanism. What our own painters have done for us in this kind has been too unworthy of their real powers, for Mr. Rossetti threw more than half his strength into literature, and, in that precise measure, left himself unequal to his appointed task in painting ; while Mr. Hunt, not knowing the necessity of masters any more than the rest of our painters, and attaching too great importance to the externals of the life of Christ, separated himself for long years from all discipline by the recognised laws of his art ; and fell into errors which wofully shortened his hand and discredited his cause—into which again I hold it no part of my duty to enter. But such works as either of these painters have done, without antagonism or ostentation, and in their own true instincts; as all Rossetti's drawing from the life of Christ, more especially that of the Madonna gathering the bitter herbs for the Passover when He was twelve years old ; and that of the Magdalen leaving her companions to come to Him ; these, together with all the mythic scenes which he painted from the *Vita Nuova* and *Paradiso* of Dante, are of quite imperishable power and value : as also many of the poems

to which he gave up part of his painter's strength. Of
Holman Hunt's "Light of the World," and "Awaken-
ing Conscience," I have publicly spoken and written,
now for many years, as standard in their kind: the
study of sunset on the Egean, lately placed by me
in the schools of Oxford, is not less authoritative in
landscape, so far as its aim extends.

248. But the School represented by the third painting, "The Bridal," is that into which the greatest
masters of *all* ages are gathered, and in which they are
walled round as in Elysian fields, unapproachable but
by the reverent and loving souls, in some sort already
among the Dead.

They interpret to those of us who can read them, so
far as they already see and know, the things that are
for ever. "Charity never faileth ; but whether there
be prophecies they shall fail—tongues, they shall cease
—knowledge, it shall vanish."

And the one message they bear to us is the
commandment of the Eternal Charity. "Thou shalt
love the Lord thy God with *all* thine heart, and thy
neighbour as thyself." As thyself—no more, even the
dearest of neighbours.

"Therefore let every man see that he love his wife
even as himself."

No more—else she has become an idol, not a fellow-
servant ; a creature between us and our Master.

And they teach us that what higher creatures exist between Him and us, we are also bound to know, and to love in their place and state, as they ascend and descend on the stairs of their watch and ward.

The principal masters of this faithful religious school in painting, known to me, are Giotto, Angelico, Sandro Botticelli, Filippo Lippi, Luini, and Carpaccio ; but for a central illustration of their mind, I take that piece of work by the sculptor of Quercia,* of which some shadow of representation, true to an available degree, is within reach of my reader.

249. This sculpture is central in every respect ; being the last Florentine work in which the proper form of the Etruscan tomb is preserved, and the first in which all right Christian sentiment respecting death is embodied. It is perfectly severe in classical tradition, and perfectly frank in concession to the passions of existing life. It submits to all the laws of the past, and expresses all the hopes of the future.

Now every work of the great Christian schools expresses primarily, conquest over death ; conquest

---

* James of Quercia : see the rank assigned to this master in *Ariadne Florentina*, p. 45. The best photographs of the monument are, I believe, those published by the Arundel Society ; of whom I would very earnestly request that if ever they quote *Modern Painters*, they would not interpolate its text with unmarked parentheses of modern information such as "emblem of conjugal fidelity." I must not be made to answer for either the rhythm, or the contents, of sentences thus manipulated.

not grievous, but absolute and serene ; rising with the greatest of them, into rapture.

But this, as a *central* work, has all the peace of the Christian Eternity, but only in part its gladness. Young children wreathe round the tomb a garland of abundant flowers, but she herself, Ilaria, yet sleeps; the time is not yet come for her to be awakened out of sleep.

Her image is a simple portrait of her—how much less beautiful than she was in life, we cannot know— but as beautiful as marble can be.

And through and in the marble we may see that the damsel is not dead, but sleepeth : yet as visibly a sleep that shall know no ending until the last day break, and the last shadow flee away ; until then, she " shall not return." Her hands are laid on her breast—not praying —she has no need to pray now. She wears her dress of every day, clasped at her throat, girdled at her waist, the hem of it drooping over her feet. No disturbance of its folds by pain of sickness, no binding, no shrouding of her sweet form, in death more than in life. As a soft, low wave of summer sea, her breast rises; no more: the rippled gathering of its close mantle droops to the belt, then sweeps to her feet, straight as drifting snow. And at her feet her dog lies watching her ; the mystery of his mortal life joined, by love, to her immortal one.

Few know, and fewer love, the tomb and its place,

—not shrine, for it stands bare by the cathedral wall : only, by chance, a cross is cut deep into one of the foundation stones behind her head. But no goddess statue of the Greek cities, no nun's image among the cloisters of Apennine, no fancied light of angel in the homes of heaven, has more divine rank among the thoughts of men.

250. In so much as the reader can see of it, and learn, either by print or cast, or beside it ; (and he would do well to stay longer in that transept than in the Tribune at Florence,) he may receive from it, unerring canon of what is evermore Lovely and Right in the dealing of the Art of Man with his fate, and his passions. Evermore *lovely*, and *right*. These two virtues of visible things go always hand in hand : but the workman is bound to assure himself of his Rightness first ; then the loveliness will come.

And primarily, from this sculpture, you are to learn what a " Master " is. Here was one man at least, who knew his business, once upon a time ! Unaccusably ; —none of your fool's heads or clown's hearts can find a fault here ! " Dog-fancier,* cobbler, tailor, or churl, look here "—says Master Jacopo—" look ! I know what a brute is, better than you, I know what a silken tassel is—what a leathern belt is—Also, what a woman is ;

* I foolishly, in *Modern Painters*, used the generic word " hound " to make my sentence prettier. He is a flat-nosed bulldog.

and also—what a Law of God is, if you care to know."
This it is, to be a Master.

Then secondly—you are to note that with all the
certain rightness of its material fact, this sculpture still
is the Sculpture of a Dream. Ilaria is dressed as she
was in life. But she never lay so on her pillow ! nor
so, in her grave. Those straight folds, straightly laid
as a snowdrift, are impossible; known by the Master to
be so—chiselled with a hand as steady as an iron beam,
and as true as a ray of light—in defiance of your law
of Gravity to the Earth. *That* law prevailed on her
shroud, and prevails on her dust: but not on herself,
nor on the Vision of her.

Then thirdly, and lastly. You are to learn that the
doing of a piece of Art such as this is *possible* to the
hand of Man just in the measure of his obedience to the
laws which are indeed over his heart, and not over his
dust : primarily, as I have said, to that great one,
" Thou shalt *Love* the Lord thy God." Which command
is straight and clear ; and all men may obey it if they
will,—so only that they be early taught to know Him.

And that is precisely the piece of exact Science
which is not taught at present in our Board Schools—
so that although my friend, with whom I was staying,
was not himself, in the modern sense, ill-educated ;
neither did he conceive me to be so,—he yet thought it
good for himself and me to have that Inscription, " Lord,

teach us to Pray," illuminated on the house wall—if perchance either he or I could yet learn what John (when he still had his head) taught *his* Disciples.

251. But alas, for us only at last, among the people of all ages and in all climes, the lesson has become too difficult ; and the Father of all, in every age, in every clime adored, is Rejected of science, as an Outside Worker, in Cockneydom of the nineteenth century.

Rejected of Science : well ; but not yet, not yet—by the men who can do, as well as know. And though I have neither strength nor time, nor at present the mind to go into any review of the work done by the Third and chief School of our younger painters, headed by Burne Jones ; * and though I know its faults, palpable enough, like those of Turner, to the poorest sight ; and though I am discouraged in all its discouragements, I still hold in fulness to the hope of it in which I wrote the close of the third lecture I ever gave in Oxford—of

* It would be utterly vain to attempt any general account of the works of this painter, unless I were able also to give abstract of the subtlest mythologies of Greek worship and Christian romance. Besides, many of his best designs are pale pencil drawings like Florentine engravings, of which the delicacy is literally invisible, and the manner irksome, to a public trained among the black scrabblings of modern woodcutter's and etcher's prints. I will only say that the single series of these pencil-drawings, from the story of Psyche, which I have been able to place in the schools of Oxford, together with the two coloured beginnings from the stories of Jason and Alcestis, are, in my estimate, quite the most precious gift, not excepting even the Loire series of Turners, in the ratified acceptance of which my University has honoured with some fixed memorial the aims of her first Art-Teacher.

which I will ask the reader here in conclusion to weigh the words, set down in the days of my best strength, so far as I know ; and with the uttermost care given to that inaugural Oxford work, to "speak only that which I did know."

252. "Think of it, and you will find that so far from art being immoral, little else *except* art is moral ;—that life without industry is guilt, and industry without art is brutality : and for the words 'good,' and 'wicked,' used of men, you may almost substitute the words 'Makers' or 'Destroyers.'

"Far the greater part of the seeming prosperity of the world is, so far as our present knowledge extends, vain : wholly useless for any kind of good, but having assigned to it a certain inevitable sequence of destruction and of sorrow.

"Its stress is only the stress of wandering storm ; its beauty the hectic of plague : and what is called the history of mankind is too often the record of the whirl-wind, and the map of the spreading of the leprosy. But underneath all that, or in narrow spaces of dominion in the midst of it, the work of every man, 'qui non accepit in vanitatem animam suam,' endures and prospers; a small remnant or green bud of it prevailing at last over evil. And though faint with sickness, and encumbered in ruin, the true workers redeem inch by inch the wilderness into garden ground ; by the help of their joined hands the order of all things is surely sustained and vitally expanded, and although with strange vacillation, in the eyes of the watcher, the morning cometh, and also the night, there is no hour of human existence that does not draw on towards the perfect day.

" And perfect the day shall be, when it is of all men understood that the beauty of Holiness must be in labour as well as in rest. Nay! more, if it may be, in labour; in our strength, rather than in our weakness; and in the choice of what we shall work for through the six days, and may know to be good at their evening time, than in the choice of what we pray for on the seventh, of reward or repose. With the multitude that keep holiday, we may perhaps sometimes vainly have gone up to the house of the Lord, and vainly there asked for what we fancied would be mercy; but for the few who labour as their Lord would have them, the mercy needs no seeking, and their wide home no hallowing. Surely goodness and mercy shall follow them, all the days of their life, and they shall dwell in the house of the Lord—For Ever."*

* *Lecture on Art,* pp. 88-9, §§ 95-6.--ED.

ART.

III.

ARCHITECTURE.

THE OPENING OF THE CRYSTAL PALACE.
(Pamphlet, 1854.)

THE STUDY OF ARCHITECTURE IN OUR SCHOOLS.
(R.I.B.A. Transactions, 1865.)

253. I read the account in the *Times* newspaper
of the opening of the Crystal Palace at Sydenham
as I ascended the hill between Veway and Chatel
St. Denis, and the thoughts which it called up haunted
me all day long as my road wound among the grassy
slopes of the Simnenthal. There was a strange
contrast between the image of that mighty palace,
raised so high above the hills on which it is built
as to make them seem little else than a basement
for its glittering stateliness, and those lowland huts,
half hidden beneath their coverts of forest, and
scattered like grey stones along the masses of far-
away mountain. Here man contending with the
power of Nature for his existence ; there commanding
them for his recreation : here a feeble folk nested
among the rocks with the wild goat and the coney,

* A pamphlet, the full title of which was "The Opening of the
Crystal Palace Considered in some of its Relations to the Progress of
Art," by John Ruskin, M.A.   London : Smith, Elder, & Co., 1854.—ED.

and retaining the same quiet thoughts from generation to generation ; there a great multitude triumphing in the splendour of immeasurable habitation, and haughty with hope of endless progress and irresistible power.

254. It is indeed impossible to limit, in imagination, the beneficent results which may follow from the undertaking thus happily begun.*   For the first time in the history of the world, a national museum is formed in which a whole nation is interested ; formed on a scale which permits the exhibition of monuments of art in unbroken symmetry, and of the productions of . nature in unthwarted growth,—formed under the auspices of science which can hardly err, and of wealth which can hardly be exhausted ; and placed in the close neighbourhood of a metropolis over-flowing with a population weary of labour, yet thirsting for knowledge, where contemplation may be consistent with rest, and instruction with enjoyment. It is impossible, I repeat, to estimate the influence of such an institution on the minds of the working-classes.   How many hours once wasted may now be profitably dedicated to pursuits in which interest was first awakened by some accidental display in the Norwood palace ; how many constitutions, almost broken, may be restored by the healthy temptation

* But see now " Aratra Pentelici," pp. 50 seqq., § 53. Ed.

into the country air ; how many intellects, once dormant, may be roused into activity within the crystal walls, and how these noble results may go on multiplying and increasing and bearing fruit seventy times seven-fold, as the nation pursues its career,—are questions as full of hope as incapable of calculation. But with all these grounds for hope there are others for despondency, giving rise to a group of melancholy thoughts, of which I can neither repress the importunity nor forbear the expression.

255. For three hundred years, the art of architecture has been the subject of the most curious investigation ; its principles have been discussed with all earnestness and acuteness ; its models in all countries and of all ages have been examined with scrupulous care, and imitated with unsparing expenditure. And of all this refinement of inquiry,—this lofty search after the ideal,—this subtlety of investigation and sumptuousness of practice,—the great result, the admirable and long-expected conclusion is, that in the centre of the 19th century, we suppose ourselves to have invented a new style of architecture, when we have magnified a conservatory !

256. In Mr. Laing's speech, at the opening of the palace, he declares that *" an entirely novel order of architecture*, producing, by means of unrivalled mechanical ingenuity, the most marvellous and beau-

tiful effects, sprang into existence to provide a building." * In these words, the speaker is not merely giving utterance to his own feelings. He is expressing the popular view of the facts, nor that a view merely popular, but one which has been encouraged by nearly all the professors of art of our time.

It is to this, then, that our Doric and Palladian pride is at last reduced! We have vaunted the divinity of the Greek ideal—we have plumed ourselves on the purity of our Italian taste—we have cast our whole souls into the proportions of pillars and the relations of orders—and behold the end! Our taste, thus exalted and disciplined, is dazzled by the lustre of a few rows of panes of glass; and the first principles of architectural sublimity, so far sought, are found all the while to have consisted merely in sparkling and in space.

Let it not be thought that I would depreciate (were it possible to depreciate) the mechanical ingenuity which has been displayed in the erection of the Crystal Palace, or that I underrate the effect which its vastness may continue to produce on the popular imagination. But mechanical ingenuity is *not* the essence either of painting or architecture, and largeness of dimension does not necessarily involve nobleness

* See the *Times* of Monday, June 12th.

of design. There is assuredly as much ingenuity required to build a screw frigate, or a tubular bridge, as a hall of glass ;—all these are works characteristic of the age ; and all, in their several ways, deserve our highest admiration, but not admiration of the kind that is rendered to poetry or to art. We may cover the German Ocean with frigates, and bridge the Bristol Channel with iron, and roof the county of Middlesex with crystal, and yet not possess one Milton, or Michael Angelo.

257. Well, it may be replied, we need our bridges, and have pleasure in our palaces ; but we do not want Miltons, nor Michael Angelos.

Truly, it seems so ; for, in the year in which the first Crystal Palace was built, there died among us a man whose name, in after-ages, will stand with those of the great of all time. Dying, he bequeathed to the nation the whole mass of his most cherished works ; and for these three years, while we have been building this colossal receptacle for casts and copies of the art of other nations, these works of our own greatest painter have been left to decay in a dark room near Cavendish Square, under the custody of an aged servant.

This is quite natural. But it is also memorable.

258. There is another interesting fact connected with the history of the Crystal Palace as it bears on

23

that of the art of Europe, namely, that in the year
1851, when all that glittering roof was built, in order
to exhibit the paltry arts of our fashionable luxury—
the carved bedsteads of Vienna, and glued toys of
Switzerland, and gay jewellery of France—in that
very year, I say, the greatest pictures of the Venetian
masters were rotting at Venice in the rain, for want of
roof to cover them, with holes made by cannon shot
through their canvas.

There is another fact, however, more curious than
either of these, which will hereafter be connected with
the history of the palace now in building; namely, that
at the very period when Europe is congratulated on the
invention of a new style of architecture, because fourteen acres of ground have been covered with glass, the
greatest examples in existence of true and noble Christian architecture are being resolutely destroyed, and
destroyed by the effects of the very interest which was
beginning to be excited by them.

259. Under the firm and wise government of the
third Napoleon, France has entered on a new epoch of
prosperity, one of the signs of which is a zealous care
for the preservation of her noble public buildings.
Under the influence of this healthy impulse, repairs of
the most extensive kind are at this moment proceeding,
on the cathedrals of Rheims, Amiens, Rouen, Chartres,
and Paris; (probably also in many other instances un-

known to me). These repairs were, in many cases, necessary up to a certain point ; and they have been executed by architects as skilful and learned as at present exist,—executed with noble disregard of expense, and sincere desire on the part of their superintendents that they should be completed in a manner honourable to the country.

260. They are, nevertheless, more fatal to the monuments they are intended to preserve, than fire, war, or revolution. For they are undertaken, in the plurality of instances, under an impression, which the efforts of all true antiquaries have as yet been unable to remove, that it is impossible to reproduce the mutilated sculpture of past ages in its original beauty.

" Reproduire avec une exactitude mathematique," are the words used, by one of the most intelligent writers on this subject,* of the proposed regeneration of the statue of Ste. Modeste, on the north porch of the Cathedral of Chartres.

Now it is not the question at present whether thirteenth century sculpture be of value, or not. Its value is assumed by the authorities who have devoted sums so large to its so-called restoration, and may therefore be assumed in my argument. The worst state of the

---

* M. l'Abbé Bulteau, Description de la Cathédrale de Chartres (8vo, Paris, Sagnier et Bray, 1850), p. 98, *note*.

sculptures whose restoration is demanded may be fairly represented by that of the celebrated group of the Fates, among the Elgin Marbles in the British Museum. With what favour would the guardians of those marbles, or any other persons interested in Greek art, receive a proposal from a living sculptor to " reproduce with mathematical exactitude" the group of the Fates, in a perfect form, and to destroy the original ? For with exactly such favour, those who are interested in Gothic art should receive proposals to reproduce the sculpture of Chartres or Rouen.

261. In like manner, the state of the architecture which it is proposed to restore may, at its worst, be fairly represented to the British public by that of the best preserved portions of Melrose Abbey. With what encouragement would those among us who are sincerely interested in history, or in art, receive a proposal to pull down Melrose Abbey, and "reproduce it mathematically"? There can be no doubt of the answer which, in the instances supposed, it would be proper to return. "By all means, if you can, reproduce mathematically, elsewhere, the group of the Fates, and the Abbey of Melrose. But leave unharmed the original fragment, and the existing ruin." And an answer of the same tenour ought to be given to every proposal to restore a Gothic sculpture or building. Carve or raise a model of it in some

other part of the city; but touch not the actual edifice, except only so far as may be necessary to sustain, to protect it. I said above that repairs were in many instances necessary. These necessary operations consist in substituting new stones for decayed ones, where they are absolutely essential to the stability of the fabric; in propping, with wood or metal, the portions likely to give way; in binding or cementing into their places the sculptures which are ready to detach themselves; and in general care to remove luxuriant weeds and obstructions of the channels for the discharge of the rain. But no modern or imitative sculpture ought *ever*, under any circumstances, to be mingled with the ancient work.

262. Unfortunately, repairs thus conscientiously executed are always unsightly, and meet with little approbation from the general public; so that a strong temptation is necessarily felt by the superintendents of public works to execute the required repairs in a manner which, though indeed fatal to the monument, may be, in appearance, seemly. But a far more cruel temptation is held out to the architect. He who should propose to a municipal body to build in the form of a new church, to be erected in some other part of their city, models of such portions of their cathedral as were falling into decay, would be looked upon as merely asking for employment, and his offer

would be rejected with disdain. But let an architect declare that the existing fabric stands in need of repairs, and offer to restore it to its original beauty, and he is instantly regarded as a lover of his country, and has a chance of obtaining a commission which will furnish him with a large and ready income, and enormous patronage, for twenty or thirty years to come.

263. I have great respect for human nature. But I would rather leave it to others than myself to pronounce how far such a temptation is always likely to be resisted, and how far, when repairs are once permitted to be undertaken, a fabric is likely to be spared from mere interest in its beauty, when its destruction, under the name of restoration, has become permanently remunerative to a large body of workmen.

Let us assume, however, that the architect is always conscientious—always willing, the moment he has done what is strictly necessary for the safety and decorous aspect of the building, to abandon his income, and declare his farther services unnecessary. Let us presume, also, that every one of the two or three hundred workmen who must be employed under him is equally conscientious, and, during the course of years of labour, will never destroy in carelessness what it may be inconvenient to save, or in cunning what it is difficult to imitate. Will all this probity of purpose preserve the hand from error, and the heart from weariness? Will it give dexterity to the awkward—sagacity to the dull—and at once invest two or three hundred imperfectly educated men with the feeling, intention, and information of the freemasons of the thirteenth century? Grant that it can do all this, and that the new building is both equal to the old in beauty, and precisely correspondent to it in detail. Is it, therefore, altogether *worth* the old building? Is the stone carved to-day in their masons' yards altogether the same in value to the hearts of the French people as that which the eyes of St. Louis saw lifted to its place? Would a loving daughter, in mere desire for gaudy dress, ask a jeweller for a bright facsimile of the worn cross which her mother bequeathed to her on her death-bed?—would a thoughtful nation, in mere fondness for splendour of streets, ask its architects to provide for it facsimiles of the temples which for centuries had given joy to its saints, comfort to its mourners, and strength to its chivalry?

264. But it may be replied, that all this is already admitted by the antiquaries of France and England; and that it is impossible that works so important should now be undertaken with due consideration and faithful superintendence.

I answer, that the men who justly feel these truths

are rarely those who have much influence in public affairs. It is the poor abbé, whose little garden is sheltered by the mighty buttresses from the north wind, who knows the worth of the cathedral. It is the bustling mayor and the prosperous architect who determine its fate.

I answer farther, by the statement of a simple fact. I have given many years, in many cities, to the study of Gothic architecture ; and of all that I know, or knew, the entrance to the north transept of Rouen Cathedral was, on the whole, the most beautiful—beautiful, not only as an elaborate and faultless work of the finest time of Gothic art, but yet more beautiful in the partial, though not dangerous, decay which had touched its pinnacles with pensive colouring, and softened its severer lines with unexpected change and delicate fracture, like sweet breaks in a distant music. The upper part of it has been already restored to the white accuracies of novelty ; the lower pinnacles, which flanked its approach, far more exquisite in their partial ruin than the loveliest remains of our English abbeys, have been entirely destroyed, and rebuilt in rough blocks, now in process of sculpture. This restoration, so far as it has gone, has been executed by peculiarly skilful workmen ; it is an unusually favourable example of restoration, especially in the care which has been taken to preserve intact the exquisite, and hitherto almost uninjured sculptures which fill the quatrefoils of the tracery above the arch. But I happened myself to have made, five years ago, detailed drawings of the buttress decorations on the right and left of this tracery, which are part of the work that has been completely restored. And I found the restorations as inaccurate as they were unnecessary.

265. If this is the case in a most favourable instance, in that of a well-known monument, highly esteemed by every antiquary in France, what, during the progress of the now almost universal repair, is likely to become of architecture which is unwatched and despised ?

Despised! and more than despised—even hated! It is a sad truth, that there is something in the solemn aspect of ancient architecture which, in rebuking frivolity and chastening gaiety, has become at this time literally *repulsive* to a large majority of the population of Europe. Examine the direction which is taken by all the influences of fortune and of fancy, wherever they concern themselves with art, and it will be found that the real, earnest effort of the upper classes of European society is to make every place in the world as much like the Champs Elysées of Paris as possible. Wherever the influence of that educated society is felt, the old buildings are relentlessly destroyed ; vast hotels, like barracks, and rows of high, square-windowed dwelling-houses, thrust themselves forward to conceal the hated antiquities of the great cities of France and Italy. Gay promenades, with fountains and statues, prolong themselves along the quays once dedicated to commerce; ball-rooms and theatres rise upon the dust of desecrated chapels, and thrust into darkness the humility of domestic life. And when the formal street, in all its pride of perfumery and confectionery, has successfully consumed its way through wrecks of historical monuments, and consummated its symmetry in the ruin of all that once prompted a reflection, or pleaded for regard, the whitened city is praised for its splendour, and the exulting inhabitants for their patriotism—patriotism which consists in insulting their fathers with forgetfulness, and surrounding their children with temptation.

266. I am far from intending my words to involve any disrespectful allusion to the very noble improvements in the city of Paris itself, lately carried out under the encouragement of the Emperor. Paris, in its own peculiar character of bright magnificence, had nothing to fear, and everything to gain, from the gorgeous prolongation of the Rue Rivoli. But I speak of the general influence of the rich travellers and proprietors of Europe on the cities which they pretend to admire, or endeavour to improve. I speak of the changes wrought during my own lifetime on

the cities of Venice, Florence, Geneva, Lucerne, and chief of all on Rouen, a city altogether inestimable for its retention of mediæval character in the infinitely varied streets in which one half of the existing and inhabited houses date from the 15th or early 16th century, and the only town left in France in which the effect of old French domestic architecture can yet be seen in its collective groups. But when I was there, this last spring, I heard that these noble old Norman houses are all, as speedily as may be, to be stripped of the dark slates which protected their timbers, and deliberately whitewashed over all their sculptures and ornaments, in order to bring the interior of the town into some conformity with the "handsome fronts" of the hotels and offices on the quay.

Hotels and offices, and "handsome fronts" in general—they can be built in America or Australia—built at any moment, and in any height of splendour. But who shall give us back, when once destroyed, the habitations of the French chivalry and bourgeoisie in the days of the Field of the Cloth of Gold?

267. It is strange that no one seems to think of this! What do men travel for, in this Europe of ours? Is it only to gamble with French dies—to drink coffee out of French porcelain—to dance to the beat of German drums, and sleep in the soft air of

Italy ? Are the ball-room, the billiard-room, and the Boulevard, the only attractions thát win us into wandering, or tempt us to repose ? And when the time is come, as come it will, and that shortly, when the parsimony—or lassitude—which, for the most part, are the only protectors of the remnants of elder time, shall be scattered by the advance of civilization —when all the monuments, preserved only because it was too costly to destroy them, shall have been crushed by the energies of the new world, will the proud nations of the twentieth century, looking round on the plains of Europe, disencumbered of their memorial marbles,—will those nations indeed stand up with no other feeling than one of triumph, freed from the paralysis of precedent and the entanglement of memory, to thank us, the fathers of progress, that no saddening shadows can any more trouble the enjoyments of the future,—no moments of reflection retard its activities ; and that the new-born population of a world without a record and without a ruin may, in the fulness of ephemeral felicity, dispose itself to eat, and to drink, and to die ?

268. Is this verily the end at which we aim, and will the mission of the age have been then only accomplished, when the last castle has fallen from our rocks, the last cloisters faded from our valleys, the last streets, in which the dead have dwelt, been

effaced from our cities, and regenerated society is left in luxurious possession of towns composed only of bright saloons, overlooking gay parterres? If this indeed be our end, yet why must it be so laboriously accomplished? Are there no new countries on the earth, as yet uncrowned by thorns of cathedral spires, untenanted by the consciousness of a past? Must this little Europe—this corner of our globe, gilded with the blood of old battles, and grey with the temples of old pieties—this narrow piece of the world's pavement, worn down by so many pilgrims' feet, be utterly swept and garnished for the masque of the Future? Is America not wide enough for the elasticities of our humanity? Asia not rich enough for its pride? or among the quiet meadow-lands and solitary hills of the old land, is there not yet room enough for the spreadings of power, or the indulgences of magnificence, without founding all glory upon ruin, and prefacing all progress with obliteration?

269. We must answer these questions speedily, or we answer them in vain. The peculiar character of the evil which is being wrought by this age is its utter irreparableness. Its newly formed schools of art, its extending galleries, and well-ordered museums will assuredly bear some fruit in time, and give once more to the popular mind the power to discern what is great, and the disposition to protect what is precious.

But it will be too late. We shall wander through our palaces of crystal, gazing sadly on copies of pictures torn by cannon-shot, and on casts of sculpture dashed to pieces long ago. We shall gradually learn to distinguish originality and sincerity from the decrepitudes of imitation and palsies of repetition ; but it will be only in hopelessness to recognize the truth, that architecture and painting can be "restored" when the dead can be raised,—and not till then.

270. Something might yet be done, if it were but possible thoroughly to awaken and alarm the men whose studies of archæology have enabled them to form an accurate judgment of the importance of the crisis. But it is one of the strange characters of the human mind, necessary indeed to its peace, but infinitely destructive of its power, that we never thoroughly feel the evils which are not actually set before our eyes. If, suddenly, in the midst of the enjoyments of the palate and lightnesses of heart of a London dinner-party, the walls of the chamber were parted, and through their gap, the nearest human beings who were famishing, and in misery, were borne into the midst of the company—feasting and fancy-free—if, pale with sickness, horrible in destitution, broken by despair, body by body, they were laid upon the soft carpet, one beside the chair of every guest, would only the crumbs of the dainties be cast

to them—would only a passing glance, a passing thought be vouchsafed to them ? Yet the actual facts, the real relations of each Dives and Lazarus, are not altered by the intervention of the house wall between the table and the sick-bed—by the few feet of ground (how few !) which are indeed all that separate the merriment from the misery.

271. It is the same in the matters of which I have hitherto been speaking. If every one of us, who knows what food for the human heart there is in the great works of elder time, could indeed see with his own eyes their progressive ruin ; if every earnest antiquarian, happy in his well-ordered library, and in the sense of having been useful in preserving an old stone or two out of his parish church, and an old coin or two out of a furrow in the next ploughed field, could indeed behold, each morning as he awaked, the mightiest works of departed nations mouldering to the ground in disregarded heaps; if he could always have in clear phantasm before his eyes the ignorant monk trampling on the manuscript, the village mason striking down the monument, the court painter daubing the despised and priceless masterpiece into freshness of fatuity, he would not always smile so complacently in the thoughts of the little learnings and petty preservations of his own im- mediate sphere. And if every man, who has the interest

of Art and of History at heart, would at once devote himself earnestly—not to enrich his own collection—not even to enlighten his own neighbours or investigate his own parish-territory—but to far-sighted and *fore*-sighted endeavour in the great field of Europe, there is yet time to do much.　An association might be formed, thoroughly organized so as to maintain active watchers and agents in every town of importance, who, in the first place, should furnish the society with a *perfect* account of every monument of interest in its neighbour-hood, and then with a yearly or half-yearly report of the state of such monuments, and of the changes pro-posed to be made upon them ; the society then furnishing funds, either to buy, freehold, such buildings or other works of untransferable art as at any time might be offered for sale, or to assist their proprietors, whether private individuals or public bodies, in the maintenance of such guardianship as was really necessary for their safety ; and exerting itself, with all the influence which such an association would rapidly command, to prevent unwise restoration and unnecessary destruction.

272. Such a society would of course be rewarded only by the consciousness of its usefulness.　Its funds would have to be supplied, in pure self-denial, by its members, who would be required, so far as they assisted it, to give up the pleasure of purchasing prints or pictures for their own walls, that they

might save pictures which in their lifetime they might never behold ; they would have to forego the enlargement of their own estates, that they might buy, for a European property, ground on which their feet might never tread. But is it absurd to believe that men are capable of doing this ? Is the love of art altogether a selfish principle in the heart ? and are its emotions altogether incompatible with the exertions of self-denial or enjoyments of generosity ?

273. I make this appeal at the risk of incurring only contempt for my Utopianism. But I should for ever reproach myself if I were prevented from making it by such a risk ; and I pray those who may be disposed in any wise to favour it to remember that it must be answered at once or never. The next five years determine what is to be saved—what destroyed. The restorations have actually begun like cancers on every important piece of Gothic architecture in Christendom ; the question is only how much can yet be saved. All projects, all pursuits, having reference to art, are at this moment of less importance than those which are simply protective. There is time enough for everything else. Time enough for teaching—time enough for criticising—time enough for inventing. But time little enough for saving. Hereafter we can create, but it is now only that we can preserve. By the exertion of great national powers, and

24

under the guidance of enlightened monarchs, we may raise magnificent temples and gorgeous cities; we may furnish labour for the idle, and interest for the ignorant. But the power neither of emperors, nor queens, nor kingdoms, can ever print again upon the sands of time the effaced footsteps of departed generations, or gather together from the dust the stones which had been stamped with the spirit of our ancestors.

THE STUDY OF ARCHITECTURE IN OUR SCHOOLS.*

274. I suppose there is no man who, permitted to address, for the first time, the Institute of British Architects, would not feel himself abashed and restrained, doubtful of his claim to be heard by them, even if he attempted only to describe what had come under his personal observation, much more if on the occasion he thought it would be expected of him to touch upon any of the general principles of the art of architecture before its principal English masters.

But if any more than another should feel thus abashed, it is certainly one who has first to ask their pardon for the petulance of boyish expressions of partial thought; for ungraceful advocacy of principles which needed no support from him, and discourteous blame of work of which he had never felt the difficulty.

* This paper was read by Mr. Ruskin at the ordinary meeting of the Royal Institute of British Architects, May 15, 1865, and was afterwards published in the Sessional Papers of the Institute, 1864-5, Part III., No 2, pp. 139-147. Its full title (as there appears) was " An Inquiry into some of the conditions at present affecting the Study of Architecture in our Schools."— ED.

275. Yet, when I ask this pardon, gentlemen—and I do it sincerely and in shame—it is not as desiring to retract anything in the general tenor and scope of what I have hitherto tried to say. Permit me the pain, and the apparent impertinence, of speaking for a moment of my own past work; for it is necessary that what I am about to submit to you to-night should be spoken in no disadvantageous connection with that; and yet understood as spoken, in no discordance of purpose with that. Indeed there is much in old work of mine which I could wish to put out of mind. Reasonings, perhaps not in themselves false, but founded on insufficient data and imperfect experience —eager preferences, and dislikes, dependent on chance circumstances of association, and limitations of sphere of labour: but, while I would fain now, if I could, modify the applications, and chasten the extravagance of my writings, let me also say of them that they were the expression of a delight in the art of architecture which was too intense to be vitally deceived, and of an inquiry too honest and eager to be without some useful result; and I only wish I had now time, and strength and power of mind, to carry on, more worthily, the main endeavour of my early work. That main endeavour has been throughout to set forth the life of the individual human spirit as modifying the application of the formal laws of architecture, no less

than of all other arts; and to show that the power
and advance of this art, even in conditions of formal
nobleness, were dependent on its just association with
sculpture as a means of expressing the beauty of
natural forms : and I the more boldly ask your per-
mission to insist somewhat on this main meaning of
my past work, because there are many buildings now
rising in the streets of London, as in other cities of
England, which appear to be designed in accordance
with this principle, and which are, I believe, more
offensive to all who thoughtfully concur with me in
accepting the principle of Naturalism than they are to
the classical architect to whose modes of design they
are visibly antagonistic.   These buildings, in which
the mere cast of a flower, or the realization of a vulgar
face, carved without pleasure by a workman who is
only endeavouring to attract attention by novelty, and
then fastened on, or appearing to be fastened, as
chance may dictate, to an arch, or a pillar, or a wall,
hold such relation to nobly naturalistic architecture
as common sign-painter's furniture landscapes, do to
painting, or commonest wax-work to Greek sculpture ;
and the feelings with which true naturalists regard
such buildings of this class are, as nearly as might be,
what a painter would experience, if, having contended
earnestly against conventional schools, and having
asserted that Greek vase-painting and Egyptian wall-

painting, and Mediæval glass-painting, though beautiful, all, in their place and way, were yet subordinate
arts, and culminated only in perfectly naturalistic work
such as Raphael's in fresco, and Titian's on canvas ;—
if, I say, a painter, fixed in such faith in an entire,
intellectual and manly truth, and maintaining that an
Egyptian profile of a head, however decoratively applicable, was only noble for such human truth as it
contained, and was imperfect and ignoble beside a
work of Titian's, were shown, by his antagonist, the
coloured daguerreotype of a human body in its naked-
ness, and told that it was art such as that which he
really advocated, and to such art that his principles, if
carried out, would finally lead.

276. And because this question lies at the very root
of the organization of the system of instruction for our
youth, I venture boldly to express the surprise and
regret with which I see our schools still agitated by
assertions of the opposition of Naturalism to Invention,
and to the higher conditions of art.   Even in this very
room I believe there has lately been question whether
a sculptor should look at a real living creature of
which he had to carve the image.   I would answer in
one sense,—no ; that is to say, he ought to carve no
living creature while he still needs to look at it.   If
we do not know what a human body is like, we
certainly had better look, and look often, at it,

before we carve it; but if we already know the
human likeness so well that we can carve it by
light of memory, we shall not need to ask whether
we ought now to look at it or not; and what
is true of man is true of all other creatures and
organisms—of bird, and beast, and leaf. No assertion
is more at variance with the laws of classical as well as
of subsequent art than the common one that species
should not be distinguished in great design. We
might as well say that we ought to carve a man so as
not to know him from an ape, as that we should carve
a lily so as not to know it from a thistle. It is difficult
for me to conceive how this can be asserted in the
presence of any remains either of great Greek or
Italian art. A Greek looked at a cockle-shell or a
cuttlefish as carefully as he looked at an Olympic
conqueror. The eagle of Elis, the lion of Velia, the
horse of Syracuse, the bull of Thurii, the dolphin of
Tarentum, the crab of Agrigentum, and the crawfish of
Catana, are studied as closely, every one of them, as
the Juno of Argos, or Apollo of Clazomenae. Idealism,
so far from being contrary to special truth, is the very
abstraction of speciality from everything else. It is
the earnest statement of the characters which make
man man, and cockle cockle, and flesh flesh, and fish
fish. Feeble thinkers, indeed, always suppose that
distinction of kind involves meanness of style ; but the

meanness is in the treatment, not in the distinction.
There is a noble way of carving a man, and a mean
one ; and there is a noble way of carving a beetle, and
a mean one; and a great sculptor carves his scarabaeus
grandly, as he carves his king, while a mean sculptor
makes vermin of both.   And it is a sorrowful truth, yet
a sublime one, that this greatness of treatment cannot
be taught by talking about it.   No, nor even by
enforced imitative practice of it.   Men treat their subjects nobly only when they themselves become noble ;
not till then.   And that elevation of their own nature
is assuredly not to be effected by a course of drawing
from models, however well chosen, or of listening to
lectures, however well intended.

Art, national or individual, is the result of a long
course of previous life and training ; a necessary result, if that life has been loyal, and an impossible one,
if it has been base.   Let a nation be healthful, happy,
pure in its enjoyments, brave in its acts, and broad in
its affections, and its art will spring round and within
it as freely as the foam from a fountain ; but let the
springs of its life be impure, and its course polluted,
and you will not get the bright spray by treatises on
the mathematical structure of bubbles.

277. And I am to-night the more restrained in addressing you, because, gentlemen—I tell you honestly—I am
weary of all writing and speaking about art, and most

of my own. No good is to be reached that way. The last fifty years have, in every civilized country of Europe, produced more brilliant thought, and more subtle reasoning about art than the five thousand before them, and what has it all come to? Do not let it be thought that I am insensible to the high merits of much of our modern work. It cannot be for a moment supposed that in speaking of the inefficient expression of the doctrines which writers on art have tried to enforce, I was thinking of such Gothic as has been designed and built by Mr. Scott, Mr. Butterfield, Mr. Street, Mr. Waterhouse, Mr. Godwin, or my dead friend, Mr. Woodward. Their work has been original and independent. So far as it is good, it has been founded on principles learned not from books, but by study of the monuments of the great schools, developed by national grandeur, not by philosophical speculation. But I am entirely assured that those who have done best among us are the least satisfied with what they have done, and will admit a sorrowful concurrence in my belief that the spirit, or rather, I should say, the dispirit, of the age, is heavily against them; that all the ingenious writing or thinking which is so rife amongst us has failed to educate a public capable of taking true pleasure in any kind of art, and that the best designers never satisfy their own requirements of themselves, unless by vainly addressing another temper of mind, and providing for another manner of life, than ours. All lovely architecture was designed for cities in cloudless air ; for cities in which piazzas and gardens opened in bright populousness and peace ; cities built that men might live happily in them, and take delight daily in each other's presence and powers. But our cities, built in black air which, by its accumulated foulness, first renders all ornament invisible in distance, and then chokes its interstices with soot ; cities which are mere crowded masses of store, and warehouse, and counter, and are therefore to the rest of the world what the larder and cellar are to a private house ; cities in which the object of men is not life, but labour ; and in which all chief magnitude of edifice is to enclose machinery ; cities in which the streets are not the avenues for the passing and procession of a happy people, but the drains for the discharge of a tormented mob, in which the only object in reaching any spot is to be transferred to another ; in which existence becomes mere transition, and every creature is only one atom in a drift of human dust, and current of interchanging particles, circulating here by tunnels underground, and there by tubes in the air ; for a city, or cities, such as this no architecture is possible—nay, no desire of it is possible to their inhabitants.

278. One of the most singular proofs of the vanity of all hope that conditions of art may be combined with

the occupations of such a city, has been given lately in the design of the new iron bridge over the Thames at Blackfriars. Distinct attempt has been there made to obtain architectural effect on a grand scale. Nor was there anything in the nature of the work to prevent such an effort being successful. It is not edifices, being of iron, or of glass, or thrown into new forms, demanded by new purposes, which need hinder its being beautiful. But it is the absence of all desire of beauty, of all joy in fancy, and of all freedom in thought. If a Greek, or Egyptian, or Gothic architect had been required to design such a bridge, he would have looked instantly at the main conditions of its structure, and dwelt on them with the delight of imagination. He would have seen that the main thing to be done was to hold a horizontal group of iron rods steadily and straight over stone piers. Then he would have said to himself (or felt without saying), "It is this holding,—this grasp,—this securing tenor of a thing which might be shaken, so that it cannot be shaken, on which I have to insist." And he would have put some life into those iron tenons. As a Greek put human life into his pillars and produced the caryatid ; and an Egyptian lotus life into his pillars and produced the lily capital : so here, either of them would have put some gigantic or some angelic life into those colossal sockets. He would perhaps have put vast winged

statues of bronze, folding their wings, and grasping
the iron rails with their hands ; or monstrous eagles,
or serpents holding with claw or coil, or strong four-
footed animals couchant, holding with the paw, or in
fierce action, holding with teeth. Thousands of grotesque
or of lovely thoughts would have risen before him,
and the bronze forms, animal or human, would have
signified, either in symbol or in legend, whatever might
be gracefully told respecting the purposes of the work
and the districts to which it conducted.   Whereas,
now, the entire invention of the designer seems to have
exhausted itself in exaggerating to an enormous size a
weak form of iron nut, and in conveying the information upon it, in large letters, that it belongs to the
London, Chatham, and Dover Railway Company.   I
believe then, gentlemen, that if there were any life in
the national mind in such respects, it would be shown
in these its most energetic and costly works.   But
that there is no such life, nothing but a galvanic
restlessness and covetousness, with which it is for the
present vain to strive ;   and in the midst of which,
tormented at once by its activities and its apathies,
having their work continually thrust aside and dishonoured, always seen to disadvantage, and over-
topped by huge masses, discordant and destructive,
even the best architects must be unable to do justice
to their own powers.

279. But, gentlemen, while thus the mechanisms of the age prevent even the wisest and best of its artists from producing entirely good work, may we not reflect with consternation what a marvellous ability the luxury of the age, and the very advantages of education, confer on the unwise and ignoble for the production of attractively and infectiously *bad* work ? I do not think that this adverse influence, necessarily affecting all conditions of so-called civilization, has been ever enough considered. It is impossible to calculate the power of the false workman in an advanced period of national life, nor the temptation to all workmen, to *become* false.

280. First, there is the irresistible appeal to vanity. There is hardly any temptation of the kind (there cannot be) while the arts are in progress. The best men must then always be ashamed of themselves ; they never can be satisfied with their work absolutely, but only as it is progressive. Take, for instance, any archaic head intended to be beautiful ; say, the Attic Athena, on the early Arethusa of Syracuse. In that, and in all archaic work of promise, there is much that is inefficient, much that to us appears ridiculous—but nothing sensual, nothing vain, nothing spurious or imitative. It is a child's work, a childish nation's work, but not a fool's work. You find in children the same tolerance of ugliness, the same

eager and innocent delight in their own work for the moment, however feeble; but next day it is thrown aside, and something better is done. Now, in this careless play, a child or a childish nation differs inherently from a foolish educated person, or a nation advanced in pseudo-civilization. The educated person has seen all kinds of beautiful things, of which he would fain do the like—not to add to their number—but for his own vanity, that he also may be called an artist. Here is at once a singular and fatal difference. The childish nation sees nothing in its own past work to satisfy itself. It is pleased at having done this, but wants something better; it is struggling forward always to reach this better, this ideal conception. It wants more beauty to look at, it wants more subject to feel. It calls out to all its artists—stretching its hands to them as a little child does—"Oh, if you would but tell me another story,"—"Oh, if I might but have a doll with bluer eyes." That's the right temper to work in, and to get work done for you in. But the vain, aged, highly-educated nation is satiated with beautiful things—it has myriads more than it can look at; it has fallen into a habit of inattention; it passes weary and jaded through galleries which contain the best fruit of a thousand years of human travail; it gapes and shrugs over them, and pushes its way past them to the door.

281. But there is one feeling that is always distinct,
however jaded and languid we may be in all other
pleasures, we are never languid in vanity, and we
would still paint and carve for fame. What other
motive have the nations of Europe to-day ? If they
wanted art for art's sake they would take care of what
they have already got. But at this instant the two
noblest pictures in Venice are lying rolled up in
outhouses, and the noblest portrait of Titian in existence is hung forty feet from the ground. We have
absolutely no motive but vanity and the love of money
—no others, as nations, than these, whatever we may
have as individuals. And as the thirst of vanity thus
increases, so the temptation to it. There was no
fame of artists in these archaic days. Every year,
every hour, saw some one rise to surpass what had
been done before. And there was always better work
to be done, but never any credit to be got by it.
The artist lived in an atmosphere of perpetual, wholesome, inevitable eclipse. Do as well as you choose
to-day,—make the whole Borgo dance with delight,
they would dance to a better man's pipe to-morrow.
*Credette Cimabue nella pittura, tener lo campo, et ora
ha Giotto il grido.* This was the fate, the necessary
fate, even of the strongest. They could only hope
to be remembered as links in an endless chain. For
the weaker men it was no use even to put their name

on their works. They did not. If they could not work for joy and for love, and take their part simply in the choir of human toil, they might throw up their tools. But now it is far otherwise—now, the best having been done—and for a couple of hundred years, the best of us being confessed to have come short of it, everybody thinks that he may be the great man once again, and this is certain, that whatever in art is done for display, is invariably wrong.

282. But, secondly, consider the attractive power of false art, completed, as compared with imperfect art advancing to completion. Archaic work, so far as faultful, is repulsive, but advanced work is, in all its faults, attractive. The moment that art has reached the point at which it becomes sensitively and delicately imitative, it appeals to a new audience. From that instant it addresses the sensualist and the idler. Its deceptions, its successes, its subtleties, become interesting to every condition of folly, of frivolity, and of vice. And this new audience brings to bear upon the art in which its foolish and wicked interest has been unhappily awakened, the full power of its riches : the largest bribes of gold as well as of praise are offered to the artist who will betray his art, until at last, from the sculpture of Phidias and fresco of Luini, it sinks into the cabinet ivory and the picture kept under lock and key. Between these highest

and lowest types, here is a vast mass of merely imitative and delicately sensual sculpture;—veiled nymphs—chained slaves—soft goddesses seen by rose-light through suspended curtains—drawing room portraits and domesticities, and such like, in which the interest is either merely personal and selfish, or dramatic and sensational ; in either case, destructive of the power of the public to sympathize with the aims of great architects.

283. Gentlemen,—I am no Puritan, and have never praised or advocated puritanical art. The two pictures which I would last part with out of our National Gallery, if there were question of parting with any, would be Titian's Bacchus and Correggio's Venus. But the noble naturalism of these was the fruit of ages of previous courage, continence, and religion—it was the fulness of passion in the life of a Britomart. But the mid-age and old age of nations is not like the mid-age or old age of noble women. National decrepitude must be criminal. National death can only be by disease, and yet it is almost impossible, out of the history of the art of nations, to elicit the true conditions relating to its decline in any demonstrable manner. The history of Italian art is that of a struggle between superstition and naturalism on one side, between continence and sensuality on another. So far as naturalism prevailed over super-

stition, there is always progress ; so far as sensuality
over chastity, death. And the two contests are
simultaneous. It is impossible to distinguish one
victory from the other. Observe, however, I say
victory over superstition, not over religion. Let me
carefully define the difference. Superstition, in all
times and among all nations, is the fear of a spirit
whose passions are those of a man, whose acts are
the acts of a man ; who is present in some places,
not in others ; who makes some places holy and not
others ; who is kind to one person, unkind to another ;
who is pleased or angry according to the degree of
attention you pay to him, or praise you refuse to him ;
who is hostile generally to human pleasure, but may
be bribed by sacrifice of a part of that pleasure into
permitting the rest. This, whatever form of faith it
colours, is the essence of superstition. And religion
is the belief in a Spirit whose mercies are over all
His works—who is kind even to the unthankful and
the evil ; who is everywhere present, and therefore
is in no place to be sought, and in no place to be
evaded ; to whom all creatures, times, and things are
everlastingly holy, and who claims—not tithes of
wealth, nor sevenths of days—but all the wealth that
we have, and all the days that we live, and all the
beings that we are, but who claims that totality because
He delights only in the delight of His creatures ;

and because, therefore, the one duty that they owe to Him, and the only service they can render Him, is to be happy. A Spirit, therefore, whose eternal benevolence cannot be angered, cannot be appeased; whose laws are everlasting and inexorable, so that heaven and earth must indeed pass away if one jot of them failed: laws which attach to every wrong and error a measured, inevitable penalty; to every rightness and prudence, an assured reward; penalty, of which the remittance cannot be purchased; and reward, of which the promise cannot be broken.

284. And thus, in the history of art, we ought continually to endeavour to distinguish (while, except in broadest lights, it is impossible to distinguish) the work of religion from that of superstition, and the work of reason from that of infidelity. Religion devotes the artist, hand and mind, to the service of the gods; superstition makes him the slave of ecclesiastical pride, or forbids his work altogether, in terror or disdain. Religion perfects the form of the divine statue, superstition distorts it into ghastly grotesque. Religion contemplates the gods as the lords of healing and life, surrounds them with glory of affectionate service, and festivity of pure human beauty. Superstition contemplates its idols as lords of death, appeases them with blood, and vows itself to them in torture and solitude. Religious proselytes

by love, superstition by war; religion teaches by
example, superstition by persecution. Religion gave
granlte shrine to the Egyptian, golden temple to the
Jew, sculptured corridor to the Greek, pillared aisle
and frescoed wall to the Christian. Superstition made
idols of the splendours by which Religion had spoken :
reverenced pictures and stones, instead of truths ;
letters and laws, instead of acts, and for ever, in
various madness of fantastic desolation, kneels in the
temple while it crucifies the Christ.

285. On the other hand, to reason resisting superstition, we owe the entire compass of modern energies
and sciences; the healthy laws of life, and the
possibilities of future progress. But to infidelity
resisting religion (or which is often enough the case,
taking the mask of it), we owe sensuality, cruelty,
and war, insolence and avarice, modern political
economy, life by conservation of forces, and salvation
by every man's looking after his own interests ; and,
generally, whatsoever of guilt, and folly, and death,
there is abroad among us. And of the two, a thousand-
fold rather let us retain some colour of superstition,
so that we may keep also some strength of religion,
than comfort ourselves with colour of reason for the
desolation of godlessness. I would say to every youth
who entered our schools—Be a Mahometan, a Diana-
worshipper, a Fire-worshipper, Root-worshipper, if

you will ; but at least be so much a man as to know
what worship means.   I had rather, a million-fold
rather, see you one of those "quibus hæc nascuntur
in hortis numina," than one of those "quibus hæc *non*
nascuntur in cordibus lumina " ; and who are, by everlasting orphanage, divided from the Father of Spirits,
who is also the Father of lights, from whom cometh
every good and perfect gift.

286. "So much of man," I say, feeling profoundly
that all right exercise of any human gift, so descended
from the Giver of good, depends on the primary
formation of the character of true manliness in the
youth—that is to say, of a majestic, grave, and deliberate
strength.   How strange the words sound ; how little
does it seem possible to conceive of majesty, and
gravity, and deliberation in the daily track of modern
life.   Yet, gentlemen, we need not hope that our work
will be majestic if there is no majesty in ourselves.
The word "manly" has come to mean practically,
among us, a schoolboy's character, not a man's.   We
are, at our best, thoughtlessly impetuous, fond of
adventure and excitement ; curious in knowledge for
its novelty, not for its system and results ; faithful
and affectionate to those among whom we are by
chance cast, but gently and calmly insolent to strangers : we are stupidly conscientious, and instinctively
brave, and always ready to cast away the lives we

take no pains to make valuable, in causes of which
we have never ascertained the justice. This is
our highest type—notable peculiarly among nations
for its gentleness, together with its courage ; but in
lower conditions it is especially liable to degradation
by its love of jest and of vulgar sensation. It is
against this fatal tendency to vile play that we have
chiefly to contend. It is the spirit of Milton's Comus ;
bestial itself, but having power to arrest and paralyze
all who come within its influence, even pure creatures
sitting helpless, mocked by it on their marble thrones.
It is incompatible, not only with all greatness of
character, but with all true gladness of heart, and it
develops itself in nations in proportion to their
degradation, connected with a peculiar gloom and a
singular tendency to play with death, which is a
morbid reaction from the morbid excess.

287. A book has lately been published on the
Mythology of the Rhine, with illustrations by Gustave Doré. The Rhine god is represented in the
vignette title-page with a pipe in one hand and a pot
of beer in the other. You cannot have a more
complete type of the tendency which is chiefly to be
dreaded in this age than in this conception, as opposed
to any possibility of representation of a river-god,
however playful, in the mind of a Greek painter.
The example is the more notable because Gustave

Doré's is not a common mind, and, if born in any other epoch, he would probably have done valuable (though never first rate) work; but by glancing (it will be impossible for you to do more than glance) at his illustrations of Balzac's "Contes Drolatiques," you will see further how this "drolatique," or semi-comic mask is, in the truth of it, the mask of a skull, and how the tendency to burlesque jest is both in France and England only an effervescence from the *cloaca maxima* of the putrid instincts which fasten themselves on national sin, and are in the midst of the luxury of European capitals, what Dante meant when he wrote "quel mi sveglio col puzzo," of the body of the Wealth-Siren; the mocking levity and mocking gloom being equally signs of the death of the soul; just as, contrariwise, a passionate seriousness and passionate joyfulness are signs of its full life in works such as those of Angelico, Luini, Ghiberti, or La Robbia.

It is to recover this stern seriousness, this pure and thrilling joy, together with perpetual sense of spiritual presence, that all true education of youth must now be directed. This seriousness, this passion, this universal human religion, are the first principles, the true roots of all art, as they are of all doing, of all being. Get this *vis viva* first and all great work will follow. Lose it, and your schools of art

will stand among other living schools as the frozen
corpses stand by the winding stair of the St.
Michael's Convent of Mont Cenis, holding their hands
stretched out under their shrouds, as if beseeching
the passer by to look upon the wasting of their death.

288. And all the higher branches of technical teaching are vain without this; nay are in some sort vain
altogether, for they are superseded by this. You
may teach imitation, because the meanest man can
imitate; but you can neither teach idealism nor composition, because only a great man can choose, conceive, or compose; and he does all these necessarily,
and because of his nature. His greatness is in his
choice of things, in his analysis of them, and his
combining powers involve the totality of his knowledge
in life. His methods of observation and abstraction are
essential habits of his thought, conditions of his being.
If he looks at a human form he recognizes the signs
of nobility in it, and loves them—hates whatever is
diseased, frightful, sinful, or *designant* of decay. All
ugliness, and abortion, and fading away; all signs
of vice and foulness, he turns away from, as inherently diabolic and horrible; all signs of unconquered
emotion he regrets, as weaknesses. He looks only
for the calm purity of the human creature, in living
conquest of its passions and of fate. That is idealism;
but you cannot teach any one else that preference.

Take a man who likes to see and paint the gambler's
rage ; the hedge-ruffian's enjoyment ; the debauched
soldier's strife ; the vicious woman's degradation ;—
take a man fed on the dusty picturesque of rags and
guilt ; talk to him of principles of beauty ! make him
draw what you will, how you will, he will leave the
stain of himself on whatever he touches. You had
better go lecture to a snail, and tell it to leave no
slime behind it. Try to make a mean man compose ;
you will find nothing in his thoughts consecutive or
proportioned—nothing consistent in his sight—nothing
in his fancy. He cannot comprehend two things in
relation at once—how much less twenty ! How much
less all ! Everything is uppermost with him in its
turn, and each as large as the rest ; but Titian or
Veronese compose as tranquilly as they would speak
—inevitably. The thing comes to them so—they see
it so—rightly, and in harmony : they will not talk to
you of composition, hardly even understanding how
lower people see things otherwise, but knowing that
if they *do* see otherwise, there is for them the end
there, talk as you will.

289. I had intended, in conclusion, gentlemen, to
incur such blame of presumption as might be involved
in offering some hints for present practical methods
in architectural schools, but here again I am checked,
as I have been throughout, by a sense of the use-

lessness of all minor means, and helps, without the
establishment of a true and broad educational system.
My wish would be to see the profession of the
architect united, not with that of the engineer, but
of the sculptor. I think there should be a separate
school and university course for engineers, in which
the principal branches of study connected with that
of practical building should be the physical and exact
sciences, and honours should be taken in mathematics;
but I think there should be another school and
university course for the sculptor and architect, in
which literature and philosophy should be the associated
branches of study, and honours should be taken *in
literis humanioribus*; and I think a young architect's
examination for his degree (for mere pass), should
be much stricter than that of youths intending to
enter other professions. The quantity of scholarship
necessary for the efficiency of a country clergyman
is not great. So that he be modest and kindly,
the main truths he has to teach may be learned
better in his heart than in books, and taught in very
simple English. The best physicians I have known
spent very little time in their libraries; and though
my lawyer sometimes chats with me over a Greek
coin, I think he regards the time so spent in the
light rather of concession to my idleness than as
helpful to his professional labours.

But there is no task undertaken by a true architect of which the honourable fulfilment will not require a range of knowledge and habitual feeling only attainable by advanced scholarship.

290. Since, however, such expansion of system is, at present, beyond hope, the best we can do is to render the studies undertaken in our schools thoughtful, reverent, and refined, according to our power. Especially, it should be our aim to prevent the minds of the students from being distracted by models of an unworthy or mixed character. A museum is one thing—a school another; and I am persuaded that as the efficiency of a school of literature depends on the mastering a few good books, so the efficiency of a school of art will depend on the understanding a few good models. And so strongly do I feel this that I would, for my own part, at once consent to sacrifice my personal predilections in art, and to vote for the exclusion of all Gothic or Mediæval models whatsoever, if by this sacrifice I could obtain also the exclusion of Byzantine, Indian, Renaissance-French, and other more or less attractive but barbarous work; and thus concentrate the mind of the student wholly upon the study of natural form, and upon its treatment by the sculptors and metal workers of Greece, Ionia, Sicily, and Magna Græcia, between 500 and 350 B.C. But I should hope that exclusiveness

need not be carried quite so far. I think Donatello,
Mino of Fiesole, the Robbias, Ghiberti, Verrocchio,
and Michael Angelo, should be adequately represented
in our schools—together with the Greeks—and that
a few carefully chosen examples of the floral sculpture
of the North in the thirteenth century should be
added, with especial view to display the treatment of
naturalistic ornament in subtle connection with constructive requirements; and in the course of study
pursued with reference to these models, as of admitted
perfection, I should endeavour first to make the
student thoroughly acquainted with the natural forms
and characters of the objects he had to treat, and
then to exercise him in the abstraction of these forms,
and the suggestion of these characters, under due
sculptural limitation. He should first be taught to
draw largely and simply; then he should make
quick and firm sketches of flowers, animals, drapery,
and figures, from nature, in the simplest terms of
line, and light and shade; always being taught to
look at the organic, actions and masses, not at the
textures or accidental effects of shade; meantime his
sentiment respecting all these things should be culti-
vated by close and constant inquiry into their
mythological significance and associated traditions;
then, knowing the things and creatures thoroughly,
and regarding them through an atmosphere of en-

chanted memory, he should be shown how the facts
he has taken so long to learn are summed by a great
sculptor in a few touches ; how those touches are
invariably arranged in musical and decorative relations ;
how every detail unnecessary for his purpose is refused ; how those necessary for his purpose are
insisted upon, or even exaggerated, or represented by
singular artifice, when literal representation is impossible ; and how all this is done under the instinct
and passion of an inner commanding spirit which it
is indeed impossible to imitate, but possible, perhaps,
to share.

291. Perhaps ! Pardon me that I speak despond-
ingly. For my own part, I feel the force of mechanism
and the fury of avaricious commerce to be at present
so irresistible, that I have seceded from the study
not only of architecture, but nearly of all art ; and
have given myself, as I would in a besieged city, to
seek the best modes of getting bread and water for
its multitudes, there remaining no question, it seems,
to me, of other than such grave business for the time.
But there is, at least, this ground for courage, if
not for hope : As the evil spirits of avarice and luxury
are directly contrary to art, so, also, art is directly
contrary to them ; and according to its force, expulsive
of them and medicinal against them ; so that the
establishment of such schools as I have ventured to

describe—whatever their immediate success or ill success in the teaching of art—would yet be the directest method of resistance to those conditions of evil among which our youth are cast at the most critical period of their lives. We may not be able to produce architecture, but, at the least, we shall resist vice. I do not know if it has been observed that while Dante rightly connects architecture, as the most permanent expression of the pride of humanity, whether just or unjust, with the first cornice of Purgatory, he indicates its noble function by engraving upon it, in perfect sculpture, the stories which rebuke the errors and purify the purposes of noblest souls. In the fulfilment of such function, literally and practically, here among men, is the only real use of pride of noble architecture, and on its acceptance or surrender of that function it depends whether, in future, the cities of England melt into a ruin more confused and ghastly than ever storm wasted or wolf inhabited, or purge and exalt themselves into true habitations of men, whose walls shall be Safety, and whose gates shall be Praise.

NOTE.—In the course of the discussion which followed this paper the meeting was addressed by Prof. Donaldson, who alluded to the architectural improvements in France under the Third Napoleon, by Mr. George Edmund Street, by Prof. Kerr, Mr. Digby Wyatt, and others. The President then proposed a vote of thanks to Mr. Ruskin, who, in acknowledging the high compliment paid him, said he would detain the meeting but a few minutes, but he felt he ought to make some attempt to explain what he had inefficiently stated in his paper; and there was hardly anything said in the discussion in which he did not concur: the supposed differences of opinion were either because he had ill-expressed himself, or because of things left unsaid. In the first place he was surprised to hear dissent from Professor Donaldson while he expressed his admiration of some of the changes which had been developed in modern architecture. There were two conditions of architecture adapted for different climates; one with narrow streets, calculated for shade; another for broad avenues beneath bright skies; but both conditions had their beautiful effects. He sympathized with the admirers of Italy, and he was delighted with Genoa. He had been delighted also by the view of the long vistas from the Tuileries. Mr. Street had showed that he had not sufficiently dwelt on the distinction between near and distinct carving—between carving and sculpture. He (Mr. Ruskin) could allow of no distinction. Sculpture which was to be viewed at a height of 500 feet above the eye might be executed with a few touches of the chisel; opposed to that there was the exquisite finish which was the perfection of sculpture, as displayed in the Greek statues, after a full knowledge of the whole nature of the object pourtrayed; both styles were admirable in their true application —both were "sculpture"—perfect according to their places and requirements. The attack of Professor Kerr he regarded as in play, and in that spirit he would reply to him that he was afraid a practical association with bricks and mortar, would hardly produce the effects upon him which had been suggested, for having of late in his residence experienced the transition of large extents of ground into bricks and mortar, it had had no effect in changing his views; and when he said he was tired of writing upon art, it was not that he was ashamed of what he had written, but that he was tired of writing in vain, and of knocking his head, thick as it might be, against a wall. There was another point which he would answer very gravely. It was referred to by Mr. Digby Wyatt, and was the one point he had mainly at heart all through—viz., that religion and high morality were at the root of all great art in all great times. The instances referred to by Mr. Digby Wyatt did not counteract that proposition. Modern and ancient forms of life might be different, nor could all men be judged by formal canons, but a true human heart was in the breast of every really great artist. He had the greatest detestation of anything approaching to cant in respect of art; but, after long investigation of the historical evidence, as well as of the metaphysical laws bearing on this question, he was absolutely certain that a high moral and religious training was the only way to get good fruits from our youth; make them good men first, and only so, if at all, they would become good artists. With regard to the points mooted respecting the practical and poetical uses of architecture, he thought they did not sufficiently define their terms; they spoke of poetry as rhyme. He thanked the President for his definition to-night, and he was sure he would concur with him that poetry meant as its derivation implied--"the *doing*." What was rightly done was done for ever, and that which was only a crude work for the time was not poetry; poetry was only that which would recreate or remake the human soul. · In that sense poetical architecture was separated from all utilitarian work. ·He had said long ago men could not decorate their shops and counters; they could decorate only where they lived in peace and rest—where they existed to be happy. There ornament would find use, and there their "doing" would be permanent. In other cases they wasted their money if they attempted to make utilitarian work ornamental. He might be wrong in that principle, but he had always asserted it, and had seen no reason in recent works for any modification of it. He thanked the meeting sincerely for the honour they had conferred upon him by their invitation to address them that evening, and for the indulgence with which they had heard him.—ED.

END OF VOL. I. PART I.

www.ingramcontent.com/pod-product-compliance
Lightning Source LLC
Chambersburg PA
CBHW020238110726
47898CB00004B/1303